Six Sigma Fundamentals

A Complete Guide to the System, Methods and Tools

By
D.H. Stamatis

PRODUCTIVITY PRESS
NEW YORK, NEW YORK

Most Productivity Press books are available at quantity discounts when purchased in bulk. For more information contact our Customer Service Department (800-394-6868). Address all other inquiries to:
Productivity Press
444 Park Avenue South, Suite 604
New York, NY 10016
United States of America
Telephone: 212-686-5900
Telefax: 212-686-5411
E-mail: info@productivityinc.com

Composed by William H. Brunson Typography Services
Printed and bound by Malloy Lithographing in the United States of America

Library of Congress Cataloging-in-Publication Data

Stamatis, D. H., 1947-
    Six Sigma fundamentals : a complete guide to the system, methods and tools / D. H. Stamatis.
        p. cm.
    ISBN 1-56327-292-X
    1. Quality control—Statistical methods.   2. Production management—Statistical methods.   3. Six sigma (Quality control standard)   I. Title.
TS156.S735 2003
658.4'013—dc22

2003017249

06 05 04 03 02   5 4 3 2 1

To
Aristea and Boula

Table of Contents

Chapter 10
Implementing Six Sigma   271

Appendices

Acknowledgments

This volume is the result of encouragement from many friends and colleagues. High on the list of the individuals who started me thinking about writing this one self-contained volume are Dr. Ranjider Kapur and Ms. Janet MacDonald. Their constant reminder of the need for a single volume addressing the general items of the six sigma methodology without the "fluffiness" resulted in the forming of not only the title of the book, but also the content and the glossary.

Mr. Stephen Stamatis for his thorough work with the computer and the generation of the tables on the Poison and binomial distribution, as well as the generation of the traditional sigma (abridged) conversion table—using the METLAB software.

For constructing the forms on the CD, I thank Cary D. Stamatis and Stephen D. Stamatis for their contribution in both designing and drawing the forms.

Drs. R. Munro and E. Rice as always were available to bounce around ideas and content at short notice and eager to suggest approaches for handling the content.

The participants of several seminars through the Detroit section of the American Society of Quality, who gave plenty of suggestions and comments to make this book a reality and more reader friendly.

To my friends Mr. Ron Butler and H. Jamal their loyalty, friendship and constant encouragement to complete this project—for their belief in me.

The editors of the text, Michael Sinocchi and Emily Pillars, whose excellent suggestions made this a better book.

Finally, my family and especially my dearest wife for understanding and putting up with me during this project—especially for the long hours in the "basement office."

Common Abbreviations Used in Six Sigma

Symbol/Acronym	Meaning	Symbol/Acronym	Meaning
ANOVA	Analysis of variance	e	Base of natural logarithm (2.718)
COPQ	Cost of poor quality	μ	Population mean
DFSS	Design for six sigma	Σ	Summation
DOE	Design of experiments	σ	Population standard deviation
Dpm (DPM)	Defects per million	σ^2	Population variance
FMEA	Failure mode and effect analysis		
LCL	Lower control limit	n	Sample size
LSL	Lower specification limit	N	Population size
PSM	Program safety management	p	Probability or sample proportion
ROI	Return on investment	r^2	Sample coefficient of determination
RPN	Risk priority number		
SOP	Standard operating procedure	s	Sample standard deviation
SPC	Statistical process control	s^2	Sample variance
UCL	Upper control limit	$\bar{x}$	Sample mean
USL	Upper specification limit		
MPIW	Mistake proofing improvement worksheet		

Preface

What do we mean by quality products, quality design, and quality improvement? Do we mean

- Fitness for function?
- Customer satisfaction?
- Conformance to design specifications?
- Conformance to requirements?
- Providing products and services that meet customer expectations over the life of the product or service at a cost that represents customer value?

While most of these words sound fine, such definitions have not been very useful in helping us do a better job. Why? Because they are attribute-based. A precise quantitative definition has not been established. In general, they prescribe that something is either in one state or another:

- Good or bad.
- Fine or not fine.
- Defective or nondefective.
- Conforming or nonconforming.

As a result, such definitions are serious inhibitors to continual and never-ending improvement. They are product-based (attribute-based) and comparative—that is, they attempt to compare the product, upon completion of manufacturing, to the input specifications of the manufacturers. As a result, they become static and passive filters through which we attempt to push product. They cannot serve as design criteria. They do not clearly distinguish between product species and product function. Species is a matter of subjective criteria (i.e., color, style, customer preference). Function, on the other hand, is a matter of loss of performance in use (i.e., useful life, power consumption, trouble in field, harmful effects, user friendliness).

A product is sold (gains market) by virtue of its species, function, and price. A product gains or loses reputation (market share) by virtue of its quality. Therefore, quality must be judged through customer loss, as a result of functional variation and harmful effects, when the product is used. Functional variation is the deviation of performance from that intended by engineering design. Harmful effects, on the other hand, are injurious effects encountered during use, which are unrelated to function. For example, if the product is a train that can go 100 miles an hour, and the function is to reduce travel time, the harmful effect might be an uncomfortable ride due to excessive vibration.

Functional variation is manifested in two basic ways:

- Failure to meet the target (average performance).
- Variability of the target (dispersion performance).

This means that the focus in any process is to be on target with the smallest variation. So, the greatest difficulty we have with the meaning of quality centers around our inability to define it in precise and quantitative terms that can then be used as design criteria rather than simply as shipping criteria.

We therefore cannot afford to use concepts and measures of quality that:

- Do not relate the achievement of quality to the engineering design process as a criterion.
- Administer "quality control" through defect detection and containment (i.e., product control).
- Promote improvement only to some acceptable plateau of performance.
- Inhibit the continual pursuit of never ending improvement.
- Have a weak and perhaps an opposing relationship to performance in terms of productivity.
- Have a producer rather than a consumer orientation.

There is a very strong relationship between quality and productivity. Adding improvement building blocks to an ideal industrial system in any arena is possible on an appropriate and sound foundation. Competitive pressures have recently caused many companies to examine the foundations on which their improvement strategies are based.

A competitive position in the marketplace, for both manufacturing and non-manufacturing companies, depends then on two components: quality and productivity. Any improvement strategy should accordingly aim for maximum advancement within these two components and progress may be measured by monitoring such advancements.

For a company to improve its long-term competitive position, it must focus on the process rather than on the product. Appropriately applied, the concepts and techniques embraced by the six sigma methodology help companies to maintain this focus and provide guidance for quality and productivity improvement.

The trilogy balance that guides the six sigma methodology to the improvement levels of 3.4 defects per million are the strategies of technology, people and business. Focusing on any one in particular shifts the balance and suboptimization will occur to the detriment of the entire organization.

This book focuses on the basics of the six sigma methodology. It covers the essential items and selected tools for pursuing excellence without getting bogged down with details. Specifically, on a chapter basis it discusses the following:

- *Chapter 1: Overview of six sigma.* The focus of this chapter is the essential core elements of the six sigma methodology. The chapter outlines what six sigma is and what the key questions or concerns surrounding it are.

- *Chapter 2: Customer satisfaction.* This is the cornerstone of every quality initiative. The aim of this chapter is to clearly explain why customer satisfaction is important and how it relates to six sigma.

- *Chapter 3: The DMAIC model.* This is the core model of six sigma. This chapter explains the process and requirements of this traditional approach to six sigma.

- *Chapter 4: Common methodologies (tools) used in the DMAIC model.* This chapter provides a selected review of tools and methodologies used in the DMAIC model for optimizing customer satisfaction and profitability.

- *Chapter 5: Design for six sigma.* This chapter explains the DCOV model, which is a much more powerful approach than the DMAIC model. It also addresses the process and requirements associated with this approach.

- *Chapter 6: Common methodologies (tools) used in the DCOV model.* This chapter reviews the tools and methodologies used in the DCOV approach for optimizing customer satisfaction and profitability in the design phase of product and service development.

- *Chapter 7: Roles and responsibilities.* This chapter explains who does what, and where they do it. The focus is to summarize the roles and responsibilities of the people directly involved with the six sigma methodology.

- *Chapter 8: Six sigma applied in non-manufacturing.* This chapter discusses the essentials of the non-manufacturing application of six sigma. Addressing the issues and concerns of non-manufacturing in a transactional environment (i.e., businesses that focus on services other than manufacturing—for example, financial, consulting, or engineering firms). An introduction to safety and environmental issues as they relate to how six sigma is also presented.

- *Chapter 9: Training and certification.* The aim of this chapter is to address the issues and concerns of training and certification for six sigma and explain the significance of both.

- *Chapter 10: Implementing six sigma.* This chapter outlines the change process from a traditional organization to a six sigma organization and examines the problems that may be experienced during the implementation process.

The accompanying CD provides the reader with a typical calculation for six sigma capability, a cascading model for identifying the customer's wants, and typical forms that may be used in the course of the six sigma implementation process. These items are of importance to the reader as they provide a cursory view of what it means to have the wants of the customer cascaded to develop the CTCs (critical to customer characteristics).

In addition, the CD includes a glossary of terms and more than 70 forms and tables that the reader may use in the process of developing the six sigma implementation process for their own organization. The forms vary from simple work sheets defining the function, to FMEA forms, to P-diagrams, gage capability and many more.

Introduction

Business methodologies, programs, and disciplines often become fashionable quickly and then drop out of fashion just as quickly. What remains constant is the relationship between people, technology and business strategy. This relationship sometimes favors one at the expense of the other two, even though the goal is always to have a balance among the three.

Rather than review a litany of past programs and methodologies, here are just a few to make the point:

1. The Allen-Bradley pyramid, which represented the structure of a manufacturing enterprise, was basic and easy to remember. It was associated with a great company but was simplistic in its top-to-bottom depiction of corporate/financial, plant, area, cell, and work units. With its clearly defined hierarchy and neatly fitting layers, the pyramid gave many people a sense of security; however, it was a false sense of security offering "good luck" rather than good judgment.

2. The CIM (computer-integrated manufacturing) wheel replaced the pyramid with integrated systems architecture at its hub and the functions and factors of CIM spread out like spokes from the hub to the wheel. It was characterized by arrows of interaction from one function and factor to another that acted as an announcement of the information age in manufacturing. The wheel reflected the great importance of computer hardware and software within the manufacturing process. It heralded the breakdown of walls between manufacturing processes. The most widely known integration in the time of the CIM wheel was between design (CAD) and manufacturing (CAM). The CIM wheel, however, was before the Internet and, like the pyramid, concentrated on manufacturing within the confines of the plant or factory. As the world hurtled toward global manufacturing, global standards, and materials procurement on an international scale, the supply chain concept was fully born.

3. The supply chain concept (SCC) supplanted the CIM wheel for many people. It is interesting to note that within the CIM wheel, there was no acknowledgment of the customer, ware-

housing, procurement, or logistics. The SCC model added a very necessary set of these dimensions. This set contained, on the input side, the supplier and procurement process; on the output side, it added the distribution and customer components. Suddenly we were out of the box—or the building—and dealing with a broadly based process from supplier's supplier to customer's customer. The model also reflected repeated phases of plan, source, make, and deliver. As time went on, it was improved by the tool kit model, which articulated more levels of detail within each zone of activity.

The key shift toward the process of work, coupled with the processing of information relating to critical factors, is easy to recognize. However, this does not come close to creating an image of the actual supply chain process and its core manufacturing function. In the six sigma methodology we talk about the supplier, input, process, output, and customer (SIPOC) model to reflect the importance of this chain.

Once again, six sigma is a methodology that attempts to create harmony between technology, people and business strategy and, at the same time, optimize each of the components with the total organization in mind. To optimize the three, it focuses on the customer and in turn on customer satisfaction. How? By adhering to the following seven principles:

1. *Always do right by the customer.* This will gratify some people and astonish the rest, including the competition. The value of customer satisfaction has been proven in many studies. Doing right by customers is both beneficial and profitable. To do this, we must understand the functionality that the customer is seeking from our products or services.

2. *It is noble to be good, and it is nobler to teach others to be good.* It is imperative that we teach the employees of our organization that keeping existing customers is easier and less expensive than finding new customers. Part of the training must be continual support of customer satisfaction initiatives including, but not limited to, customer recognition.

3. *When in doubt, tell the truth.* Indeed, it is a novel idea. However, unless there is trust in the culture of the organization, there can be no expectation of results. It is of paramount significance that employees should be trained to be truthful, and a simple job aid, for example a procedure guide-

line, may be all that is needed. This may help to remind us that we are all working to please the customer. Without a customer, we have no reason to work!

4. *It is better to listen.* We must be cognizant of the old Spartan saying: "To speak less is a true philosophy." Train your employees to listen to their customers and respond appropriately, keeping in mind that body language may be just as acceptable a response as the verbal kind.

5. *Always set a good example.* Employees and customers both constantly appraise your behavior and performance; the former we hope will emulate it, while the latter will appreciate it and ultimately repay it with more business. Setting standards is always a challenging task; the lack of standards results in failure.

6. *Where possible, a compliment should always precede a complaint.* A compliment softens resentment and ensures a courteous and gentle reception for the complaint. To be sure, we all know that the customer quite often is wrong, unreasonable and difficult to deal with. However, it is not smart to make that distinction immediately. When appropriate, the customer should be retrained to your corporate values. For any change to be successful, the customer must be on your side first.

7. *Do not let schooling interfere with education through experience.* In the final analysis all levels of management are responsible for the success of the organization—they are the ones that have to decide what level of customer satisfaction is required, how to train for it and how to nurture it. It usually requires both knowledge learned in formal education and through real world experiences. The balance between the two depends on the occasion and the specific goal. The truly educated know that education alone is not enough—experience is equally important.

In our modern world, one can see that businesses (manufacturing and non-manufacturing alike) are being put to the test. They must pursue customer satisfaction through quality initiatives, yet at the same time these programs must contribute to the organization's bottom line. Six sigma can help in this initiative, because it focuses on real improvement rather than finding scapegoats for the failures. It forces us to look at actual situations with real potential of improvement for the entire organization rather than the following:

Looking for the next sale. Looking for the next sale as a tactic for organizational survival is a sign of serious trouble. The question "Where are our sales going to come from?" is haunting most companies. While just-in-time deliveries make sense in manufacturing, expecting the next sale to come through the door at just the right moment does not. Unfortunately, too many companies insist on short-circuiting the selling process. All they want is the order. A severe disconnect, such as a terrorist attack or an economic downturn, causes sales to hit the wall, and many companies do not bounce back quickly. Before you can own the customer's wallet, you must own the customer's head. Yet many companies think expert marketing or salesmanship is the solution, and they want to make a sale before they actually have a customer. To gain and sustain the customer, an organization must have a good product or service and satisfied customers.

Deliver on false expectations. The moral here is that we must deliver on trust, or the customer will not follow through on the order. Honda Motors has long recognized that winning customer trust is the key to selling cars. Honda vehicles are very good, but they are not great. They are, however, what millions of consumers want—vehicles that are incredibly trustworthy. Once again, many other companies try to do it backward—they push to build sales before they build customer trust. They fail to recognize that trust keeps customers buying—no matter what the economic environment or competition—because they don't want to risk making the wrong purchase. Even though the economy falters and new competitors like Kia and Hyundai have assaulted its market segment, Honda sales continue to be virtually unaffected. General Motors, DaimlerChrysler and Ford are not as fortunate.

Pull the wool over the customer's eyes. Customers are more sophisticated today than they were in the past, due to the volumes of information accessible to them through the media and the Internet. Customers demand the truth from companies. With the Firestone-Ford tire debacle in 2000, we realized that our lives and those of our families were on the line, and we wanted facts, not corporate PR fluff—a lesson Ford learned far faster than Bridgestone/ Firestone. The 9/11 attacks, the ENRON, Worldcom, Merck, Johnson and Johnson, XEROX and other fiascoes, have only escalated customers' demand for the truth.

Baffle the customer with jargon and fluffiness. Customers are emboldened! Every salesperson has noted that customers have become far more aggressive in the last five years, again coinciding with the Internet's emergence. The 9/11 attacks, however, have brought out America's more serious side. We have all noted the signs—less small talk, a more no-nonsense attitude and an even higher value placed on time. This suggests that we need to probe more when dealing with customers, letting them talk more than we have in the past. Furthermore, companies can enhance the sales process by forgoing the usual corporate marketing materials that can obfuscate the facts, avoid competitor qualities and steer the customer in one direction. Customers want objective and comprehensive information that helps them become more productive.

Postpone any future problems or concerns. Take charge of the future. With the future so uncertain, this may seem like a strange suggestion. However, look at what is happening in business. Management's top priority is to address current issues, such as meeting quotas and stock analysts' (and shareholders') expectations, and trying to outdo the competition. Thinking about the future is not even on the radar screen. Yet, it's the future that fuels the present. To ignore what lies ahead spells trouble for the present. To avoid the disruptions caused by economic contractions and other changes, companies must create a constant, long-term flow of new customers by continually identifying and cultivating prospects. The future can never be known for certain, of course, and unforeseen events will surely arise, but creating a framework for the future is very much in our hands. While some company executives and business owners are panicking, the more astute are taking charge of their destiny.

Six sigma is indeed a methodology that will allow suppliers, organizations and customers to work toward robust products and services giving measurable value to the customer. This value is customer satisfaction and ultimately customer loyalty. However, in order for that satisfaction and loyalty to exist and be consistent, organizations must strive to understand customer functionality so that they can deliver to customer requirements.

Chapter 1

Overview of Six Sigma

Few quality-focused initiatives have generated as much interest and debate as six sigma. This methodology, developed at Motorola, has been adopted by companies such as General Electric, Allied-Signal, Ford Motor Company and others. It is routinely debated in periodicals, and dozens of books, courses and consulting firms promote it. However, many executives, managers and engineers still do not understand what six sigma is or how it can help them.

The basic elements of six sigma are not new—statistical process control, failure mode effects analyses, gage repeatability and reproducibility studies and other tools and methodologies have been in use for some time. Six sigma offers a framework that unites these basic quality tools with high-level management support. The keys to the program's success are the commitment of resources and a rigorous methodology to identify and eliminate sources of variability.

The practitioner of the six sigma methodology in any organization should expect to see the use of old and established tools and approaches in the pursuit of continual improvement and customer satisfaction. So much so that even TQM (total quality management) is revisited as a foundation of some of the approaches. In fact, one may define six sigma as "TQM on steroids." However, it must be emphasized over and over again that the difference between the established quality initiatives and six sigma is the packaging of the tools, the systematic implementation of the tools, a commitment to extensive training and, perhaps the most important ingredient of them all, the commitment of the executives in the organization. This commitment is quite unique—quality initiatives in the past have been identified and promoted but were never made available to the boardrooms of American organizations, until the six sigma.

It is this presence in the boardroom that has made the difference, because suddenly we are all looking at specific ROI (return on investment) that can help the organization through specialized projects. This is indeed a new approach.

However, what is six sigma? In the narrow statistical sense, six sigma is a quality objective that identifies the variability of a process in terms of the specifications of the product, so that product quality and reliability meet and exceed today's demanding customer requirements. Specifically, six sigma refers to a process capability that generates 3.4 defects per million opportunities. Most organizations today operate in the four-to-five sigma range (6,000–67,000 defects per million opportunities); moving to six sigma is a challenge. The DMAIC (define, measure, analyze, improve and control) process is the key to achieving this breakthrough improvement in performance. It is a nonlinear process—if any step yields new information, earlier steps in the process must be reevaluated.

Successful use of the data-driven six sigma concepts helps organizations to eliminate waste, hidden rework and undesirable variability in their processes, resulting in quality and cost improvements, driving continued success. The following sections examine the six sigma methodology in detail.

What are the most important ingredients in the six sigma methodology?

To successfully implement the six sigma methodology, executives and practitioners in the organization must have the following characteristics:

- *A realistic outlook*. We all have a tendency to avoid reality, so we try many things in the name of problem-solving, but realistically we are not accomplishing very much. Six sigma is a data-driven methodology that helps the organization to see the true picture and act accordingly. In other words, it helps us to identify and accept good as well as bad results. It forces us to be realistic.

- *A positive approach.* Six sigma encourages us to try something risky before complaining about it.
- *The habit of questioning the status quo.* Action does not take place unless something changes. Unless you question the way things are done today, you are unlikely to devise ways of doing them better in the future. It is that simple.
- *Flexibility.* Dealing successfully with change requires flexibility. Six sigma is a drastic change on many fronts, but perhaps the most important one is the notion of making decisions on data. (Data is the engine that makes six sigma what it is.)
- *The desire to follow up.* Although in the six sigma methodology the ability to delegate is one hallmark of effective management, it does not end there. At some point delegation must be succeeded by some kind of follow-up for best results. Managers must remember that good plans by themselves do not ensure good results, that the job that gets followed-up is less apt to get fouled up.

What are the goals of six sigma?

Among the many goals of this methodology, six stand out:
- Reduce defects.
- Improve yield.
- Improve customer satisfaction.
- Reduce variation.
- Ensure continual improvement.
- Increase shareholder value.

In some organizations the concept of "defect" has many legal ramifications, therefore the term "non-conformance" may be substituted.

What is the typical methodology of six sigma?

There are several approaches to six sigma. The three predominant ones are:
- *The Motorola approach.* Motorola was the first company to develop the methodology and they focused on six steps:
  1. Identifying the product you create or the service you provide.
  2. Identifying the customers for your product or service and determining what they consider important.

3. Identifying your needs (i.e., to provide products or services that satisfy the customer).

4. Defining the process for doing the work.

5. Mistake-proofing the process and eliminating wasted effort.

6. Ensuring continual improvement by measuring, analyzing and controlling the improved process.

- *The Six Sigma Academy approach.* This is the first commercially accepted methodology of six sigma, with minor variations, from the original Motorola approach. Indeed, it is the first six sigma methodology to which most organizations were exposed early in the life of the methodology. It is a simple, popular and straightforward approach. It focuses on four major phases:

1. Measure.

2. Analyze.

3. Improve.

4. Control.

- *The General Electric approach.* General Electric was the company that continued the progress of Motorola and standardized the methodology. GE's approach has become the de facto approach of most organizations with some very small variations. GE focused on the following five steps, which together make up the DMAIC model:

1. Define—identify the improvement opportunity.
2. Measure—account for the current performance.
3. Analyze—evaluate the primary contributors.
4. Improve—enhance the operation or process.
5. Control—regulate (verify) the improved operation or process.

Yet another approach to six sigma is the understanding that improvement may be attained in current and future products and services. As a result of this thinking, design for six sigma (DFSS) came to be an addition to the traditional approach. The traditional approach is the DMAIC model and the define, characterize, optimize, verify (DCOV) is the newer addition.

Where did six sigma begin?

Six sigma started as an improvement program at Motorola in 1982. At the time, Motorola needed new analytical tools to help reduce costs and improve quality. As a result, the initial six sigma tools were developed. In the meantime, General Electric started to use them (with some modifications) in 1995. Since then, other companies such as Polaroid, DuPont, Crane, Ford Motor Company, American Express, Nokia and others have followed.

Is six sigma a problem-solving methodology?

The simple answer is that six sigma is a very formal, systematic approach to solving problems. It follows a somewhat generic pattern. However, it takes a more holistic approach for the entire organization. Rather than sub-optimizing the solution to a specific problem or concern, it forces the experimenter to see the whole solution and its effects. The problem-solving approach that six sigma takes is basically:

- *Defining the problem.* Listing and prioritizing problems, defining the project and the team.
- *Diagnosing the problem.* Analyzing the symptoms, formulating theories of causes, testing these theories, and identifying root causes.
- *Remedying the problem.* Considering alternative solutions, designing solutions and controls, addressing resistance to implementation, implementing solutions and controls.
- *Holding the gains.* Checking performance and monitoring the control system.

What exactly is six sigma?

Sigma (σ) is the Greek letter associated with standard deviation. However, in six sigma it takes on various definitions and interpretations, such as, a metric of comparison, a benchmark comparison, a vision, a philosophy, a methodological approach, a symbol, a specific value, or a goal. All of these present the holistic definition of what six sigma can do, but none of them accurately depict what six sigma really means. This convoluted explanation has contributed to the confusion of a standard definition, and that is why there are so many different interpretations.

In simple terms, six sigma engages each employee of the organization from the top executive to the employee on the manufacturing or service floor. It focuses on quality improvement, cost reduction, cycle time reduction and improved delivery performance. This results in higher profits and customer satisfaction. It also improves the relationship between the management and employees. Consistency of quality at all levels of the organization is easy through the use of common metrics that compare the quality of both technical and transactional processes. In addition, this powerful approach to improvement focuses on critical to customer (CTC) characteristics. The CTC is the first step of understanding in pursuing the six sigma methodology. It all starts with the functionality that the customer is seeking from either a product or a service. The more we understand this functionality (the Y in the six sigma equation $Y = f(x)$, which is discussed later in this chapter), the more accurate will be our focus on the variables that control this functionality (the $F(x)$). However, we must not forget that this methodology is an approach that has borrowed many systems, tools and best practices from previous approaches and has combined them in a bundle called six sigma. It is precisely this bundle of tools and methodologies, in addition to the management commitment and overall attitude change, that has contributed to why the six sigma approach may be applied to every process in any organization.

Finally, six sigma integrates technology, company assets, management and employees with continual improvement practices such as:

- Project management.
- Team problem-solving.
- Statistical process control.
- Measurement system assessment.
- Process FMEA (Failure Mode and Effect Analysis).
- Mistake-proofing.
- Team-building.
- Applied statistics.
- Design of experiments.
- Cost of quality.
- Process mapping.
- Product reliability and other disciplines.

What are the major objectives in the six sigma methodology?

In the six sigma methodology there are three broad levels of objectives. They are:

- *Problem-solving.* These are fixes of specific areas.

- *Strategic improvement.* These are targets of key strategic or operational weakness or opportunity.
- *Business transformation.* This is a major shift in how the organization works (i.e., a culture change).

Is six sigma another quality fad?

This is a very difficult question to answer. Many professionals and practitioners have opinions about the status of the six sigma methodology. For example, five years ago, there were consultants who thought that the life cycle of six sigma would be about 10 years. There are other consultants who claim that six sigma is going to be here for good, but will be constantly adapting. Regardless of the long-term outcome, the systematic approach of the six sigma methodology can indeed produce results. The fact that upper management has embraced it shows that commitment, at least for now, is strong and, therefore, it offers the possibility of longevity.

Is six sigma compatible with other methodologies and tools?

Six sigma is extremely compatible with other quality initiatives that may already be in place in an organization. It has the capacity to be implemented as a macro and in the micro level of an organization. More important, it can be successful with both elementary graphical tools as well as very advanced statistical tools.

What are the levels of responsibility in a typical six sigma organization?

In a typical organization, the levels of responsibility are:

- Executives, who authorize and follow up the program.
- Champions, who mediate resources and eliminate roadblocks for the projects.
- Master black belts, who are the technical resource and experienced in the six sigma methodology.
- Black belts, who are the project managers for the project.
- Green belts, who are the helpers of the black belts in the work environment.

More is discussed regarding these levels in chapter 7. However, it is very important to note that the essential participants of any six sigma implementation process are the black belt and the green belt.

Their role is extremely important, so here we identify the core minimum requirements for each of the roles.

The green belt must be familiar with and competent in the following concepts:

- The six sigma approach.
- Basic statistical process control.
- Classical design of experiments.
- Basic measurement system assessment.
- Statistical analysis for process improvement.
- Process FMEA.
- Team problem-solving.
- Cost of quality.

In addition to the requirements of the green belt, the black belt
must have expertise in the following areas:

- Advanced statistical process control.
- Taguchi and classical design of experiments.
- Advanced measurement system assessment.
- Project management fundamentals.
- Short run SPC.
- Mistake-proofing.
- Lean manufacturing.
- Advanced product quality planning (APQP).

Is it the intent of the six sigma methodology to reduce the number of employees in the organization?

Strictly speaking, not at all. The intent of the methodology is to
reduce variation and to increase the profitability of the organization. However, if in the scope of the project too many employees
are identified, then perhaps re-engineering the process could cause
reduction in the work force.

Can six sigma be applied equally to both manufacturing and non-manufacturing organizations?

Yes. Six sigma methodology may be introduced to any organization
that deals with processes, variation and customer complaints.

How long does it take to implement a six sigma program in a typical organization?

For the organization to be following the six sigma methodology, a critical mass must be present. Critical mass is when enough personnel have been trained to carry out the methodology of six sigma in the organization. The initial steps are to select key individuals for black belt training and then progressively train more employees until there are enough trained individuals to attack problems throughout the organization. Some organizations have not recuperated their costs within two to three years. On the other hand, some have claimed that the payoff of implementation came in less than a year.

Is there anything that can derail the six sigma methodology?

Successful six sigma implementation is an issue of understanding and support. If we are not careful to generate that understanding and provide that support, the methodology is not only not going to be implemented successfully in the organization, but it is also going to leave a bad taste. There are many things that can derail the process. Some of the key ones are:

- Success is not fast enough, so the organization gives up.
- There is no priority for selected projects.
- Too many projects are identified and the methodology is overloaded, so no results are apparent.
- Undoable objectives and timelines are established and the organization expects the methodology to deliver results from the impossible.
- Past experience is ignored, including organizational cultural issues. Unless the organization recognizes the shortcomings of the past and is willing to address new cultural objectives, the six sigma methodology will fail.
- The organization lacks flexibility; it must be prepared for the unexpected. Interruptions will occur, but organizers should not give up, instead, they should focus on the goal and target of the improvement.
- The organization doesn't devote enough resources and/or training to the project. Without a commitment for personnel, training and other appropriate resources, the six sigma transformation will not be successful.

- False euphoria—that is, the tendency to think that you reached six sigma prematurely (usually after the first or second completed project)—leads to less attention paid to six sigma, less follow-up, and fewer benefits achieved.

What does the "1.5σ shift" mean?

Without getting into a statistical and lengthy discussion on what the famous "shift" is, let us say that all processes produce variations over time. In the six sigma methodology (at least in the electronics industry), it was empirically validated that the shift of the distribution was about 1.5σ. This does not mean that with all processes, and in all industries, this shift is always within this ±1.5σ. It does vary. For example, in the automotive industry we know, at least since 1980, that the shift is ±1σ and not ±1.5σ. Convention now has it that everyone follows the 1.5σ. One may simplify the interpretation of the shift as a drift of the process in the long term.

What is the difference between 3σ and 6σ?

Most companies have been following a standard of performance for ±3σ. There is nothing wrong with ±3σ for certain products and certain industries. However, there is a tremendous difference between ±3σ and ±6σ. For example, a ±3σ capability accounts for 93.32 percent long-term yield (this is the historical standard for most organizations). By comparison, a ±4σ accounts for 99.38 percent long-term yield (this is a standard that some organizations operate currently). If an organization wants to account for 99.99966 percent long-term yield, then the move to ±6σ is inevitable. When the ±6σ philosophy is implemented, expect your organization to perform at 3.4 defects per million opportunities. That is truly a breakthrough in performance! The percentages presented here have been adjusted for the long-term shift.

What is the DMAIC model?

The DMAIC model is the official methodology for the six sigma problem resolution approach. It stands for define, measure, analyze, improve, control. Fundamentally, the model helps in the following:

- Knowing what is important to the customer.
- Identifying the target.
- Minimizing variation.
- Reducing concerns.

Chapter 3 is devoted to explaining this model.

What is the DCOV model?

The DCOV model is the official model methodology design for six sigma. It stands for define, characterize, optimize and verify. Fundamentally, the model helps in the following:

- Defining what the customer needs, wants and expects.
- Defining the specifications for those needs, wants and expectations.
- Optimizing the specifications for the specific needs, wants and expectations.
- Verifying that the needs, wants and expectations are indeed what the customer wanted.

Chapter 5 is devoted to looking at this model in depth.

Is there a real difference between the DMAIC and DCOV models?

Yes, the DMAIC model focuses on appraising quality—it identifies and then tries to "fix" the problem. One may say it is a formal approach to solving problems when they occur. On the other hand, the DCOV model is a proactive approach trying to prevent problems from happening. The DCOV model would give a better return on investment and better customer satisfaction.

What does the $Y = f(x)$ expression mean?

In simple mathematical terms, this means that the Y is a function of x. In plain language, it means that changes in the x (i.e., inputs and processes) will determine how the Y (i.e., the output) will turn out. In the six sigma methodology the Y may mean profits, customer satisfaction, strategic goal, efficiency and so on. On the other hand, the x may mean actions that achieve the strategic goals, influences on customer satisfaction, process variables and so on. Another way of thinking about this equation is to think of the Y as the dependent variable and the x as the independent variable.

What does the $Y = f(x,n)$ expression mean?

In simple mathematical terms this means that the Y is a function of x and n. In plain language it means that changes in the x (inputs and processes) and some noise (n) will determine what will happen to the Y. (Noise means factors that are uncontrollable or that the experimenter chooses not to control.) In the six sigma methodology, the Y may mean any company aim, such as profits, customer satisfaction, strategic goal and efficiency. The x may mean actions that are important enough in the presence of noise that achieve the strategic goals, influences customer satisfaction, processes variables and so on. The n is a noise that is present in the process, however, it does not effect the x in any significant way. This is called the principle of robustness. Finally, the formula $Y = f(x,n)$ is used primarily in the DFSS approach of the methodology

Is six sigma just a version of TQM or another cost-efficiency program?

TQM principles are scattered throughout the six sigma methodology and one will have a difficult time separating the two. We like to think that the six sigma methodology is TQM on steroids, primarily because it uses the tools and approaches of TQM, but it takes them one step further, in terms of effectiveness, analysis and profitability. As for six sigma being just another cost-efficiency program—that is not quite accurate. Cost of quality is used through the six sigma methodology, as well as a cost/benefit analysis. However, both of these devices play a much greater role than other tools/devices in the context of the total organization and the optimization of the particular process under evaluation. The efficiency through cost is optimized through the elimination of the hidden factory (see the next question).

What is the hidden factory?

The hidden factory is the hidden cost of a process, due to unaccounted and unrelated costs associated with the standard process. Examples are inspection, delays, rework, and extra processing. The hidden factory deals with throughput in the process and tries to calculate the probability of an item passing through the process the first time without any defects. Anything else is a loss, and therefore should be counted as the hidden factory.

What does the equation Q x A = E have to do with six sigma?

This equation was introduced first by Eckes (2001, p. 3) and refers to the acceptance of the methodology within organizations. It means: Q = quality of the technical and strategic six sigma activities; A = cultural acceptance, and E = excellence of the six sigma results.

In relation to this success, we must also be cognizant of the change and paradigm shift. In other words, we must be aware that the acceptance is a function of how we see our future. In an earlier work (Stamatis 1996, p. 52), I pointed out that, to want to bring about a change, you must be dissatisfied with the way things are right now and have a positive vision of the future following such change. This may be shown with the mathematical equation of $D \times V \times F > R$ where: D = dissatisfaction with the current situation, V = vision of a better future, F = the first step of a plan to convert D to V, and R = resistance to change.

What is the SIPOC model?

Traditionally, in the quality field we talk about a process model which is the input, process and output. In the six sigma methodology we talk about SIPOC. SIPOC is a variation of the process model—supplier, inputs, process, output and customer. It is through this model and process mapping that we identify the hidden factory and throughput yield. Throughput yield is the probability that all defect opportunities produced at a particular step in the process will conform to their respective performance standards. Roled throughput yield is the probability of being able to pass a unit of product or service through the entire process defect-free. These definitions of course, have to be understood in light of a) the normalized yield which can be thought of as the average throughput yield result one would expect at any given step of the process b) first time yield, which measures how well companies process units and c) final yield which reports on the proportion of product or service units that pass inspection. In other words, it tells us what we did. The reader may want to see item 75 in the CD for an example.

What is defects per opportunity (DPO)?

Defects per opportunity is the proportion of non-conformities (defects) within the total number of opportunities in a particular unit. For example, 43 errors (defects) were found in reviewing 445 leasing contracts. There are 5 items that present themselves as possible errors. In other words, the reviewer must make sure that these 5 items are correct. The DPO can be calculated as: 43/445x5 = .019 DPO. The opportunity has to be correlated with the critical to quality (CTQ) requirement. The CTQ characteristic is closely related to the customer, and it is this relationship that we want to maximize, free of any defects. A caution is necessary here. The opportunity identified and calculated can have a direct impact on the sigma value. Therefore, make sure that the opportunity identified and evaluated is the same before and after the analysis, otherwise the experimenter may be comparing apples and apricots.

What is defects per million opportunity (DPMO)?

This is the classic standard measure of the six sigma methodology, which indicates how many defects would arise if there were one million opportunities. It is calculated as:

DPMO = 1,000,000 x (total defects) / (total opportunities)

In our example from the previous question the
DPMO $= 106 \times .019 = 19,000$

What are the CTX (process) and CTY (product) trees?

CT stands for critical to, and this characteristic is always a function of the $Y = f(x)$, where Y is the product requirement that impacts quality delivery or cost, and $f(x)$ is one of the vital few process variables that can influence the Y. Another way to view this relationship is to think of Y as the dependent variable and x as the independent variables (factors) that define Y. In other words, as the experimenter defines and understands the x or multiple xs, the better the chance that the Y will be understood, controlled or predicted. On the other hand, CTY is a visual representation of the individual levels of the product. It must be remembered that both the CTX and CTY trees give the opportunity to select the strategy for improvement. Whereas the CTY will help in the area of defect opportunity, the CTX will help in controlling the opportunities in the process. Therefore, it is imperative that we understand both trees, as they will guide us to better results in our analysis. For example, if we consider the Ys and Xs involved in a good meal the CTY and CTX trees will look like: A good meal = Y = service, quality, price, location, ambiance and so on. Now if we take the quality of food as our new Y then we have. Quality of food as the new Y= freshness, wait time for meal, preparation, presentation and so on. On the CD we also have a similar example of cascading the requirements.

What is the significance of the project?

The aim of the six sigma methodology is improvement in specific projects, authorized by the management, which black belts attack with the intention to remove the "specific" problem. The project has to be worth pursuing with regard to ROI, as well as customer satisfaction. The project is the lifeblood of the entire methodology, and it requires very rigorous investigation, analysis, implementation and follow-up to make sure that the gains claimed become gains realized. It usually follows this pattern:

- Develop the problem statement.
- Determine the problem objective.
- Determine the COPQ parameters.
- Identify CTQ and operational definitions.
- Determine which tools should be used to measure the current status and to prioritize the input variables that contribute to the problem as defined.
- Validate improvement to determine the relationship of $Y = f(x...)$.
- Institutionalize the results in such a way that the gains are sustained.

A suitable project may be identified in various ways. However, the main factors that make a project a suitable candidate for six sigma are that it has:

- Recurring events.
- Narrow scope.
- Available metrics or measurements that can be developed quickly.
- Control of the process.
- Customer satisfaction.
- An annual cost savings target of 250K.

For the project to be effective there are two issues of concern: the project objective and the problem statement. The project objective provides a clear macro statement of the problem. This allows the process owner and team members to focus on what needs to be improved (Y variables). Team members should be specific about the defect, but not include possible solutions. A useful problem statement must have the condition, the criteria, and the measurement. For example, product returns will be reduced to 4% of sales, resulting in a profit impact of $4 million and customer dissatisfaction of 5 percent decrease in the next 12 months.) The problem statement states the goal(s) of the project. It also links to the business objectives through expected output variable performance, ROI impact and project timing. It is important to use enough detail to define success.

What is the cost of poor quality (COPQ)?

The costs of poor quality are the items that drive the project's ROI improvement. Typical examples may be the cost of scrap, the cost differential of reduced quality material, headcount reduction, and transportation costs, both to receive defective products and to send new.

What is customer and CTQ identification?

The customer is typically the one who dictates your output specifications (Y's in the statement $Y = f(x)$). That is why it is very important to specify project customers (and to prioritize if there are more than one). In other words, the more you know about the customer's needs, wants and expectations, the more precise and accurate the project requirements will be to satisfy them. Customers may be internal or external. In conjunction with the appropriate customer, it is imperative that we also specify and operationally define the project in terms of critical to quality (CTQ) and variable measurements. This means that the more we know about the customer's needs, wants and expectations, the more we can align our project to satisfy the CTQ requirements as well as focus on variable measurements for evaluating our success

What is the significance of a data collection plan?

Data is the driving force for any analysis. Therefore, it is important to know and identify a data plan, explaining what data you will need to collect and how you will collect it. Without appropriate and applicable data, project results may be questionable.

Is six sigma related to Deming's philosophy?

Yes, very much so. Deming, through his fourteen obligations for top management, communicated the need for improvement of quality, productivity, and competitive position. For the list of the fourteen points see the glossary.

It is very important to recognize that, even though Deming never mentions six sigma, he was very well attuned to the benefits of ever-improving quality. Deming also wrote about some of the negative forces that would stop an organization from embracing the fourteen points and the notion of continual improvement, in general. He called them the seven deadly sins and they are:

- Lack of constancy of purpose.
- Emphasis on short-term profits.
- Evaluation of performance, merit rating or annual review.
- Mobility of management.
- Management by use of visible figures.
- Excessive medical costs.
- Excess costs of liability.

These deadly sins are the same as the deadly sins for the six sigma initiative. Any one of these can torpedo six sigma beyond repair.

In six sigma, there is much talk about quality needs and over-all strategic plans. What does this mean?

In order for six sigma to survive, quality needs and overall strategic plans must exist in the organization. That is, there must be a system established in the organization to address the following:

- *The link between quality function needs and overall strategic plan.* Perhaps this is the most important issue in six sigma, but also in any endeavor that tries to address improvement of any kind. The focus here is on the quality function needs and the plan to support these needs, both now and in the future. Of course, these needs have to be in line with organizational aims, policies and plans. Some key considerations are: competition, cost, differentiation of product and usage of appropriate tools.

- *The link between strategic plan and quality plan.* The second most important issue in six sigma methodology is to correlate the strategic plans with an actual quality plan. That means that the organization either has, or is willing to develop, programs that deal with feedback, corrective action, data collection, processing and analysis and process and product development. In addition, it means that the organization has, or is willing to develop, an infrastructure to address such issues as organization, administrative support, control processes, internal audits, processes that identify customer needs and policies for inspection and testing.

- *The theory of variation (common and special causes).* It is beyond the scope of this book to have a lengthy discussion on variation.

However, it is imperative that common (inherent) variation and special (assignable) variation are clearly understood. We associate common variation with random, material, prevalent, or normal variation; stable process; predictability; and process improvement through management intervention. On the other hand, we associate special variation with abnormal activity, unpredictability; and specific knowable causes. To understand variation we must also understand the components of variation: total variation = variation due to factor A + variation due to factor B + variation due to interaction AB + variation due to sampling error. Typical examples of common variation are:

- Slight variation in raw material.
- Slight machine vibration.
- Lack of human perfection.
- Variation in gage readings.
- Variation in tooling.
- Variation in operator skills.

- Special cause variations include:
  - Difference in machines or processes.
  - Batch of defective raw material.
  - Faulty machine setup.
  - Test equipment out of calibration.
  - Unqualified operator.
  - Part-time seasonal help.
  - Variable work force.

- Sometimes, it is possible to have variation due to a combination of both types, for example:
  - Major recession.
  - Equipment failure.
  - Price roll-back.
  - Employee downsizing.

- Some typical problems that the six sigma methodology may tackle, which confirm Deming's intuitive knowledge about variation and system thinking, include:
  - Poor design of product.
  - Poor instruction and poor supervision.
  - Failure to measure the effects of common causes and to reduce them.

- Failure to provide the production workers with information in a statistical form.
- Procedures not suited to the requirements.
- Machines not suited to the requirements.
- Settings of the machines chronically inaccurate.
- Poor lighting.
- Vibration.
- Mixing product from streams of production.
- Uncomfortable working conditions.
- Shift of management's emphasis from quality to quantity.
- Management's failure to face the problem of inherited defective material.

- The quality function mission is very important in strategic planning. The focus here is to make sure that the mission is aligned with the business strategy of the organization. In other words, the goal should be to establish an organizational mission statement in clear and simple language, so that it is understood by everyone in the organization (and by others) and so that the key driving forces to achieve customer satisfaction are identified in such a way that improvement must begin with:
  - Establishing priorities.
  - Defining organizational policies.
  - Analyzing trade-offs to resolve conflict with cost, delivery dates and other parameters. Maintaining continual improvement activity.

To appreciate even further the power and influence of the mission, let us look at its hierarchy:

- *The mission.* This is the broad policy of what the organization is existing for. The focus is on defining the quality mission and policy and providing quality awareness in the organization. It also involves setting goals to meet the mission, training and team concepts; measuring mission accomplishments, and determining the mission's relationship with vision, values and goals.
- *The vision.* This is made up of the key processes that assist in fulfilling this mission.
- *The values.* These are the key indicators to affirm the vision and the mission.

♦ *The goals*. The goals provide reinforcement to accomplish the mission.

In the context of the six sigma methodology, it is imperative to recognize that no organization can function without some (written or unwritten) quality principles and policies. So management must champion, if not outright, the key principles and policies for the entire organization. Typical issues are:

♦ The need for quality principles and the right policies (creed, beliefs, truths, rules, moral and ethical standards as they relate to the uniqueness of the organization's history, management and state of development).

♦ Appropriate approval from executive management (practiced by everyone).

♦ Participation by key managers.

♦ Understanding the need for customer relations (internal and external).

♦ Understanding the need for continual improvement.

♦ Understanding that everyone should be involved and concerned.

♦ Understanding the importance of quality.

♦ Understanding the importance of planning and organization.

• *The metrics and goals that drive organizational performance.* We cannot talk about performance in the abstract. Performance is always the result of a function. Therefore, for performance to be of value, the organization must have metrics and goals. The goals should be attainable, realistic, measurable and related to customer usage. The metrics, on the other hand, must be identified as real measures for these goals. Do not be afraid to take a risk if the risk is commensurable with the anticipated benefit. Fundamental requirements used as metrics may be the following items

♦ Customer satisfaction.

♦ The voice of the customer.

♦ Economic ramifications.

♦ Environmental and legal impact.

♦ Worthiness.

♦ Applicability.

A visual representation of the link between metrics and goals may be seen in Figure 1.1.

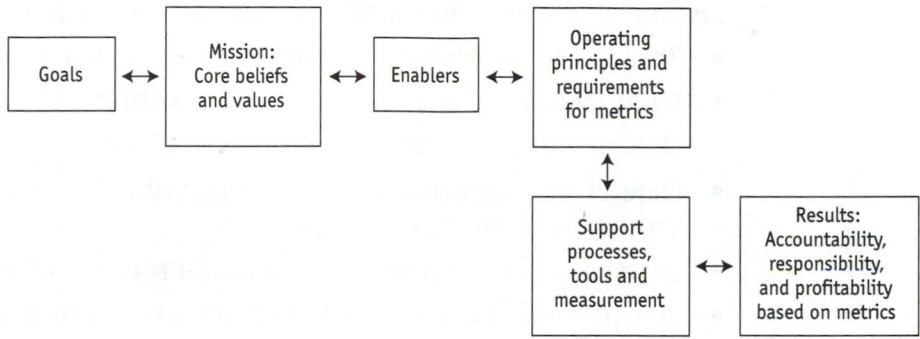

Figure 1.1 Links of metrics and goals

- Resource requirements to manage the quality function. The last item in strategic planning is resources. It must be recognized and understood that a typical organization embracing the six sigma philosophy requires everyone directly involved to be appropriately trained, especially at the managerial levels. So the issues associated with resource requirements are quite important for the organization. Typical items of concern are:
  - ♦ Appropriate and applicable training.
  - ♦ Knowledgeable personnel.
  - ♦ Adequate leadership commitment.
  - ♦ Inspection and testing availability.
  - ♦ Work performance personnel.
  - ♦ Verification capability.

How is robustness incorporated into the six sigma methodology?

Robustness is an issue of both design and process. The aim is to identify factors that are important enough in the presence of noise so that satisfaction is the result. A typical strategy for robustness is to:

- Change the technology to be robust.
- Make basic current design assumptions insensitive to noise.
- Reduce or remove the noise factors.
- Insert a compensation device.
- Send the error state or noise somewhere else where it will be less harmful—in other words, disguise the effect.

What are some of the common formulas used in six sigma?

In addition to the statistical formulas, there are some basic formulas that everyone should be familiar with. They are:

- Proportion defective = [number of defectives]/[number of units].
- Final yield (noted as Y_{final}) = 1 – Proportion defective.
- Defects per unit (DPU) = [number of defects]/number of units].
- Defects per opportunity (DPO) = [number of defects]/number of units $\times$ number of opportunities].
- Defects per million opportunities (DPMO) = DPO $\times$ 1,000,000.
- first pass yield = 1 – [number of units reworked]/[number of units input].

References

Eckes, G. *Making Six Sigma Last*. New York: John Wiley & Sons, 2001.

Stamatis, D. H. *Total Quality Service*. Delray Beach, FL: St. Lucie Press, 1996.

Selected Bibliography

Pande, P. S., L. Holp, and P. Pande. *What Is Six Sigma?* New York: McGraw-Hill, 2001.

Stamatis, D. H. *Six Sigma and Beyond: Foundations of Excellent Performance*. Boca Raton, FL: St. Lucie Press, 2002.

Chapter 2

Customer Satisfaction

Perhaps the strongest argument for using the six sigma methodology is the notion of customer satisfaction. It is the driving force behind the improvement initiative of excellence. Customer satisfaction is created through knowledge of the customer, overall customer service systems, responsiveness and the ability to meet all customer requirements and expectations.

The basic aim of a quality process is to consistently improve value to customers. To identify this value we must also identify the types of customer. A customer is someone who is influenced by the product (goods or service). Therefore, within any company there are departments and personnel (i.e., internal customers) that supply products or services to each other. If the service to internal customers is unsatisfactory, it is unlikely that the expectations of external customers will be met. External customers are the clients who buy the product or service. Products or services may be sold to end users by intermediaries, such as dealers, retail stores, distributors and so on, thus determining the ultimate customer. Organizations should take into account both intermediaries and end users when defining their customers.

Knowing customer expectations and priorities is essential in product development. Product development translates customer expectations for functional requirements into specific engineering and quality characteristics. This means starting with a desired product and then identifying the necessary characteristics for raw materials, parts, assemblies and process steps.

Two of the most common techniques for documenting the voice of the customer in their own terms are the Kano model and quality function deployment (QFD). Whereas the Kano model allows us to identify and differentiate the basic, performance and excitement items that the customer perceives as important, QFD is a specific technique consisting of a series of interlocking matrices that translate customer functionality into product or service or process characteristics. Specifically, QFD provides a systematic methodology that helps the organization to:

- Thoroughly translate customer functionalities into requirements.
- Prioritize those requirements.
- Benchmark characteristics against competition and best practices.
- Decide how to meet or exceed the requirements by incorporating those features into the product, process or service.

If the appropriate and applicable definition of quality, as it relates to customer expectations, is not introduced early in the concept or design phase, there is a risk that the customer will recognize this lack of quality in the market place and not be satisfied. Because the maintenance of quality is so important, it is imperative that management must continually review the process. This means that management must always be aware of the company's interactions and relationships with the customers, including how the information gained from customers is used to improve products, processes or services. Management must also be familiar with the process by which the organization manages its customer relationships. Management can do this by:

- Ensuring easy access for customers to seek assistance, to comment and to complain.
- Following up with customers on products to determine satisfaction with recent transactions, to seek feedback and to help build relationships.
- Creating customer-contact employees. This involves selecting employees and providing them with special training so they have complete knowledge of a specific product and are empowered to make decisions regarding the product and the customer.

They must also be given the technology and logistics support necessary for them to offer reliable and responsive service satisfaction to the customer.

- Analyzing feedback and complaint data for policy development, planning and resource allocations. In other words, a commitment to customers by the organization:
  - ♦ To promote trust and confidence in its product, even when failure occurs.
  - ♦ To make sure they are free from unusual conditions or exceptions.
  - ♦ To be open and honest in communications.
  - ♦ To improve on competitors' commitment.

Why put such emphasis on customer satisfaction in the six sigma methodology? Because, as we remove the dissatisfaction, we decrease variation, and thereby increase profitability. However, what is the source of dissatisfaction? Simply stated, it is a complaint. It is the recognition of a breakdown in quality. The complaint may concern the product or it may concern other activities, such as incorrect invoicing or the shipment of incorrect goods. As the number of complaints increases, a systematic approach from a centralized location to register all complaints, summarize the complaints and route the complaint to the concerned department must be put in place. The information gained should be viewed as feedback, and appropriate and applicable action should be taken to fix the problems. To enable customers to comment freely on an organization's products, processes, or services, the organization should have a company representative visit each customer frequently, or ask the customer for feedback at frequent intervals. The key is to make sure that feedback is easy for the customer to provide. Typical ways in which to do this are to:

- Provide personnel with well designed standard data sheets for easy and accurate recording of complaints.
- Provide incentives to customers to encourage adequate feedback.
- Provide a glossary of terms to improve communications and code numbers to simplify the data entry analysis.
- Provide training in how to do something and why it is being done.
- Conduct audits of the feedback process to identify and eliminate any roadblocks customers may encounter when giving feedback.

- Use technology to collect the field information (data) from the customer and to provide the appropriate and applicable analysis and summaries to managers, so that they can make optimum decisions.
- Make use of the *sample* concept.
- Make use of the *control* concept.

Furthermore, information about customer satisfaction may be obtained through warranty records. A warranty is a form of assurance that a product, process, or service is fit for use or, failing this, that the user will receive some kind of compensation. In most situations there are two kinds of warranties: a general warranty of merchantability—that is, fitness for the customary use of the product—and a special warranty for a specific use of the product, provided the seller knows these special conditions.

These special conditions may be defined through:

- The comprehensiveness of warranty coverage.
- The terms and conditions of warranties, including exclusions.
- The clarity and understandability of written warranties. Both the legal jargon and fine print (footnotes) should be kept to a minimum.
- How customers value the extra commitments the organization makes for customer satisfaction.
- How the organization compares to competitors or best class leaders.
- How innovative the organization's effort to show its commitment to the customer is.

Written guarantees are helpful to both the customer and supplier. They protect the buyer by setting out the seller's obligations to the customer and they protect the seller by clearly stating the limit of the seller's obligation.

In addition to feedback and warranties, an organization can better know its customers by using a proper and applicable segmentation strategy. The organization should first identify and list its current and potential customers (some organizations differentiate this by calling them "customer" and "consumer" respectively.) The next step is to divide the customer group (consisting of all the current and potential customers) into different market segments. While it is true that all of the customers have some common requirements and expectations about the products, those in different markets have their own unique requirements as well. For example, if more than half of your business comes from the automotive industry and the rest from many other different types of industries, it might make sense to segment your customer into two groups: automotive and non-automotive. Once this differentiation has taken place, each customer group can be considered unique. The following are important elements to consider during the segmentation process:

- The thoroughness of the process used in identifying market segments and potential customers.
- The degree to which customer requirements have been identified for each market segment.
- The identification of the common and unique requirements and expectations for each market segment.
- The frequency of data collection for each market segment.

As you can see, customer understanding and satisfaction are of great interest and importance to every organization. However, those organizations' suppliers also play a major role in customer satisfaction. The relationship obviously varies from adversarial to supporting and everything else in between, but the fact remains that unless organizations have a good relationship with their supplier base, the satisfaction they in turn provide to their customers will be short-lived or not present at all. It is imperative that the relationship be cultivated and developed to the point at which both the organization and the supplier see it as a win-win relationship. To do that, some of the following concepts and principles must be followed:

- The supplier must become an extension of the buyer's organization.
- The supplier and buyer organization must work closely together for the mutual benefit of both parties.
- They must establish a long-term purchase agreement.
- They must initiate joint quality-related activities (training, planning, etc.).

Even this short list of requirements demonstrates that communication and teamwork between supplier and buyer organization are essential. The following are some communication techniques that may help this process:

- *Warranty cards*. Upon purchase of the product, the purchaser is asked to return a card stating the condition of the product when it was received.

- *Telephone calls*. Customers are called and asked for their impressions of the quality of the item they purchased.

- *Individual customer visits*. Another form of collecting customer data is the periodic visit to major customers by a marketing or engineering representative of the company.

- *Mail surveys*. For most of the questions, the customer is asked to respond by checking a box with a description such as excellent, very good, good, fair or poor.

- *Special arrangements with individual customers*. A simple but effective approach to gaining field intelligence is to establish a special arrangement with a few customers to obtain information in depth. This approach is heavily based on interviewing skills on a one-to-one basis.

- *Focus groups*. This technique is conducted in order to better understand a customer's perception of a company's product. It consists of about eight to ten current or potential customers who meet for a few hours to discuss a specific product. Depending on the goals of the focus group, the participants may be average customers, non-customers or special customers. The following are some key features of a focus group:

  - The discussion can focus on current products, proposed products or future products.
  - A moderator, who is skilled on group dynamics, guides and facilitates the discussion.
  - The moderator has a clear goal as to the information needed and a plan for guiding a discussion.
  - A company employee often observes and listens in an adjacent room, shielded by a one-way mirror.

In the discussion of data-driven customer satisfaction, many questions must be answered regarding how the data should be gathered and interpreted. For example, how can customer-related data be combined with other key data to create actionable information and develop prompt solutions to customer-related problems? Are the customer data and other key data related? Do they have the same statistical significance? Is the combination appropriate? Or, how do we decide how to interpret and analyze the data? Or, how do we decide what data is appropriate? Conflicts arise because the people collecting and analyzing the data often have differing views about the answers to these questions. Handling these disagreements professionally, using appropriate and applicable conflict resolution practices, is essential. There are three minimum requirements for conflict resolution. They are:

- The existence of a formula and a logical process for resolving customer complaints.

- A clearly defined escalation procedure, for situations when customers do not feel their complaint has been resolved satisfactorily by lower-level personnel.

- A distinct level of empowerment. This means that the authority and responsibility to carry out the assigned task should be clearly defined.

How can six sigma help create customer satisfaction? What are the specific items that six sigma provides that benefit the organization and increase customer satisfaction and loyalty? We believe that the following outcomes are directly related to the effort of implementing six sigma:

- *Improved product and service planning.* This involves creating a long-term focus that is based on prevention activities rather than appraisal activities and developing a customer-driven strategic planning process.

- *Measurable performance improvements.* Six sigma can increase customer satisfaction, market share, long-term profitability, and total productivity.

- *Improved attitude toward customers.* This involves recognizing the importance of the voice of the customer and devoting time to the professional treatment of customer needs, wants and expectations.

- *Higher quality of products and services.* This is provided according to customer requirements and needs.

- A *more informed marketing focus.* This results in increased market share and financial growth, which is achieved through increased customer satisfaction.

- *Improved process management approach.* With six sigma the focus is on:
  - ◆ Error and defect prevention not on appraisal techniques and justification.
  - ◆ A product and service delivery attitude—the realization that fast time to market is important.
  - ◆ A people orientation—processes are customer-driven.
  - ◆ Management by data—this means that management makes its decisions based on quantitative facts.
  - ◆ Mode of operation—management-supported advancement occurs through teamwork between suppliers, process owners and customers.
  - ◆ Improvement strategy—this is the result of total process management and a focus on continual progress.

Chapter 3

The Six Sigma DMAIC Model

Every methodology has a conceptual approach to work with. Six sigma is no different and, in fact, has two lines of approach. The first is to address existing problems, and the second, to prevent problems from happening to begin with. The six sigma methodology has adopted the old plan-do-study-(check)-act (PDS(C)A) approach, with some very subtle variations in that break-through strategy. This approach is a functional one—it clearly shows the correct path to follow once a project has been selected. In its entirety, the approach is the define, measure, analyze, improve and control (DMAIC) approach.

The stages of the DMAIC model

Define

The first stage—define—serves as the platform for the team to get organized, determine the roles and responsibilities of each member of the team, establish team goals and milestones and review the process steps. The key points to be defined at this stage are the voice of the customer, the scope of the project, the cause and effect prioritization (a list that the team creates for pursuing the specific project based on cause and effect criteria) and project planning.

(aligning to the business strategy and the preliminary definition of the project).

Each of these points can be linked to the customer (some obviously and others not so), and it is essential to appreciate and understand this link to the customer before and during this stage of the model. The following are the steps to take to complete the define phase of the DMAIC model:

- *Define the problem.* The problem is based on available data, is measurable and excludes any assumptions about possible causes or solutions. It must be specific and attainable.

- *Identify the customer.* This is more demanding as we systematically begin the process of analysis. We must identify who is directly impacted by the problem and at what cost. We begin by conducting a random sample analysis to identify the overall impact and then we proceed with a detailed analysis of the cost of poor quality (COPQ). The focus of the team here is to identify a large base of people affected by poor quality.

- *Identify critical to quality (CTQ) characteristics.* By identifying CTQ characteristics, the project team determines what is important to each customer from the customer's point of view. Identification of CTQ characteristics ascertains how these particular features appear when meeting customer expectations. Typical questions here are: What is "good condition?" and What is "on time?"

- *Map the process.* Mapping of the process in this stage of the define phase of the six sigma methodology is nothing more than a high level visual representation of the current process steps leading up to fulfillment of the identified CTQ characteristics. This "as is" process map will be useful throughout the process as:
  - A method for segmenting complex processes into manageable portions.
  - A way to identify process inputs and outputs.
  - A technique to identify areas of rework.
  - A way to identify bottlenecks, breakdowns and non-value-added steps.
  - A benchmark against which future improvements can be compared with the original process.

Any organization is a collection of processes, and these processes are the natural business activities you perform that produce value, serve customers and generate income. Managing these processes is the key to the success of the organization. Process mapping is a simple yet powerful method of looking beyond functional activities and rediscovering core processes. Process maps enable you to peel away the complexity of your organizational structure and focus on the processes that are truly the heart of your business. Armed with a thorough understanding of the inputs, outputs and interrelationships of each process, you and your organization can understand how processes interact in a system, evaluate which activities add value for the customer and mobilize teams to streamline and improve processes in the "should be" and "could be" categories. It should be noted that understanding the process is an important objective of the process map. However, something that is just as important, and usually undervalued from constructing a process map, is the benefit of the alignment of the team to the process at hand. Once this alignment occurs, and everyone in the team understands what is expected, the conclusion of a successful project is a high probability.

- *Scoping the project.* The last step of the define stage is scoping the project and if necessary, updating the project charter. During this step the team members will further specify project issues, develop a refined problem statement and brainstorm suspected sources of variation. The focus of this step is to reduce the scope of the project to a level that ensures the problem is within the team's area of control, that data can be collected to show both the current and improved states and that improvements can be made within the project's timeframe.

At the end of this stage, it is not uncommon to revisit the original problem statement and refine it in such a way that the new problem statement is a highly defined description of the problem. Beginning with the general problem statement and applying what has been learned through further scoping, the team writes a refined problem statement that describes the problem in narrow terms and indicates the entry point where the team will begin its work. In addition, a considerable amount of time is taken at this step to identify the extent of the problem and how it is measured.

Ultimately, the purpose of this stage is to set the foundations for the work ahead in solving a problem. This means that an excellent understanding of the process must exist for all team members, as well as complete understanding of the CTQ characteristics. After

CTQ factors are identified, everyone in the team must agree on developing an operational definition for each CTQ aspect. Effective operational definitions:

- Describe the critical to quality characteristics accurately.
- Are specific so that the customer expectation is captured correctly.
- Are always written to ensure consistent interpretation and measurement by multiple people.

Whereas typical methods of identifying CTQ characteristics include but are not limited to focus groups, surveys and interviews, the outputs are CTQ characteristics, operational definitions and parameters for measuring.

Measure

The second stage of the DMAIC model—measure—is when the team establishes the techniques for collecting data about current performance that highlights project opportunities and provides a structure for monitoring subsequent improvements. Upon completing this stage, we expect to have a plan for collecting data that specifies the data type and collection technique, a validated measurement system that ensures accuracy and consistency, a sufficient sample of data for analysis, a set of preliminary analysis results that provides project direction and baseline measurements of current performance.

The focus of this stage is to develop a sound data collection plan, identify key process input variables (KPIV), display variation using Pareto charts, histograms, run charts, and baseline measures of process capability and process sigma level. The steps to carry through this stage are:

- *Identify measurement and variation.* The measure subsets establish the requirements of measurement and variation, including: a) the types and sources of variation and the impact of variation on process performance, b) the different types of measures for variance and the criteria for establishing good process measures, and c) the different types of data that can be collected and the important characteristics of each data type. As part of this step the types of variation must be defined. There are two types of causes of variation:

- ♦ *Common causes*. These are conditions in a process that generate variation through the interaction of the 5Ms (machine, material, method, measurement, manpower) and 1E (environment). Common causes affect everyone working in the process, and affect all of the outcomes. They are always present and thus are generally predictable. They are generally accepted sources of variation and offer opportunities for process improvement.

- ♦ *Special causes*. These are items in a process that generate variation due to extraordinary circumstances related to one of the 5Ms or 1E. Special causes are not always present, do not affect everyone working in the process and do not affect all of the outcomes. Special causes are not predictable.

- *Determine data type*. In this step the team must be able to answer the question, "What do we want to know?" Reviewing materials developed during the previous stage, the team determines what process or product characteristics they need to learn more about. A good start is the definition of the data type. This is determined by what is measured. Two types of data can be collected by measuring:

  - ♦ *Attribute data*. One way to collect data is to merely count the frequency of occurrence for a given process characteristic (e.g. the number of times something happens or fails to happen). Data collected in this manner is known as attribute data. Attribute data cannot be meaningfully subdivided into more precise increments and is discrete by nature. "Go/no go" and "pass/fail" data are examples of this category.

  - ♦ *Variable data*. A different way to look at data is to describe the process characteristic in terms of its weight, voltage or size. Data collected in this manner is known as variable data. With this type of data, the measurement scale is continuous–it can be meaningfully divided into finer and finer increments of precision.

- *Develop a data collection plan*. In developing and documenting a data collection plan the team should consider:

  - ♦ What the team wants to know about the process.
  - ♦ The potential sources of variation in the process (Xs).
  - ♦ Whether there are cycles in the process and how long data must be collected to obtain a true picture of the process.
  - ♦ Who will collect the data.

- ♦ How the measurement system will be tested.
- ♦ Whether operational definitions contain enough detail.
- ♦ How data will be displayed once collected.
- ♦ Whether data is currently available, and what data collection tools will be used if current data does not provide enough information.
- ♦ Where errors in data collection might occur and how errors can be avoided or corrected.

- *Perform measurement system analysis.* This step involves performing graphical analysis and conducting baseline analysis. During this step, the team verifies the data collection plan once it is complete and before the actual data is collected. This type of analysis is called a measurement system analysis (MSA). A typical MSA indicates whether the variation measured is from the process or the measurement tool. The MSA should begin with the data collection plan and should end when a high level of confidence is reached that the data collected will accurately depict the variation in the process. By way of a definition, MSA is a quantitative evaluation of the tools and processes used in making data observations. Perhaps the most important concept in any MSA study is that if the measurement system fails to pass analysis before collecting data, then further data should not be collected. Rather, the gauge should be fixed, the measurement system should be fixed and the measurement takers should be trained.

- *Collect the data.* During this step, the team must make sure that the collected data is appropriate, applicable and accurate, and that it provides enough information to identify the potential root cause of the problem. It is not enough to plan carefully before actually collecting the data and then assume that everything will go smoothly. It is important to make sure that the data continues to be consistent and stable as it is collected. The critical rules of data collection are:
- ♦ Be there as the data is collected.
- ♦ Do not turn over data collection to others.
- ♦ Plan for data collection, design data collection sheets and train data collectors.
- ♦ Stay involved throughout the data collection process.

The outcome of this step must be an adequate data set to carry into the analyze stage.

Analyze

The third stage—analyze—serves as an outcome of the measure stage. The team at this stage should begin streamlining its focus on a distinct group of project issues and opportunities. In other words, this stage allows the team to further target improvement opportunities by taking a closer look at the data. We must remember that the measure, analyze and improve stages quite frequently work hand in hand to target a particular improvement opportunity. For example, the analyze stage might simply serve to confirm opportunities identified by graphical analysis in the measurement stage. Conversely, the analyze stage might uncover a gap in the data collection plan that requires the team to collect additional information. Therefore, the team makes sure the appropriate recognition of data is given and applicable utilization is functional, as well as correct. Yet another important aspect of this stage is the introduction of the hypothesis testing for attribute data. On the other hand, in the case of variable data we may want to use: analysis of means (1 sample t-test or 2 sample t-test), analysis of variance for means, analysis of variance (F-test, homogeneity of variance), correlation, regression and so on.

At the end of this stage the team should be able to answer the following questions:

- What was the improvement opportunity?
- What was the approach to analyzing the data?
- What are the root causes contributing to the improvement opportunity?
- How was the data analyzed to identify sources of variation?
- Did analysis result in any changes to the problem statement or scope?

We are able to do this by performing the following specific sequence of tasks:

- *Perform capability analysis.* This is a process for establishing the current performance level of the process being. This baseline capability will be used to verify process improvements through the improve and control phases. Capability is stated as a short-term sigma value so that comparisons between processes can be made.
- *Select analysis tools.* This step allows the team to look at the complete set of graphical analysis tools to determine how each tool

may be used to reveal details about process performance and variation.

- *Apply graphical analysis tools.* This refers to the technique of applying a set of basic graphical analysis tools to data to produce a visual indication of performance,

- *Identify sources of variation.* This refers to the process of identifying the sources of variation in the process under study, using statistical techniques, so that significant variation is identified and eliminated.

The analyze stage continues the process of streamlining and focusing that began with project selection. The team will use the results produced by graphical analysis to target specific sources of variation.

As an outcome of the analyze stage, the team should have a strong understanding of the factors impacting their project including:

- Key process input variables (the vital few Xs that impact the Y).

- Sources of variation—where the greatest degree of variation exists.

Improve

The fourth stage—improve—aims to generate ideas; design, pilot and implement improvements; and validate the improvements. Perhaps the most important items in this stage are the process of brainstorming, the development of the "should be" process map, the review and/or generation of the current FMEA (failure mode and effect analysis), a preliminary cost/benefit analysis, a pilot of the recommended action and the preliminary implementation process. Design of experiments (DOE) is an effective methodology that may be used in both the analyze and improve stages. However, DOE can be a difficult tool to use outside a manufacturing environment, where small adjustments can be made to input factors and output can be monitored in real time. In non-manufacturing, other creative methods are frequently required to discover and validate improvements.

The following steps should be taken at this stage:

- Generate improvement alternatives. The emphasis here is to generate alternatives to be tested as product or process improvements. The basic tools to be used here are brainstorming and DOE. With either tool, a three-step process is followed:

1. Define improvement criteria—develop CTQ characteristics.
2. Generate possible improvements—the best potential improvements are best evaluated based on the criteria matrix.
3. Evaluate improvements and make the best choice.

As a result of these steps, several alternatives may be found and posted in a matrix formation. The matrix should have at least the following criteria: "must" criteria (the basic items without which satisfaction will not occur) and "desirable" criteria (items that are beyond the basic criteria and do contribute to performance improvement). Once these are identified a weight for each is determined, either through historical or empirical knowledge, and appropriately posted in the matrix. At that point each criteria is cross-multiplied by the weight and the appropriate prioritization takes place. This is just one of many prioritization methods. Other prioritization methods may be based on cost, frequency, effect on customer and other factors.

- *Create a "should be" process map.* This map represents the best possible improvement the project team is able to implement. It is possible that a number of changes could be made to improve a process. The individual process map steps will serve as the input function of the FMEA.

- *Conduct FMEA (failure mode and effect analysis).* The FMEA is meant to be a "before the failure" action, not an "after the fact" reaction. Perhaps the most important factor in any FMEA is the fact that it is a living document and therefore it should be continually updated as changes occur or more information is gained.

- *Perform a cost/benefit analysis.* This analysis is a structured process for determining the trade-off between implementation costs and anticipated benefits of potential improvements.

- *Conduct a pilot implementation.* This step is a trial implementation of a proposed improvement, conducted on a small scale under close observation.

- *Validate improvement.* One of the ways to validate the effectiveness of the changes made is to compare the sigma values before and after the changes have been made. Remember, this means to compare the same defects per million opportunity.

Control

The fifth stage—control—is to institutionalize process or product improvements and monitor ongoing performance. This stage is the place where the transition from improvement to controlling the process and ensuring that the new improvement takes place. Of course, the transition is the transferring of the process from the project team to the original owner. The success of this transfer depends upon an effective and very detailed control plan. The objective of the control plan is to document all pertinent information regarding the following:

- Who is responsible for monitoring and controlling the process.
- What is being measured.
- Performance parameters.
- Corrective measures.

To make the control effective, several factors must be identified and addressed. Some of the most critical are:

- *Mistake-proofing.* This is to remove the opportunity for error before it happens. Mistake-proofing is a way to detect and correct an error where it occurs and avoid passing the error to the next worker or the next operation. This keeps the error from becoming a defect in the process and potentially impacting the customer CTQ characteristics.
- *Long-term MSA (measurement system analysis) plan.* Similar to the original MSA conducted in the measure stage, the long-term MSA looks at all aspects of data collection relating to the ongoing measurement of the Xs and high level monitoring of the Ys. Specifically, the long term MSA documents how process measurements will be managed over time to maintain desired levels of performance.
- *Appropriate and applicable charts (statistical process control).* A control is simply a run chart with upper and lower control limit lines drawn on either side of the process average. Another way to view the control chart is to see it as a graphical representation of the behavior of a process over time.
- *Reaction plan.* A reaction plan provides details on actions to be taken should control charts indicate the revised process is no

longer in control. Therefore, having a reaction plan helps ensure that control issues are addressed quickly and that corrective actions are taken.

• *The new or revised standard operating procedures (SOPs).* Updating SOPs and training plans is the practice of revising existing documentation to reflect the process improvements.

At the end of the control stage, the process owner will understand performance expectations, how to measure and monitor Xs to ensure performance of the Y, and what corrective actions should be executed if measurements drop below the desired and anticipated levels. Furthermore, the team is disbanded while the black belt begins the next project with a new team.

Typical tools and deliverables for each of the stages of the DMAIC model are shown in Table 3.1

Table 3.1 Typical tools/methodologies and deliverables for the DMAIC model

Stage	Tools/methodologies	Deliverables

Define	• Brainstorming
	• Cause and effect diagram
	• Process mapping
	• Cause and effect matrix
	• Current failure mode and effect analysis (FMEA)
	• Y/X diagram
	• CT matrix
		• The real customers
		• Data to verify customers' needs collected
		• Team charter—with emphasis on:
		  ♦ problem statement
		  ♦ project scope
		  ♦ projected financial benefits
		• High-level process map—"as is"

Measure	• Process mapping • Cause and effect • FMEA • Gauge R&R (repeatability and reproducibility) • Graphical techniques	• Key measurements identified • Rolled throughput yielded • Defects identified • Data collection plan completed • Measurement capability study completed • Baseline measures of process capability • Defect reduction goals established

Continued on next page

Table 3.1 (*Continued from previous page*)

Stage	Tools/methodologies	Deliverables
Analyze	• Process mapping • Graphical techniques • Multi-vari studies • Hypothesis testing • Correlation • Regression	• Detailed "as is" process map completed • The sources of variation and their prioritization • SOPs reviewed • Identify the vital few factors KPIVs with appropriate and applicable data to support such KPIVs (Key process input variables) • Refined problem statement to the point where the new understanding is evident • Estimates of the quantifiable opportunity represented by the problem
Improve	• Process mapping • Design of experiments • Simulation • Optimization	• Alternative improvements • Implementation of best alternative for improving the process • "Should be" process map developed • Validation of the improvement—especially for key behaviors required by new process • Cost/benefit analysis for the proposed solutions • Implementation plan developed—a preliminary preparation for the transition to the control stage • Communication plan established for any changes

Table 3.1 *(Continued from previous page)*

Stage	Tools/methodologies	Deliverables
Control	• Control plans • Statistical process control • Gage control plan • Mistake-proofing • Preventive maintenance	• Control plan completed • Evidence that the process is in control • Documentation of the project • Translation opportunities identified • Systems and structures changes to institutionalize the improvement • Audit plan completed

Selected bibliography

Eckes, G. *Making Six Sigma Last.* New York: John Wiley & Sons, 2001.
Harry, M., and R. Schroeder. *Six Sigma.* New York: Doubleday, 2000.
Stamatis, D. H. *Six Sigma and Beyond: Foundations of Excellent Performance.* Boca Raton, FL: St. Lucie Press, 2002.

Chapter 4

Common Methodologies Used in the DMAIC Model

The common methodologies and some typical tools used in the DMAIC model for six sigma are:

- Benchmarking.
- Statistical process control.
- Measurement system analysis.
- Poka-yoke.
- Failure mode and effect analysis.
- Project management.
- Cost of quality.
- Teams.
- Statistics.

Each of these is discussed in the following sections.

Benchmarking

Benchmarking is a continuous, systematic process that uses metrics to find practices that will enable and direct real change, leading to best-in-class (BIC) performance. In addition, benchmarking is recognized as a proactive, positive, structured process that affords value to the company, its employees, customers and shareholders.

Benchmarking is a recurring process of defining critical success factors (CSFs), comparing CSFs with the toughest competitors or BIC performers and using comparison results to develop strategies and plans to change.

The objective of benchmarking is to make effective and verifiable changes that achieve BIC performance. Large improvements of up to 100% can be realized. If you have a specific problem, it may already have a solution. Find and apply the solution quickly and reduce the cycle time. Change is accepted more readily when benchmarking metrics prove that techniques, methods and processes are being used successfully in BIC organizations. Good leaders realize benchmarking is not a delegated process, but consider it an energizing learning event, especially when done as a team.

The expected results from applying successful benchmarking processes include:

- Gaining valuable knowledge and insight to help appraise business decisions, strategic options and business opportunities that impact shareholder value.

- Identifying the gaps between your performance and BIC organizations' performance. This result should support the organization's objective of comparing key business indicators to those of competitors and other non-competitive organizations. The comparison helps to determine the organization's position in the industry and marketplace.

- Identifying ways to close these gaps through improved knowledge, process and practices that support the overall organizational strategy—fastest time to market and quickest implementation of new ideas in the industry.

A benchmarking process to close these gaps requires a combination of management, organization and employee allegiance—all critical to achieving the superior performance necessary for a true commitment to change. The benchmarking process and findings must be understood by the entire organization to obtain a commitment to change. Organized management support and careful communication are essential to successful benchmarking. Employee involvement is needed to smoothly implement the findings. These criteria lead to excellence and superior performance.

It is of paramount importance to recognize that BIC is not necessarily referring to your competitors. Rather, best-in-class achievement is defined as the reference metric that best describes the appropriate level of achievement for a project. Therefore, in benchmarking we may pursue the BIC in a variety of situations and sources, such as in:

- Best-in-city.
- Best-in-company.
- Best-in-industry.
- Best-in-country.
- Best-in-world.

For benchmarking to be effective it must support the effort to compare the organization's key business indicators to those of competitors and BIC performers, and identify in-house performance by comparing business practices to best practices within the company and other organizations. Ultimately, to realize overall value, best practices and lessons learned must be shared continuously with others throughout the company.

Why would anybody use benchmarking? Because by learning from several BIC organizations and adding your own innovative ideas, it is possible to surpass the BIC performance. By using benchmarking, an organization may become more flexible, learn to use less to do more and become faster, more agile and more competitive. What better way to accomplish this strategy than by identifying and implementing the best practices within the company and those employed by BIC organizations? The benchmarking process is learning and doing things that other BIC organizations are already doing. There is nothing theoretical or futuristic here. Many of the answers you need are in another company, perhaps another industry. It is faster to find these proven solutions and add your innovative ideas than to reinvent. Therefore, the power of benchmarking is truly in the application and transfer of knowledge from other BIC organizations to your own.

In addition to the obvious benefits, benchmarking can also contribute to the following:

- Achieving organizational objectives.
- Establishing baseline measurements.
- Meeting and exceeding competitor's strengths.
- Bringing best practices into the company, quickly.

- Stimulating and motivating learning from outside the company.
- Breaking down barriers to change.

Benchmarking types

Different situations require different benchmarking processes to attain reliable results, best practices and a commitment for change from the team. The following benchmarking process types may be used individually or combined as necessary:

Process or generic benchmarking. This type of benchmarking focuses on:

- Improving processes, practices, methods and techniques.
- Improving organizational strategies that link projects to customer driven functionalities.
- Improving value added improvements for a wide range of applications

Specialized benchmarking. The following types of benchmarking are used similarly to process benchmarking but each for a more specific objective:

- Strategic benchmarking helps with strategic decisions (high level) as opposed to tactical decisions (lower level).
- Functional benchmarking usually looks only within a specific function of an organization.
- Competitive benchmarking is product- or process-focused, but only competitors are looked at. The emphasis here is on competitors and not process. For example, when an automobile company is looking at the preventive maintenance of Toyota, that company is interested only on the issues of preventive maintenance as they relate to Toyota and not necessarily to the BIC practices.
- Performance benchmarking is usually comparing the product or service performance with that of its competitors.
- Best practices benchmarking is similar to process benchmarking and is sometimes used synonymously, however it can add to process benchmarking a focus on management practices that allow for superior processes.

- Internal benchmarking looks at other internal operations to find best-in-company practices.
- Product benchmarking is a form of performance or competitive benchmarking that concentrates on product design evaluations and manufacturing and assembly methods.
- Camera benchmarking uses photography (i.e., taking pictures of a process or product) to obtain product ideas and competitive information.

Benchmarking model

Benchmarking encourages systemic thinking by recognizing interdependencies and aspects of a process to attain BIC status. Benchmarking allows individuals and teams to identify the most critical things to change. Ultimately, it encourages new ideas and motivates people to take an innovative approach to business problems.

There are several models to follow. However, here we will only describe one of the most common models, known as the Motorola model. (Actually, the model was developed by DEC, Motorola, Boeing and XEROX.) The model has five phases, begins with deciding what to benchmark and concludes with the actual implementation of change.

Phase 1. Phase 1 answers the question, What to benchmark? This involves selecting a focused project and studying the current process or project. Phase 1 may take up to about 10 percent of the total time of the Motorola model. The steps to follow to achieve the goal of selecting a benchmarking topic are:

- List the critical success factors.
- Review the strategic plan (identify elements that support the organizational objectives in it).
- Determine whether the team can link the CSFs to elements in the strategic plan.
- Choose an area of strengths or weaknesses to focus on.
- List the CSFs by priority.
- Divide the highest priority CSFs into components and prioritize, if necessary.

At the end of this phase, the team should agree on a benchmarking topic.

Phase 2. This phase answers the question, "How do we do it?" It helps determine how best to benchmark whatever project was selected during Phase 1 by analyzing the internal process data. It may take up to 40 percent of the total project time and involves the following steps:

- Identify the people who are critical to the benchmark process.
- Get team agreement on definitions as they relate to the task at hand.
- Contact people critical to the project.
- Define the process for which benchmarking is being undertaken (through documentation, flowcharting and organizational mapping, etc.).
- Define at least two different ways to quantify the internal data and break it down into smaller sections.
- Normalize data (this allows the experimenter to compare different data on the same scale) and apply over time to make the data process dependent as opposed to time dependent.
- Contact internal people to verify internal data.

At the end of this phase, the team should have agreed on how the process is defined—that is, how the benchmarking should be done.

Phase 3. Phase 3 answers the question, "Who is best?" This involves finding the BIC process and setting up learning partnerships with your benchmarking partner. It may take up to 15 percent of the total time. Corporate values are paramount, especially during this phase. You must be honest, ethical and open about your motives when selecting benchmarking partners using the following steps:

- Create a list of criteria for selection of potential benchmark partners.
- Select a pool of partner candidates.
- Secure preliminary data.
- Narrow candidate pool to between three to five candidates.

By the end of this phase, the team should have agreed on the selection of benchmark partners.

Phase 4. This phase answers the question, "How do they do it?" It determines why the performance of those chosen in Phase 3 is superior. This phase may take up to 15 percent of the total time; it compares our methods and practices against the BIC by taking the following steps:

- Review the Dos and Don'ts and the legal considerations for information exchange.
- Gather public information.
- Create a partner profile.
- Generate a list of questions to drive the benchmark project, using documentation.
- As much as possible, answer all the questions with public information.
- Determine methods needed to gather non-public information.
- Create a project plan to gather information.
- Get help—if needed to create tools.
- Pilot the tools internally.
- Create a contingency plan.
- Gather data, debrief and finalize data gathering.
- Normalize the BIC data to your process.
- Identify the gap and calculate.

At the end of this phase, the team should have agreed on what enables the BIC to create and maintain the gap.

Phase 5. This phase involves analyzing the enablers, adding innovations, setting improvement goals and developing action plans to achieve them. This phase deals with the implementation of best practices discovered as a result of a benchmarking process. The strategy is to create and follow through on an action plan to close the gaps the benchmarking team identified. The time allotted for this phase is approximately 20 percent of the total time. It involves the following steps:

- Define what has to be done, when it should be done (i.e., project timelines), and who has the authority and responsibility to carry out the action plan.
- List the recommendations based on your findings. What do you recommend to improve your organization so that the differences are closed or even eliminated?
- Select a method to close the gap.

- Implement the action plan.
- Measure the results.
- Recalibrate—determine if the changes targeted in the action plan are taking place.
- Determine whether partners are performing as predicted.
- Determine whether there are new performers. When you get to this point you recycle—start again.

Another way to look at the deliverables of a typical benchmarking is shown in Table 4.1.

Table 4.1 Deliverables of the five-phase benchmarking model

Inputs	Outputs	Outputs	Outputs	Outputs	Outputs
Customer needs Strategic Information Internal/ external data Market trends	Champion identified Project description Plan (title, purpose, scope, etc.) Critical success factors CSF rationale	Stakeholder list Terms/ definitions List of processes Macro flow chart Process map Cross- functional map	Clients for selection List of BIC candidates Information collection plans Preliminary look at GAP (where are they and where are we?) List of partners (3 to 5)	Public data Partner Project plan to gather information Contingency plan Surveys Interview plan Letter of introduction Interview agenda Trip report List of best practices List of enablers Gap analysis	List of recommen- dations Benchmarking report Presentation plan Implementa- tion plan Measured results Recognition Recalibate decisions
Phase 1	Phase 2	Phase 3	Phase 4	Phase 5	Phase 6

Benchmarking project partners

Here are some tips to help you convince a BIC organization to partner with you on a benchmarking project:

- Find the person that can approve your request—large projects usually require a higher level of authorization.
- Explain that they will learn by participating.
- Offer an agreement that they can benchmark your company—reciprocity.

- Let them know that you anticipate a long-term relationship because your companies have common interests.
- Explain why this project is important to your company.
- Take advantage of any connections between the companies, such as customers, suppliers, or subsidiaries.
- List which disciplines you would anticipate being involved in and for how long.
- Make sure that they know that you have a benchmarking process and that you will be considerate of their time—that you will be focused and surgical.
- Confirm that they understand that you will act as project manager and provide to them all data collected from all the benchmarking partners during the project. This includes your own answers to any questions the partners are asked.
- Verify that all the benchmarking partners being considered can work together—there might be competitive or other reasons why the BIC candidate list will have to be adjusted.

Statistical process control (SPC)

SPC really addresses three distinct items—statistics, process and control. To appreciate the essence of SPC, one must think of employing the language of statistics, focused on a process for the purpose of control. An overview of what each aspect contributes to the total concept will prove helpful, but it is important to note that SPC is really a methodology to study the behavior of the process rather than to control anything.

Statistics. Statistics has frequently been described in a broad sense as a universal language, which is most useful in describing physical variability. Any group of data or numbers can be described and analyzed through statistical methods. Effective use of the language is enhanced by choosing the most pertinent data and handling it in the most efficient manner to best describe the physical variability of interest.

A familiar analogy involves engineering drawing as a universal language employed to describe the physical shape of a product, for example, a blueprint. In an analogous sense, a control chart (a central tool of SPC) is a document utilizing statistics as a universal language to describe the physical variability of a process.

Process. A process may be defined as a combination of inputs, both durable and convertible resources, for the purpose of obtaining desired quality outputs. The transformation (value added) of the inputs into the outputs is the process. Figure 4.1 shows such a process.

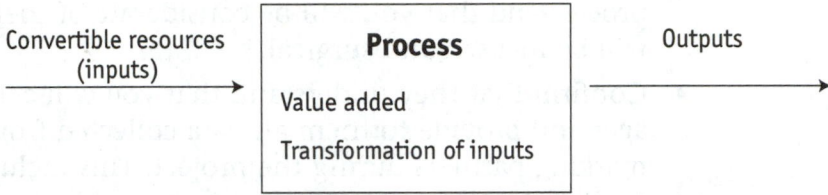

Figure 4.1 A typical process

The convertible resources are the inputs: materials, energy and information. Traditionally speaking, they have been called manpower, machine, material, method, measurement and environment. Output, on the other hand, indicates products, information and services. The transformation itself may be part of the durable resources or a combination of the durable as well as the convertible resources including environment.

Using this definition, a process may be thought of in global terms as collectively all the operations of a business, or in a much more narrow sense as a particular operation of a specific machine. Both views are appropriate. Typically, opportunities for improvement are illuminated by removing as much of the noise as possible by narrowing the focus to smaller elements of the total process.

Control. Control, the final word of SPC, is frequently misconstrued as a misnomer. The question arises, Does SPC control anything? Strictly speaking, it does not. However, control is not only an appropriate term, but also the key to the successful implementation of SPC. The classical control cycle consists of at least four actions: observing or measuring, comparing, diagnosing and correcting. Any time these four actions are successfully accomplished, a control cycle may be applied to many different systems in various ways.

Organizational improvement strategies can be condensed into two generic applications of such a control cycle: product control and process control. Successful completion in either case may lead to improvement. However, improvement is significantly better through process control.

Process control versus product control

The distinction between process control and product control is depicted in Figure 4.2. Product control orients the classical control cycle in a feed-forward [in time] mode. Process control is oriented towards a backward mode emphasizing the process.

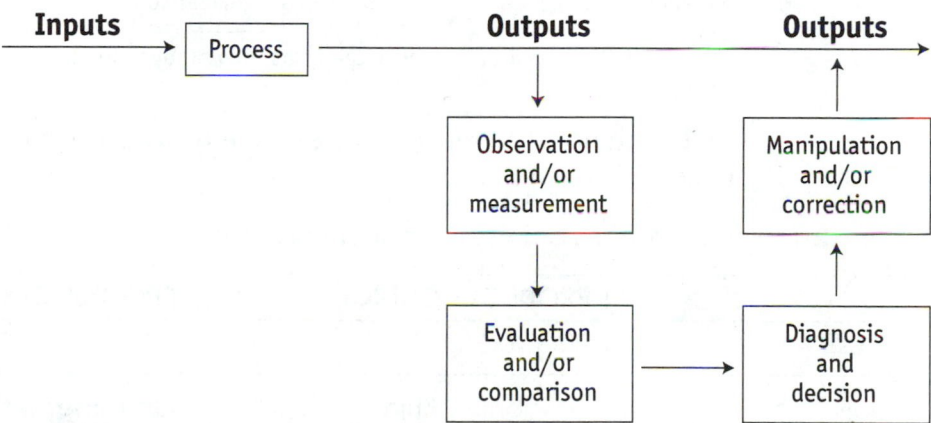

Figure 4.2a The classical control cycle—Product control

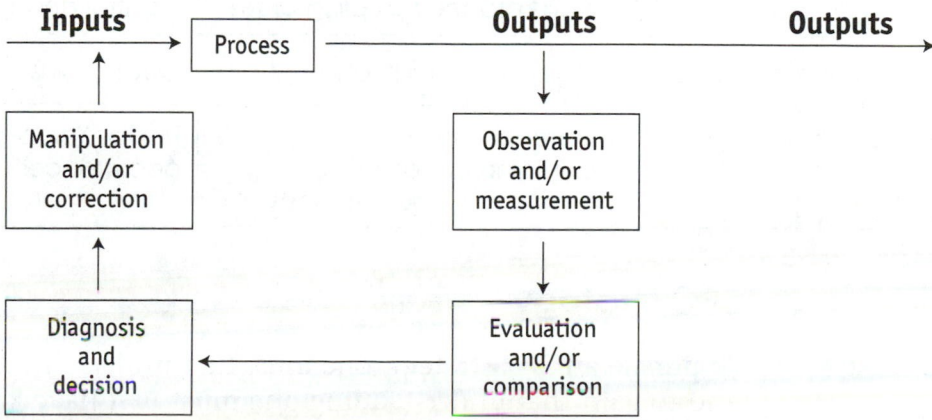

Figure 4.2b The classical control cycle—Process control

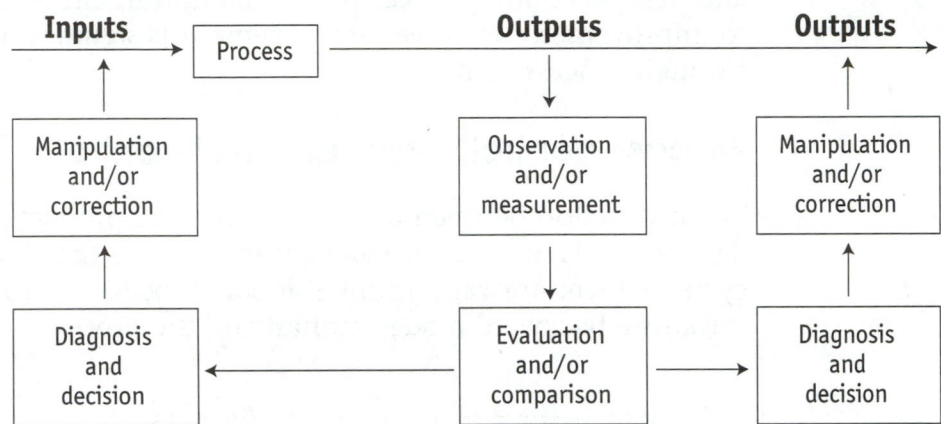

Figure 4.2c The classical control cycle—Combining product and process control

The major differences between the two approaches are summarized in Table 4.2.

Table 4.2 Major differences between product and process control

	PRODUCT CONTROL	PROCESS CONTROL
Focus	PRODUCT	PROCESS
Goal	Variability within specification limits	On target with smallest variation
Typical Tools	Acceptance sampling plans	Control charts
Improvement Nature	Outgoing quality only	Quality plus productivity
Philosophy	Detection and containment of problematic occurrences	Prevention of problematic occurrences

SPC strategy

To pursue an SPC strategy, one must first understand the process, and to gain that understanding one must first have knowledge of the process. The knowledge is generated through the definition, collection and analysis of data. Without data, nothing will happen.

The first step of the process control strategy involves the definition of the data—that is, the operational definition of what is to come. The second is the actual collection of data. Careful thought about how to obtain the most pertinent data should precede data gathering. The data should be collected accurately and precisely to maximize the information richness with respect to the process.

Measurements of one set of components are listed below. The components were all measured at the same location with the same measuring instrument by the same person.

.0138	.0150	.0164	.0132	.0119	.0144	.0144	.0140
.0146	.0158	.0140	.0125	.0147	.0149	.0163	.0135
.0161	.0138	.0126	.0147	.0153	.0157	.0154	.0150
.068	.0173	.0142	.0148	.0142	.0136	.0165	.0145
.0146	.0135	.0145	.0176	.0156	.0152	.0135	.0128

Since it is difficult to see how the data arises in a frequency sense, a more meaningful presentation of the data is desired. A simple raw tally sheet might be constructed where each x represents a frequency of one measurement: (The data have been coded as whole numbers.)

```
                      X

                      X  X  X  X  XXXX   X

X        XX X     X   XX X X X XXXXXXX XXX XXX   X XXX X      X  X
_____
120    125   130   135   140   145   150   155   160   165   170   175
                            MEASUREMENT SCALE
```

While it is helpful to unscramble the numbers and present them graphically, the question for the simple raw tally sheet presentation is, "How information rich is it?" A more informed view may be obtained through several steps for grouping the data into class intervals and presenting the data as a "frequency histogram," a "frequency polygon," or a "frequency curve." The following steps are useful in grouping the data into a frequency distribution for presentation in any of these three pictures. The actual use of each is dependent upon the preference of the experimenter and whether or not he or she is interested in the individual representation or the shape of the distribution.

1. Count the number of measurements or observations (N).
2. Determine the number of class intervals (K) (see Table 4.3).

Table 4.3 Guide for determining the number of class intervals

NUMBER OF OBSERVATIONS	NUMBER OF CLASS INTERVALS
(N)	(K)
30–50	5–7
51–100	6–10
101–250	7–12
Over 250	10–20

3. Determine the data range (R). R = Highest value minus lowest value.

4. Divide the data range by the number of class intervals to obtain an estimated class size (R/K).

5. Round estimated class size to a convenient number.

6. Determine class boundaries.

7. Determine one-half number accuracy.

8. Adjust class boundaries.

9. Tabulate data.

For our example, the frequency distribution for group data is shown as:

138	150	164	132	119	144	144	140
146	158	140	125	147	149	163	135
161	138	126	147	153	157	154	150
168	173	142	148	142	136	165	145
146	135	145	176	156	152	135	128

1. $N = 40$

2. K = 5 to 7

3. $R = 176 - 119 = 57$

4. $R/K = 57 / 7 = 8.14$

5. 9

6. 117, 126, 135, 144, 153, 162, 171, 180

7. .5

8. 117.5, 126.5, 135.5, 144.5, 153.5, 162.5, 171.5, 180.5

9. ... ...

THICKNESS X	TALLY	FREQUENCY f
117.5–126.5	///	3
126.5–135.5	/////	5
135.5–144.5	/////////	9
144.5–153.5	////////////	12
153.5–162.5	/////	5
162.5–171.5	////	4
171.5–180.5	//	2

Frequency histogram

A frequency histogram or histogram is a special type of column graph consisting of a set of rectangles where:

- The bases are on a horizontal axis (x-axis) with centers at the class marks.
- The width of the rectangles represents the class size.
- The height of the rectangles reflects the respective class frequency.

And consequently,

- The areas of the rectangles are proportional to the class frequencies. The following is a visual representation:

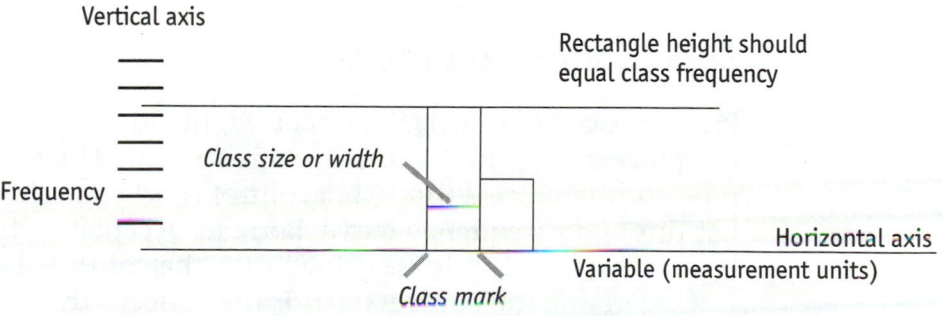

Label either class marks (more common) or class boundaries on the horizontal axis.

Interpretation

Each of the foregoing steps to group data distribution will generate graphs of the data to clarify the data and to provide a clear picture. The interest should center upon how the data illuminates the process. With some additional information the experimenter can calculate the capability of the process, the amount of rejects and the statistical confidence of the data. For example, the desired target value may be calculated—in this case, it is 150; the desired boundary may be worked out—in this case, any component measuring greater than 195 will be cost prohibitive; and we can calculate the capability—in this case, any component measuring less than 105 will not be functional.

How should one assess process behavior?

Fundamentally there are two ways of looking at data: by measuring or by observing. With each one there are two approaches for analysis: compress the data into an instant of time, thereby creating a frequency plot, or view how data arises over time, thereby creating a control chart. An experienced experimenter should know how to maximize the information by using the appropriate tools and techniques. In either case, the objective is to understand variation. Variation is the difference between each piece. However, collectively each piece variation contributes to a set pattern, which is called a distribution. This distribution may differ depending on location, spread, shape or in any combination.

Behavior of the process

Process control charts. As discussed, the idea of understanding the process is a function of a specific strategy. The strategy is to monitor the process through a control chart or evaluate the product through a frequency curve. Both are acceptable; however, there is more information to be gained with the control chart.

Underlying the control chart is the concept that variability can be separated into two arenas with respect to nature or source. Distinguishing the unstable variability from inherent or stable variability of the process is the role of the control chart, the product of statistical thinking and the foundation from which potential quality improvement stems.

The control chart is a graphic portrayal of how data of interest arises over time. Special causes of variability (process instabilities) arise or evolve in unusual manners. Distinguishing such a source of variability (special cause) from the stable variability (common causes) is possible by identifying unusual patterns and unexpected data points on the control chart.

The control chart concept is consistent for the various quantities of interest from the output. Awareness of the reference distribution underlying a particular control chart (depending upon the quantity being plotted) is paramount. A graphical representation of a control chart for sample averages (Xs) is depicted in Figure 4.3.

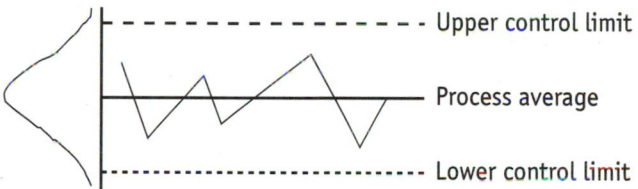

Figure 4.3 A typical control chart

While certainly not the only statistically based tool in the quest for never-ending quality improvement, the control chart provides a clear documentation of process variation in a form that guides appropriate diagnostic actions. As reduction of variability occurs, the same variability is witnessed by the data on the control charts. As variability is reduced, less masking of the smaller effects of improvements results and verification of even subtle and small improvements provides further benefits.

The main applications of control charts are:

- To monitor process performance over time.
- To aid in the quest for process improvement by verifying the authenticity of improvement actions.
- To establish the basis for true process capability assessment.

Many types of control charts exist, and choosing the most efficient and appropriate chart for a particular characteristic of interest is paramount. Two general classifications of control chart types are:

- Variable control charts.
- Attribute control charts.

Variable charts should be employed when data from a continuous scale (measurements) are of interest. Attribute charts are used when discrete data are of interest. In general, the attribute data are countable data pertaining either to the number of non-conformities (defects) or non-conforming units (defectives).

A more complete control chart selection matrix has been provided in Figure 4.4. While this matrix does not include all possible types and variations of control charts, those in current major use in industry have been included.

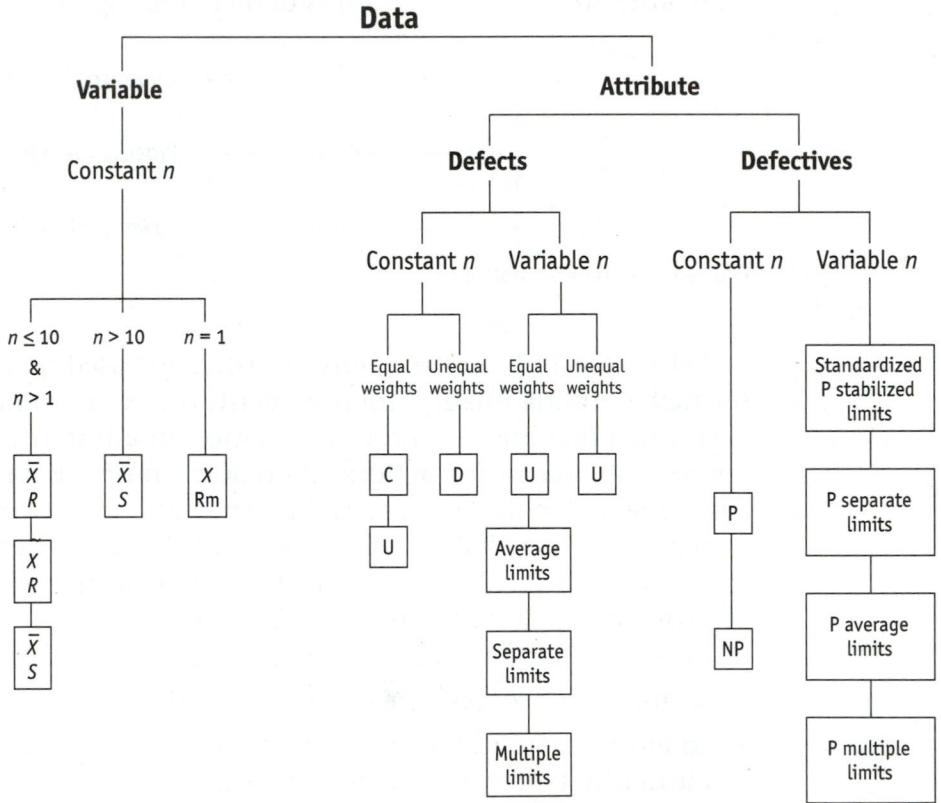

Figure 4.4 Control chart selection matrix

Process variation. The purpose of a control chart is to view the behavior of the process over time. However, we can also view the behavior of a process in specific time with a histogram. That behavior may be due to either common or special causes. In either case, improvement in quality (reduction in variation) of the output may come as a result of either removing or reducing either or both types of causes.

Special cause. A source of variation that influences some (or all) of the measurements, but in different ways. (If special causes of variation are present, the output of a process will not be stable over time and cannot be predicted!) Therefore, special causes can be characterized as assignable, chaotic and unnatural.

Common cause. A source of variation that influences all of the measurements in the same way. (If only common causes of variation are present, the output of a process forms a distribution pattern that is stable over time and that pattern can be predicted!) Therefore common causes can be thought of as chance, random and natural.

What is the problem with variation? Variation is waste. Therefore, as variation increases so does the waste. Consequently, when one wants to determine, from the variability pattern in the data, which deviations from the target have been produced by special causes and which have been produced by just the common causes, they are interested in identifying the source of waste. Why is this important? Because the responsibility for corrective actions rests with different authority levels. Special causes frequently can be corrected at the process by the operator or the supervisor at the local level. On the other hand, common causes represent a system fault, which requires the attention of management to improve the process as necessary.

How can this be done? Has all the data come from the same process? The answer is to apply appropriate and applicable statistical techniques that have the ability to separate the presence of special causes in light of the ever present common causes. When this is done, improvement is the result. A pictorial representation of the process is shown in Figure 4.5. Table 4.4 represents some of the typical characteristics of variation.

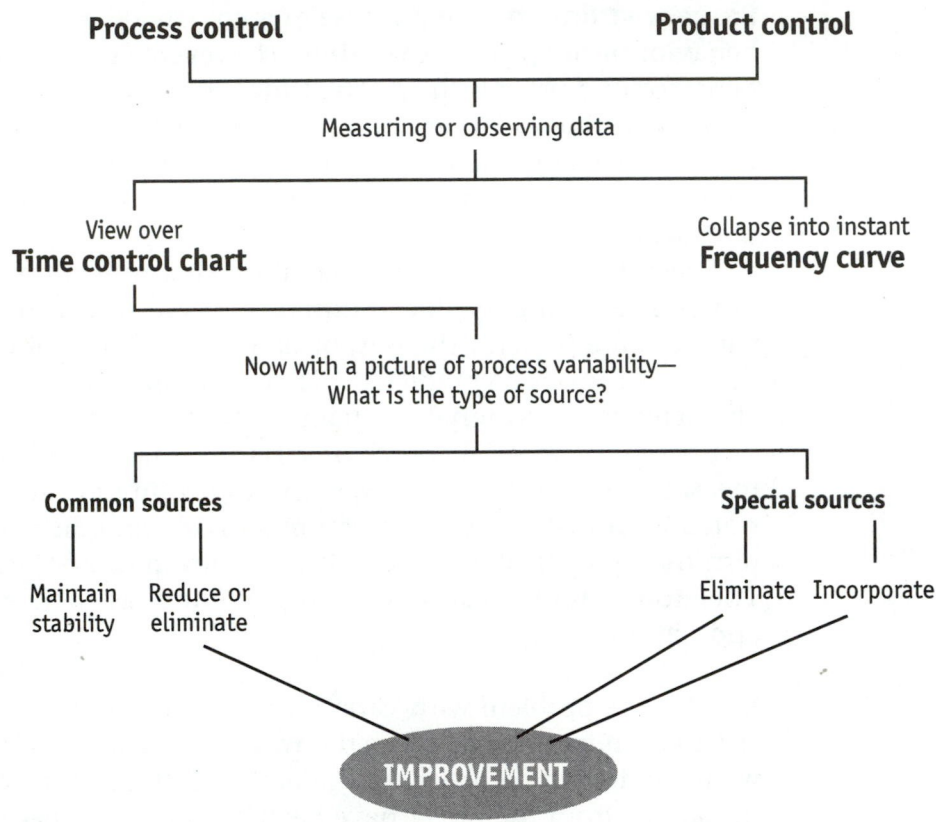

Figure 4.5 Process versus product control improvement

Table 4.4 Typical characteristics of variation

	COMMON CAUSE	**SPECIAL CAUSE**
Scope of Influence	All data in similar manner	Some (or all) data in dissimilar manner
Typical Identity	Many small sources	One or a few major sources
Nature	Stable and collective pattern is predictable. It is what is inherent or natural to the process	Sporadic irregular Unpredictable Appears & disappears
Improvement Action	Reduce common cause(s) Variability	Incorporate or eliminate
Improvement Responsibilty	SYSTEM fault Management	LOCAL fault Operator/supervisor

Steps and phases of implementation

The objectives of any statistical process control program must be to:

- Decrease quality costs by reducing scrap, rework and inspection costs by controlling the processes.
- Decrease operating costs by optimizing the frequency of process adjustments and changes.
- Improve productivity by identifying and eliminating the special causes.
- Reduce variability and establish a predictable and consistent level of quality.
- Increase customer satisfaction by reducing production variability, thereby producing a more trouble-free product.
- Eliminate the dependence on mass inspection to achieve quality. Build the quality into the product or service.
- Provoke process thinking among all levels of the organization.

For these items to be successful in any organization, they must be assessed, planned, supported and monitored through:

- An official organization for SPC.
- Training.
- Implementation.
- A philosophy of statistical and problem-solving techniques.

It is extremely important to recognize that the paths of product versus process control are quite different and they demand different approaches. In either case, a natural evolution of the need for the tools is paramount and we must never forget or become complacent about it.

So important is this natural evolution that one must understand that each input/process/output has its own level of involvement. This can be seen in Figure 4.6.

The process of involvement is done through at least the following activities:

Identify the team

Identify team members and titles

Identify area

Identify the initiation date

Levels of Involvement

Level	Key tools	Prime activity
Eyewitness	Control charts Process logs	Special cause(s) Alarm and investigation
Technical person	Control charts Design of experiments	Special cause activity Support common Cause reduction

Management and sales	All of above...
	Pertinent summaries
		Timely support of
		  above motivation,
		  recognition, and
		  accountability
		Permanent consolidation
		  of results

Figure 4.6 Levels of involvement

Identify the problem

Identify initial situation

Identify the objectives

Identify the analysis of the problem(s)

Identify the actions and resolutions including:

- ◆ Date initiated
- ◆ Description
- ◆ Responsible persons
- ◆ Date completed

Identify appropriate and applicable graphical presentations of results.

Identify appropriate and applicable permanent consolidation of results.

On the other hand, the control charting process is carried out through ten steps, which are:

1. Identify area of study.
2. Operationally define quality characteristics.

3. Assess measurement or observation system.

4. List potential special causes.

5. Determine sampling procedure size, frequency, by whom, etc.

6. Carefully record sample data by documenting important processes and noting conditions at the time the samples are drawn.

7. Continue charting to monitor process.

8. Analyze charts.

9. Reduce variability sources: special causes; common causes.

10. Plot charts.

Initiating control charts—variable data (pursuit of common cause characterization)

The following is a list of important considerations to keep in mind when initiating control charts when using variable data—that is, when attempting to characterize common cause variations.

1. Collect at least 25 samples prior to calculation of trial control limits.

2. Attain stability of the R chart prior to addressing the X-bar chart.

3. Remove sample values and revise limits if and only if special causes are identified.

4. Extend control limits as the process model only after statistical control has been established.

5. Establish stability (statistical control) prior to assessment of process capability.

Remember: The following guidelines are essential to keep in mind when initiating control charts.

- The control limits at any given time should be the best estimate of common cause variability of the process.

- The default position should generally be a sample size of five, taken once an hour. This typically works well as an initial plan.

- At least 25 samples across at least a week should provide an initial characterization of the common cause variability for most processes.

Management responsibilities

The purpose of SPC in problem-solving and process control is to continually improve quality, productivity and costs. Management plays a key part in achieving this continual improvement. In this regard, an SPC initiative must have:

1. Top management commitment.
2. Top management involvement.
3. Team approach to problem identification and solving.
4. Statistical training at all levels.
5. Implementation of plans with supportive resources.

Perhaps the most important requirement in any organization embarking on an improvement initiative is the organization itself. That means its culture, attitude and approach are items of concern. The reason for this is that a total SPC approach stresses statistical thinking as a management tool, but combines that with substantive knowledge of the processes to yield improvement results. A coordinated effort to identify and to appropriately act upon sources of variability is paramount. Proper organization is the starting point; while a number of scenarios might accomplish the objectives, a model that has performed well in various industries is discussed in the following sections.

Establish a steering committee. This group has the authority to designate and oversee SPC efforts. Setting the structure for efficient closure of the process control loop should be an aggressive goal. This group should be active in setting goals, monitoring progress and ensuring that efforts are directed in a useful manner and that the various SPC efforts of different departments or groups are compatible.

Specific responsibilities are to:

- Determine which areas should be addressed.
- Ensure smooth movement of implementation.
- Facilitate momentum-building by ensuring timely and appropriate follow-up action to requests.
- Involve each stakeholder in specific tasks following the reports.
- Recognize accomplishments.

Organize process teams. Teams integrated vertically around the processes, due to their levels of authority, work most efficiently. Collection and analysis of data, conducting of experiments and the pursuit of improvement for a particular process are all responsibilities of these groups. Specific initial responsibilities are:

- Planning the process control charts, proper type and logistics appropriate and applicable.
- Installing the control charts, training and providing suitable materials and routines for the production personnel.
- Monitoring the process control data collection and process information gathering to ensure smooth and effective use of the tools.
- Acting upon instabilities (irregularities of any kind in the team environment) and making sure that these instabilities are diffused and the team progresses as planned.
- Monitoring and reporting progress, inhibitors, etc.

Institute an educational phase. The knowledge that is needed to improve any process has to be learned. Therefore, the goals of this step are to:

- Familiarize the teams with the SPC, the cultural language of the organization, the jargon for the problem at hand and any other communication initiative that is required for the participants to function appropriately and effectively.
- Provide the teams with some basic knowledge. Problem solving techniques, seven quality tools, and team dynamics are some examples.
- Provoke thinking on an individual basis as to how this new knowledge fits into daily work.
- Provoke thinking of possible positive, as well as negative, implications of this new knowledge on a system basis.

The prerequisites for this knowledge are:

- Management awareness and understanding of the basic SPC philosophy.
- Commitment of resources.
- Organization for implementation.

Use the knowledge. The fourth step of the model is the utilization phase. The knowledge that has been learned has been (or is in the process of being) implemented. There are two stages to this phase of the model: the pilot application stage and the mature utilization stage.

The goals of the pilot application stage are to:

- Build technical confidence and maturity in the critical mass (the amount of people that the organization needs for change to occur) that is responsible for implementation.

- Demonstrate utility of the techniques to the teams.

- Bring more structure or order to problem-solving.

The goals of the mature utilization stage are to:

- Bring statistical/process thinking on board with new products and processes.

- Solve the major problems based on your criteria of importance during the definition stage.

- Realize the major gains.

- Integrate improvement programs with existing programs or with the organization's objectives.

- Transfer ownership to the system as a whole the process owner(s).

Institutionalize the knowledge. The final step is the institutionalization phase. At this stage, what has been learned must become part of the organizational culture, and this must be done as an automatic response. It creates the new status quo for improvement. Specifically, institutionalization means:

- Gathering data, charting, analysis and taking action based on that data and analysis are now a daily discipline.

- Relying on facts and statistical data are natural reactions.

- Everyone speaks the common language of SPC.

- SPC is an integral part of conducting business.

- Everyone applies process control thinking in his or her job every day.

- Statistical process control is perpetual because the benefits are recognized by all.

While some elements that need to be in place before an organization moves into this phase can be (and have been) enumerated, the timing of this phase is difficult to assess. With a clear vision of where the organization is headed, efforts for attaining the goal can be better directed.

Whereas SPC is an important element in the six sigma endeavor, the following problems associated with it are not uncommon:

- Misunderstanding the concepts of process control versus product control as they relate to both quality and productivity.

- A misconception of the physical difference between special and common causes as they relate to process performance.

- A lack of understanding of what control charts are telling an operator versus what they are telling management.

- An absence of a framework and methodology that rigorously identifies where statistical charting can best be employed for the most pertinent process diagnostic information.

- A failure to accept the absolute importance of closing the process control loop, diagnosing root causes, following through with appropriate countermeasures and solidifying the improvement gains.

- A lack of understanding of loss function. Use of the loss function concept serves as a means to evaluate quality in terms of loss due to variation in function on economic grounds, to articulate the economic interpretation of a specification limit and to assess the economic performance of a process.

Statistics used in control charting

This section provides the professional practitioner with some simple approaches to statistical understanding for the every-day application of some common charts, rather than an extensive litany of statistical tools. The section addresses computing an average, control limits for X and R charts, control limits for p charts, general formulae, capability, control chart construction guides for variable data and for attribute data and testing for normality and exponentiality. Also, some instructions for calculator usage is addressed.

Computing an average. There is a formula for computing averages. Knowing this formula is useful because it follows a pattern you will see in other statistics formulas. Here is what it looks like:

$$\bar{X} = \frac{\Sigma X}{n}$$

This is what the terms mean:

$\bar{X}$ is the symbol for the average. Average is the sum of the observations in a given experiment divided by the total amount of observations in the experiment. A bar over a letter always means average. If it has two bars ($\bar{\bar{X}}$), then it indicates the grand average or the overall average.

Σ is the summation sign. This symbol means you need to find the sum (total) of the numbers. Σ is always followed by a letter or letters to let you know which numbers to sum up.

ΣX is the symbol indicating the total sum of what you are trying to measure.

n is the symbol for how many numbers you added to get the ΣX total.

If you can remember this formula, you will have an easier time using your calculator.

An average alone does not tell you anything about the data used to find it. The two methods SPC uses to show how the average relates to the data are range and standard deviation.

Range is the difference between the highest and lowest values of data used for the average. The abbreviation for range is **R**. The formula for finding the range is:

$$R = \text{Highest} - \text{Lowest}$$

Standard deviation is a statistical unit of measure computed from all the data used for the average. There are two abbreviations for standard deviation: **s** and **σ**.

s is the standard deviation used when you use samples from a production run. This is called the **sample standard deviation**.

σ is the standard deviation used when you use an entire production run. This is called the **population standard deviation**.

Although standard deviations can be computed through longhand, it is easier to use a calculator.

For example, some calculators have statistics programs built into them. Once you learn to use this feature, you will appreciate how the calculator does number crunching for you. Calculators are not all the same. This example is based on Sharp EL-509S.

Getting into STAT mode:

Look above the ON key. STAT is outlined in brown. Anything in brown means you have to press the second function key **first**. (Every calculator has a key that is a different color and it has "2nd" printed on it. That is the second function key. It implies that the user must use this key before entering the function of choice to be calculated. When the second function key is activated, the functions shown in yellow are enabled.) To use STAT mode, press the second function key and then the ON key.

You should see STAT above the zero on your screen. Your calculator is now a statistics computer and a calculator. Make sure you use the keys identified in blue.

Find the three memory keys outlined in blue, and the gray key just above them. These are the four statistics keys. The top three statistics keys give you answers. The bottom statistics key enters data into the computer.

DATA key   M+

This is the bottom statistics key. Numbers used to compute averages, totals, and standard deviations are called data. After you punch in a piece of data, pressing the DATA key by itself enters it into the STAT program.

Standard deviation key   RM

This key can give you the two different standard deviations. Pressing it by itself will give you the sample standard deviation (abbreviated as **s**). **s** is the calculation you want when you deal with samples from an entire production run.

Pressing the second function key will give you the **population standard deviation** (abbreviated as **σ**). **σ** is the calculation you want when you deal with an entire production run.

Average key   X ➡ M

Pressing this key by itself will give you the average (also known as X-bar or X) of the numbers in the STAT program.

Total key   )

Pressing this key by itself will tell you how many numbers are in the STAT program (abbreviated **n**). This helps you keep track of where you are as you enter data.

To get the **total** (abbreviated **Σx**), you have to press the second function key and then press the key with the dot.

See how **Σx** is written in brown ink? Remember—brown ink always means you have to press the second function key first.

IMPORTANT: When you have completed the calculations for one set of data, you **must** clear out the old data before punching in new data. If you don't, the calculator will add the new data to the old data.

The easiest way to clear out old data is to turn the calculator off, turn it back on and get back into STAT mode.

If you happen to make a mistake using STAT mode, it is best to start again by clearing out the bad data.

Advanced STAT Mode

If you have data from a frequency distribution chart, you can use a shortcut method of entering data. Like all shortcuts, you have to be careful when you use it.

Frequency distributions tell you how often a certain value comes up in your data. To enter this data into the STAT program:

- Punch in the value.
- Press the multiply key.
- Punch in the frequency.
- Press the data key.

Make sure **n** (how many numbers are in your STAT program) on your screen is the same as **n** from your data.

Control limits for X and R charts. Sometimes you will see this control limits formula:

$$CL_{\bar{X}} = \bar{\bar{X}} \pm A_2\bar{R}$$

This is really two formulas in one. Here is what the different parts mean:

$CL_{\bar{X}}$ is "The control limits for X-bar." This is an abbreviation for the upper **and** lower control limits for X-bar (the average bar).

$\bar{\bar{X}}$ is called the grand average or the average of averages.

± is a math symbol that means add and subtract. Whenever you see this sign, it means there are two equations to solve. Do not confuse it with the + / - key on your calculator.

A_2 is an SPC factor you get from a table on your charts. The number you use depends on your sample size. For instance, if your sample size is 5, A_2 will always be 0.577.

$\bar{R}$ is the average range. This is read "R-bar."

Since the ± sign means there are two equations to solve, break this formula down. The two equations look like this:

$$UCL_{\bar{x}} = \bar{\bar{X}} + A_2\bar{R} \quad \text{AND} \quad LCL_{\bar{x}} = \bar{\bar{X}} - A_2\bar{R}$$

$UCL_{\bar{x}}$ is the upper control limit for X-bar.

$LCL_{\bar{x}}$ is the lower control limit for X-bar.

To find control limits, you need values for $\bar{\bar{X}}$ and $\bar{R}$. If you do not have them, calculate them. The sample size determines what A_2 will be.

For this example, the sample size is 5, $\bar{\bar{X}} = 0.5643$, and $\bar{R} = 0.0133$.

Step 1	Write down both formulas.
	$UCL_{\bar{x}} = \bar{\bar{X}} + A_2\bar{R} \quad LCL_{\bar{x}} = \bar{\bar{X}} - A_2\bar{R}$
Step 2	Substitute values (numbers) for variables (letters).
	$UCL_{\bar{X}} = 0.5643 + (0.577)(0.0\ 133)$
	$LCL_{\bar{X}} = 0.5643 - (0.577)(0.0133)$
Step 3	Complete the multiplication.
	$UCL_{\bar{x}} = 0.5643 + 0.0076741$
	$LCL_{\bar{x}} = 0.5643 - 0.0076741$
Step 4	Complete the addition and subtraction.
	$UCL_{\bar{x}} = 0.5719741 \quad LCL_{\bar{x}} = 0.5566259$
Step 5	Round off the answers as needed.
	$UCL_{\bar{x}} = 0.5720 \quad LCL_{\bar{x}} = 0.5566$

With your calculator, you can find both control limits without a great deal of extra writing. There are eight steps to follow. You have to be careful in following them, but once you get into the practice of it, you will be able to calculate these control limits with speed, accuracy, and confidence.

Because A_2 and $\bar{R}$ are written together in the equation, this means you **must** multiply them before you can solve the rest of the equations. As you will need this answer to solve both equations, store the answer in your calculator's memory. Leave this answer on the screen.

To find the upper control limit, **add** the value for $\bar{\bar{X}}$ to the value on the screen. For the lower control limit, **subtract** the saved value twice.

The eight steps to find the control limits using the calculator are:

STEPS	KEYSTROKES
Step 1. Multiply the value of A_2 times the value of $\bar{R}$	A_2 X $\bar{R}$ =
Step 2. Put the answer in memory.	X→M
Step 3. Add $\bar{\bar{X}}$ X	+ =
Step 4. Round off your answer for the upper control limit.	
Step 5. Subtract the memory.	– RM =
Step 6. Check the answer. If the answer is the same as $\bar{\bar{X}}$, go to step 7. If the answer is different, you have made a mistake somewhere. Clear the calculator and start again at step 1.	
Step 7. Hit the equals key again. This will subtract the memory.	=
Step 8. Round off the answer for the lower control limit.	

Control limits for p charts. Sometimes you will see the control limits formula like this:

$$CL_p = \bar{p} \pm 3\sqrt{\frac{\bar{p}(1-\bar{p})}{n}}$$

This means the control limits for p charts are three standard deviations both sides of the average.

Just like the control limits formula for the X-bar charts, it is really two formulas in one. And once you know what the individual parts mean, you will know what the formula means. Here is what the parts mean:

CL_p is "The control limits for p." This an abbreviation for the upper **and** lower control limits for p charts.

p is the **average proportion defective**. A proportion is the decimal answer to a fraction. This is read "pbar".

± is a math symbol that means add and subtract. Whenever you see this sign, it means there are two equations to solve. **Do not confuse it with the + / - key on your calculator**.

√ is a math sign meaning the square root. There is a key for this on the calculator.

n is the sample size.

If you know what pbar is, this formula is seven different math problems—nine if you include rounding.

Since there are always two control limits, the first thing to do is break the formula down into the upper control limit formula and the lower control limit formula.

The upper control limit formula looks like this:

$$CL_p = \bar{p} + 3\sqrt{\frac{\bar{p}(1-\bar{p})}{n}}$$

This is an addition problem. It tells us that the upper control limit on a p chart is the average plus three standard deviations.

The lower control limit formula looks like this:

$$CL_p = \bar{p} - 3\sqrt{\frac{\bar{p}(1-\bar{p})}{n}}$$

This is a subtraction problem. It tells us that the upper control limit on a p chart is the average **minus** three standard deviations.

The trick is to find the three standard deviations. That is five math problems right there—two multiplication, one square root, a division, and a subtraction. Ground rules in math tell you in what order to solve the problems. Once you find the three standard deviations, you can find both control limits. To master the trick:

- Find the answer to 1 minus pbar.
- Multiply by pbar.
- Divide by **n**.
- Find the square root.
- Multiply by three.

Now you have the values of three standard deviations. Add this number to pbar for the upper limit. Subtract this number **from** pbar for the lower limit. Both limits should be rounded off to the same number of decimal places as pbar.

With the help of your calculator, you can work out these control limits.

The calculator instructions for control limits are:

STEPS	KEYSTROKES
Step 1. Put pbar in memory.	X→M
Step 2. Find one minus pbar.	1− =
Step 3. Multiply by pbar.	X =
Step 4. Divide by **n**.	÷ n =
Step 5. Find the square root.	√
Step 6. Multiply by three.	X 3 =
Step 7. Put the answer in memory.	X→M
Step 8. Add pbar.	+ $\bar{p}$ =
Step 9. Round off the answer for the upper control limit.	
Step 10. Subtract the memory.	− RM =
Step 11. Check the answer against pbar. If the answer and pbar are the same, go to step 11. If the answers are different, you will have to start again.	
Step 12. Hit the equals key again.	=
Step 13. Round off answer to give you the lower control limit.	

General formulas. The following general formulas are useful in SPC.

1. Arithmetic mean (average) from ungrouped data.

For a population:

$$\mu = \frac{\Sigma X}{N}$$

For a sample:

$$\bar{X} = \frac{\Sigma X}{n}$$

For the average of the average

$$\bar{\bar{X}} = \frac{\Sigma \bar{X}}{n}$$

where ΣX is the sum of all observed population (or sample) values. N is the number of observations in the population and n is the number of observations in the sample. The $\Sigma \bar{X}$ is the average of the samples.

2. Arithmetic mean (average) from grouped data.

For a population:

$$\mu = \frac{\Sigma fX}{N}$$

For a sample:

$$\bar{X} = \frac{\Sigma fX}{n}$$

Where fX is the sum of all class-frequency (f) times class-midpoint (X) products. N is the number of observations in the population, and n is the number of observations in the sample.

3. Median from ungrouped data.

For a population: $M = X \frac{N+1}{2}$ in an ascending ordered array

For a sample: $m = X \frac{n+1}{2}$ in an ascending ordered array

Where X is an observed population (or sample) value, N is the number of observations in the population, and n is the number of observations in the sample.

4. Median from grouped data.

For a population:
$$M = L + \frac{(\frac{N}{2}) - F}{f}\, w$$

For a sample:
$$m = L + \frac{(n/2) - F}{f}\, w$$

Where L is the lower limit of the median class, f is its absolute frequency, and w is its width, while F is the sum of frequencies up to (but not including) the median class, N is the number of observations in the population and n is the number of observations in the sample.

5. Mode from grouped data.

For a population or a sample:
$$MO \text{ or } mo = L + \frac{d_1}{d_1 + d_2}\, w$$

Where L is the lower limit of the modal class, w is its width, and d_1 and d_2, respectively, are the differences between the modal class frequency density and that of the preceding or following class.

6. Weighted mean from ungrouped data.

For a population:
$$\mu w = \frac{\Sigma wX}{w}$$

For a sample:
$$\bar{x}w = \frac{\Sigma wX}{w}$$

Where $\Sigma w_1 X$ is the sum of all weight (w) times observed-value (x) products, while w equals N (the number of observations in the population) or n (the number of observations in the sample).

7. Mean absolute deviation

From ungrouped data

For population:
$$MAD = \frac{\Sigma |X - \mu|}{N}$$

For a sample:
$$MAD = \frac{\Sigma |X - \bar{x}|}{n}$$

Where $\Sigma|X - \mu|$ is the sum of the absolute differences between each observed population value, X, and the population mean, μ, while N is the number of observations in the population, and where $\Sigma|X - \bar{X}|$ is the sum of the absolute differences between each observed sample value, X, and the sample mean, $\bar{X}$, while n is the number of observations in the sample.

From grouped data:

Denoting absolute class frequencies by f and class midpoints by X, substitute $\Sigma f|X - \mu|$ or $\Sigma f|X - \bar{X}|$ for the numerators given here.

Note: occasionally, absolute deviations from the median rather than from the mean are calculated; in which case μ is replaced by M, and $\bar{X}$ is replaced by m.

8. Variance from ungrouped data.

For a population: $\qquad \sigma^2 = \dfrac{(x - \mu)^2}{N}$

For a sample: $\qquad s^2 = \dfrac{(x - \bar{x})^2}{n - 1}$

Where $\Sigma(x - \mu)^2$ is the sum of squared deviations between each population value, X, and the population mean, μ, with N being the number of observations in the population, while $\Sigma(x - \bar{x})^2$ is the sum of squared deviations between each sample value, x, and the sample mean, $\bar{x}$, with n being the number of observations in the sample.

9. Variance from grouped data.

For a population: $\qquad \sigma^2 = \dfrac{\Sigma f(x - \mu)^2}{N}$

For a sample: $\qquad s^2 = \dfrac{\Sigma f(x - \bar{x})^2}{n - 1}$

Where absolute class frequencies are denoted by f, class midpoints of grouped population (or sample) values by x, the population (or sample) mean by μ (or $\bar{x}$), and the number of observations in the population (or sample) by N (or n).

10. Standard deviation from ungrouped data.

For a population: $\sigma = \sqrt{\dfrac{\Sigma(x - \mu)^2}{N}}$

For a sample: $s = \sqrt{\dfrac{\Sigma(x - \bar{x})^2}{n - 1}}$

Where $\Sigma(x - \mu)^2$ is the sum of squared deviations between each population value, x, and the population mean, μ with N being the number of observations in the population, while $\Sigma(x - \bar{x})^2$ is the sum of squared deviations between each sample value, x, and the sample mean, $\bar{x}$, with *n* being the number of observations in the sample.

11. Standard deviation from grouped data.

For a population: $\sigma = \sqrt{\dfrac{\Sigma f(x - \mu)^2}{N}}$

For a sample: $s = \sqrt{\dfrac{\Sigma f(x - \bar{x})^2}{n - 1}}$

Where absolute class frequencies are denoted by f, class midpoints of grouped population (or sample) values by *x*, the population (or sample) mean by μ (or $\bar{x}$), and the number of observations in the population (or sample) by *N* (or *n*).

12. Variance from ungrouped data—shortcut method.

For a population: $\sigma^2 = \dfrac{x^2 - N\mu^2}{N}$

For a sample: $s^2 = \dfrac{x^2 - n\bar{x}^2}{n - 1}$

Where Σx^2 is the sum of squared population (or sample) values, μ^2 is the squared population mean and $\bar{x}^2$ the squared sample mean, *N* is the number of observations in the population, and *n* is the number of observations in the sample.

13. Variance from grouped data—shortcut method.

For a population: $\sigma^2 = \dfrac{\Sigma f x^2 - N\mu^2}{N}$

For a sample:
$$s^2 = \frac{\Sigma fx^2 - n\bar{x}^2}{n - 1}$$

Where Σfx^2 is the sum of absolute-class-frequency (f) times squared-class-midpoint (x) products, μ^2 is the squared population mean and $\bar{x}^2$ the squared sample mean, N is the number of observations in the population and n is the number of observations in the sample.

Capability. There are four aspects of capability: process capability, capability ratio, capability index and target ratio percent. Each is outlined here.

1. Process capability

$$C_p = \frac{USL - LSL}{6\sigma_x}$$

Where USL and LSL are the upper and lower specifications and σ_x is the standard deviation.

2. Capability ratio

$$C_r = \frac{6\sigma_x}{USL - LSL}$$

Where USL and LSL are the upper and lower specifications and σ_x is the standard deviation.

3. Capability index

$$C_{pk} = \frac{Z_{min}}{3}$$

Where Z_{min} is the less value of (USL-Xbar)/3σ and (Xbar-LSL)/3σ

4. Target ratio percent

$$TR_p = \frac{3\sigma}{Z_{min}} \times 100$$

Special note: Capability in six sigma is a very important issue. Therefore, even though the above formulas are the generic ones, the practitioner for the six sigma project should be aware of the following conditions:

For variable data: we use the C_p or C_{pk} for short-term capability and for long capability we use the P_p or P_{pk}. The difference between the two is the calculation of the sigma in the denominator of the for-

mula. That is for C_{pk} we use $\sigma = \dfrac{\bar{R}}{d_2}$ and for P_{pk} we use the actual value of σ.

For attribute data, we use the ppm, DPU, or the DPM value.

The universal metric for capability has been the sigma value. However, more and more companies are reporting the actual Z value without discriminating for short or long capability.

Control chart construction guide for variable data. This is shown in Table 4.5.

Table 4.5 A guideline for constructing variable control charts

QUANTITY	CENTRAL LINE	UPPER CONTROL LIMIT	LOWER CONTROL LIMIT	SAMPLE	NOTES
Statistic	Average	UCL Average $\pm 3\ \sigma$ statistic	LCL	n	Generic form
$\bar{X}$ Sample average	$\bar{\bar{X}}$	$\bar{\bar{X}} + A_2\bar{R}$	$\bar{\bar{X}} - A_2\bar{R}$	Small: Prefer $n < 10$ typ: $n = 5$	Normal distribution w/R chart
R: Range	$\bar{R}$	$D_4\bar{R}$	$D_3\bar{R}$	Same (above)	Analyze 1st
$\bar{X}$ Sample average	$\bar{\bar{X}}$	$\bar{\bar{X}} + A_3\bar{S}$	$\bar{\bar{X}} - A_3\bar{S}$	$7 < n < 25$	Normal distribution w/S chart
Std. Dev.	$\bar{S}$	$B_4\bar{S}$	$B_3\bar{S}$	Same (above)	Analyze 1st
X Individual values	$\bar{X}$	$\bar{X} + E_2\bar{R}m$	$\bar{X} - E_2\bar{R}m$	$n = 1$	Normality assumed < Sensitive
Rm Moving range	$\bar{R}m$	$D_4\bar{R}m$	$D_3\bar{R}m$	Small usually $n = 2$	Correlated w/X chart
Median X	$\tilde{\tilde{X}}$	$\tilde{\tilde{X}} + \tilde{A}_2\tilde{R}$	$\tilde{\tilde{X}} - \tilde{A}_2\tilde{R}$	typ: $n = 5$	< Sensitive
Range $\tilde{R}$	$\tilde{R}$	$\tilde{D}_4\tilde{R}$	$\tilde{D}_3\tilde{R}$	Same (above)	Analyze 1st

Control chart construction guide for attribute data. This is shown in Table 4.6.

Table 4.6 A guideline for constructing attribute control charts

QUANTITY	CENTRAL LINE	UPPER CONTROL LIMIT	LOWER CONTROL LIMIT	SAMPLE	NOTES
Statistic	Average	UCL LCL Average $\pm 3\ \sigma$ statistic		n	Generic form
p Proportion defective	$\bar{p}$	$\bar{p}+3\sqrt{\dfrac{\bar{p}(1-\bar{p})}{n}}$	$\bar{p}-3\sqrt{\dfrac{\bar{p}(1-\bar{p})}{n}}$	Prefer $n\bar{p}\,?\,2$ typ: $n \geq 50$	Binomial distribution LCL < 0 = >0
np Number of defectives	$N\bar{p}$	$n\bar{p}+3\sqrt{\bar{p}(1-\bar{p})}$	$n\bar{p}-3\sqrt{\bar{p}(1-\bar{p})}$	Prefer $n\bar{p}\,?\,2$ typ: $n \geq 50$	Binomial distribution LCL < 0 = >0
Standardized $p = (p - \bar{p})\,/\,\sigma p$	O	+3	−3	Variable	Standardize p: Stabilize UCL & LCL
c Number of defects per inspection unit	$\bar{c}$	$\bar{c}+3\sqrt{\bar{c}}$	$\bar{c}-3\sqrt{\bar{c}}$	Prefer $\bar{c} \geq 2$	Poisson distribution Expected # small: great opportunity
u Number of defects per inspection unit	$\bar{u}$	$\bar{u}+3\sqrt{\bar{u}/n}$	$\bar{u}-3\sqrt{\bar{u}/n}$	Prefer $\bar{c} \geq 2$	Poisson distribution Expected # small: great opportunity

Testing for Normality and Exponentiality. Table 4.7 demonstrates this test.

Table 4.7 Testing for normality and exponentiality

CONDITION	TEST FOR NORMALITY	TEST FOR EXPONENTIALITY	REMARKS
$n > 8$ and $n < 25$	1. Probability plot / histogram *and* 2. Anderson-Darling (A^{2*}) Test *or* 3. Moment tests	1. Probability plot / histogram *and* 2. Shapiro-Wilk W(E) *or* 3. Anderson-Darling (B^{2*}) test	1. Anderson-Darling A^{2*} a. Distance test b. $A^{2*} = A^2 (1+.75/n + 2*25/n^2)$ c. Useful for very small sample sizes 2. Moment tests a. Based on 3rd + 4th standardized moments b. Become more useful as n increases beyond 15–20 c. 3rd Moment: Index of skewness $\gamma_1 = \mu_3 / \mu_2^{2/3}$ d. 4th Moment: Index of kurtosis $\gamma_2 = \mu_4 / \mu_2^{2} - 3$ 3. Shapiro-Wilk W(E) a. Useful up to sample sizes of 90–110 b. Not desirable as B^{2*} for very small samples c. $W(E) = b^2/s^2$ 4. Anderson-Darling B^{2*} a. Distance test b. Requires that origin parameter is known

$n > 25$ and $n < 125$	1. Probability plot / histogram and
	2. Moment tests
		1. Probability plot / histogram and
		2. Shapiro-Wilk W(E)
			Chi-Square Goodness-of-Fit test
			 a. Optimum interval/cell (k) count:
			
			$K = 4(0.75(n-1)^2)^{1/5}$
			
			 b. Use Cochran's procedure where:
			
			$UCL = \mu + z_{ilk''}$
			   (Test of normality)
			
			or
			
			$UCL = \dfrac{1}{\lambda} \ln(1- \dfrac{i}{k}) + \mu$
			   and
			
			$X^2 = (\dfrac{k}{n}\sum\limits_{i=1}^{k} f_o^z) - n$

$n > 125$	1. Probability plot / histogram and 2. Moment tests 3. Chi-Square Goodness-of-Fit test (Cochran's procedure)	1. Probability plot / histogram *and* 2. Chi-Square Goodness-of-Fit test (Cochran's procedure)	

Not recommended: (1) Kolmogorow-Smirnov (2) Standard Chi-Square Goodness-of-Fit test over pretabulated data

Measurement system analysis (MSA)

The purpose of performing a measurement system analysis (MSA) is to ensure the information collected is a true representation of what is occurring in the process. Perhaps the most important item to remember is that total variation in a process is equal to the sum of the process variation and the measurement system variation. Therefore, minimizing measurement variation ensures that variation reflected by the data collected represents only process variation. As a consequence, MSA is performed on a regular basis to ensure that data is valid and reliable. Typical questions answered by conducting MSA include:

- Is the measurement system capable for this study?
- How big is the measurement error?
- How much uncertainty should be attached to a measurement when interpreting it?
- Are the measurements being made with measurement units that are small enough to properly reflect the variation present?
- What are the sources of measurement error?
- Can we detect process improvement if and when it happens?
- Is the measurement system stable over time?

Measurement

People measure product characteristics or process parameters so they can assess the performance of the system of interest. The measured values provide feedback of the process, so that people may adjust settings, replace tools, redesign fixtures or allow the operation to continue on its current course. The measurements are indeed the data that will allow people to make decisions critical to improvement efforts.

As critical as these measurements are, no measurement process is perfect. Sometimes different numbers or readings result when the same part or sample is measured a second time. Different readings may be made by different people, gauges or even by the same person using the same gauge. The difference in successive measurements of the same item is called measurement error. This source of variation must be analyzed, because the validity of the data directly affects the validity of process improvement decisions.

The measurement system is a major component of the process. In fact, studying variation within the parameters of the measurement system is of paramount importance for two reasons:

- Measurement error contributes to process variation and has a negative influence upon the process capability level.

- Measurement error is present whenever measurements are made. The effects of measurement error influence the assessment of all other items of the process.

In addition to being a part of the process or system, measurement activities may also form a process. It is totally inappropriate to view measurement error as merely a function of measurement hardware or instruments. Other components of the measurement process are equally important to measurement error or validity. For example, people contribute to measurement error by having different levels of tactile, auditory or visual perception. These characteristics account for calibration and/or interpretation differences.

Another example in measurement error is the contribution of a method change. This kind of error is one of the largest sources of variation in the measurement process. The significance of this is compounded when different people or instruments are used to evaluate the same item or process. Obviously, a standard procedure is needed for every measurement activity. Only this procedure should be used by all the people who operate test equipment. Measurement errors that are sometimes attributed to the different people collecting the data are actually due to differences in methodology. People are usually able to produce similar readings when they use the same methods for operating the measurement equipment. Other examples where measurement error may be introduced are: changes in environment, changes in test equipment, changes in standards and so on. In dealing with measurement error, one must be familiar with the concepts of true value, accuracy and precision. Each of these is discussed in the following sections.

True value. The true value is a theoretical number that is absolutely the "correct" description of the measured characteristic. This is the value that is estimated each time a measurement is made. The true value is never known in practice because of the measurement scale resolution, or the divisions that are used for the instrument's output. For example, someone may be satisfied with a dimension of up to tenth of an inch (0.1). However, someone else may define that dimension with a different instrument up to the ten thousandth of an inch (0.1043), which, of course, is closer to the true value. The appropriate level of measurement resolution is determined by the characteristic specifications and economic considerations. A common practice and rule of thumb calls for tester resolution that is equal to or less than one-tenth of the characteristic tolerance (the upper specification limit minus the lower specification limit). The true value is considered as part of tester calibration and discussions of measurement accuracy.

Accuracy. The accuracy of a measurement system is the relationship between the average of a number of successive measurements of a single part and that of the true value. When the measurement process yields a mean of successive measurements that is different than the true value, the instrument is not calibrated properly.

Precision. The precision of a measurement system is quantified by the spread of readings that result from successive measurements of the same part or sample. The standard deviation of measurement error is used to quantify the spread of the precision distribution. The common variation that creates the precision distribution comes from two different sources:

- *Repeatability (RPT)*. Repeatability is a measurement system variation that is due to a specific situation or set of conditions. The differences in successive measured readings for one item, made by one person, using one instrument, in one setting or environment, using one calibration of reference is error due to repeatability. This is the variation within a situation. Repeatability is present in every measurement system.
- *Reproducibility (RPD)*. Reproducibility describes the difference in successive measurements for the same item that are due to differences of hardware, people, methods or environments. This source of variability is quantified as the spread (range or standard deviation) between several repeatability distributions—the distributions generated from repeated tries. Reproducibility exists only when there is more than one measurement situation.

Any study that quantifies repeatability and reproducibility contains much diagnostic information. This information should be used to focus measurement system improvement efforts. There are two basic ways of determining the repeatability and reproducibility. The first is the graphical way and the second is the calculation method via (a) standard deviation of measurement error, (b) the precision/tolerance (P/T) ratio, and (c) the long and short method. Although the methods for determining repeatability and reproducibility are beyond the scope of this book, standard deviation and P/T ratios are briefly discussed in the following sections. The reader is encouraged to see forms 13–15 in the CD for an example of the long and short repeatability and reproducibility. For additional reading on these items see Stamatis (2003), AIAG (2002), and Bothe (1997). However, the following statements should be remembered:

- When the error due to repeatability is smaller than the error due to reproducibility, there is a good chance that the error is due to people using different calibration or measurement methods.
- When both errors are almost equal, this indicates a very small degree of reproducibility error. The error that is inherent in each measurement situation is very large. In this case, all of the measurement activities are using the same calibration and measurement procedures. In spite of these similarities, all of the distributions experience a high degree of repeatability error. This signals a source of error common to each of the measurement situations. The measurement hardware or anything else common to each of the distributions should be investigated as a major source of measurement error.

The standard deviation of measurement error. Because precision is separated into repeatability and reproducibility, the spread of the precision distribution is calculated as a composite. The standard deviation for measurement error is calculated as:

$$S_e = (S_{RPT} + S_{RPD})^{1/2}$$

Six standard deviations (6σ) of measurement error describe the spread of the precision distribution. The magnitude of this spread is evaluated with the precision/tolerance (P/T) ratio.

P/T ratio. A measurement system is declared adequate when the magnitude of measurement error is not too large. One way to evaluate the spread of the precision distribution is to compare it to the product tolerance. This is an absolute index of measurement error, because the product specifications should not change. A measurement system is acceptable if it is stable and does not consume a major portion of the product tolerance. The ratio between the precision distribution (six standard deviations of measurement error) and the product tolerance (upper specification limit and lower specification limit) is called the P/T ratio and quantifies this relationship.

$$P/T \text{ Ratio} = (6\sigma_{error})/ \text{ USL-LSL}$$

σ_{error} = standard deviation of measurement error

USL = upper specification limit

LSL = lower specification limit

The following general criteria are used to evaluate the size of the precision distribution:

P/T ratio level of measurement error:

0.0 – 0.10 excellent

0.11 – .020 good

0.21 – .030 marginal

0.31 plus unacceptable

Stability and **linearity** are also measures of measurement and integral part of the repeatability and reproducibility (R & R). Repeatability and reproducibility are indices of measurement error based on relatively short periods of time. Stability describes the consistency of the measurement system over a long period. The additional time period allows further opportunities for the sources of repeatability and reproducibility error to change and add errors to the measurement system. All measuring systems should be able to demonstrate stability over time. A control chart made from repeated measurements of the same items documents the level of a measurement system's stability. On the other hand, linearity is the difference in bias errors over the expected operating range of the measurement system.

Poka-yoke—Mistake proofing

Shigeo Shingo is considered the father of poka-yoke, and is often quoted as saying, "The idea behind poka-yoke is to respect the intelligence of workers by taking over repetitive tasks or actions that depend on the vigilance of memory." This process includes adding features to a design or process to assist the operator in the performance of the task.

Poka-yoke, in any of the various spellings, is another name for error- or mistake-proofing a design or process. The focus of poka-yoke is to sensitize us about the differences between prevention and detection and to do something about it. Prevention prevents errors from occurring or prevents those errors from causing defects. Detection identifies a defect and immediately initiates a corrective action to prevent multiple defects from leaving the workstation.

Detection devices are used to deal with an error that is difficult to eliminate, or is in the process of being located. The main idea of a prevention approach is to keep an error from producing multiple defects. Sometimes the error (or root cause) of the defect is hard to find. In this case, it is often profitable to create solutions that detect and react to an error or a defect instead of preventing an error or a defect. Such devices are detection devices.

Using detection devices in error-proofing is different from regular product or process inspection. Error-proofing initiates a corrective action once an error or defect has been detected. Regular product or process inspection should not be referred to as error-proofing unless the inspection is tied to an immediate corrective measure. An example of inspection that is not tied to an immediate corrective action is SPC (statistical process control) or a continual inspection with a process controller.

A number of criteria should be considered when choosing between a prevention or detection approach. The proposed device must be considered for its ability to:

- Prevent an error that causes the defect, or initiate a corrective action before multiple defects occur.
- Be designed and installed quickly and easily.
- Be cost-effective to implement and easy to maintain.

The need for poka-yoke

History shows that no matter how much we train the operator or document the process, human error occurs. Poka-yoke is the methodology of reducing or eliminating human error, which causes defects. The methodology is based on two essential attitudes about human behavior: mistakes are inevitable, and errors can be eliminated. Based on these attitudes the following corollary assumptions may be made about work processes and workers:

• Few workers make errors intentionally.

• Error is inherent in the nature of humans.

• Human errors are invited to occur by processes that do not use error-proofing.

A poka-yoke methodology alters the work environment with a goal of reducing human errors and their defects.

What is the current use of poka-yoke?

Poka-yoke is currently incorporated into the design and manufacturing processes and products used by many companies as a tool to stay globally competitive. It improves product quality for both internal and external customers by preventing defects from getting into the product. (In some cases, the distinction is made between error-proofing and mistake-proofing. The first is associated with design, the second with manufacturing.)

Mistake-proofing reduces costs primarily by reducing waste, because when less material is scrapped, more material is transformed into saleable product. Error-proofing improves the design by allowing a greater quantity of good products to reach the final customer without rework. Error-proofing also improves the quality of the workers' lives by improving worker safety. It is not always necessary to create all designs and processes with error-proofing in mind. Trade-offs among quality, price and delivery must be considered. Sometimes focusing on mistake-proofing is just as acceptable.

Error-proofing benefits

The earlier an error is identified, the less cost is invested in that part. If a bad or defective part is not identified until final inspection, it will go through all areas of the plant pointlessly, as it is not able to be used. All of the labor and material used in the plant operations will have been wasted. Therefore, one of the goals of error-proofing is to identify errors as close as possible to the point at which they are created.

For example, consider a door that has a defect. If the defect is not caught at the time it occurs, the door will travel through all areas of the plant, be installed, painted and have trim applied. All of those processes will waste time and material on a defective part that should have been spent on usable parts.

When analyzing the cost of defective parts versus the cost of implementing a mistake-proofing solution, consider the following factors in the equation:

- Cost of time to work on the defective parts at all stations between the point where the error is made and the point where the error is identified.

- Cost of all materials used at the stations between the point where the error is made and the point where the error is caught.

- Cost of time spent in rework.

- Cost of material used for rework.

- Cost of time spent inspecting defective parts and/or inspection processes that would no longer be necessary with the proposed error-proofing solution.

- Lost production due to time spent on defective parts.

- Impact of lower customer satisfaction and lower worker morale resulting from producing defective parts.

Definitions

To understand poka-yoke, we must first distinguish between errors and defects. The two are not the same.

Errors. An error is any deviation from a specified manufacturing process. Errors can be made by machines or people and can be caused by previous errors. Not all errors result in defects, but all defects are created by errors. This means that if errors can be prevented, defects will be avoided. Errors that cause defects are located and eliminated through the use of error-proofing tools and procedures. The following items are examples of errors:

- The wrong option package in a vehicle is sequenced into the assembly.
- An oil sender unit is defective.
- A hose clamp is not positioned correctly during the assembly.
- A worn installation tool causes molding clips to be installed incorrectly.
- A door is left open on an assembly finishing line.

Defects. A defect is the result of any deviation from product specifications that may lead to customer dissatisfaction. (In some industries the word *defect* is unacceptable for legal reasons. If that is an issue, then the term *non-conformance* is used). Product specifications are set by customer requirements, which are translated into design and manufacturing requirements. A "deviation from product specifications" means the product is not produced according to the manufacturing plan or requirements. A product must fall into one of two categories to be classified as a defect:

- The product has deviated from manufacturing or design specifications.
- The product does not meet internal and/or external customer expectations.

Note that the definition of a defect applies whether the receiver of the defective part is the final customer to receive the product (external customer), or the first operator outside of a group of processes in the manufacturing system (internal customer). Examples of defects (the result of errors) include:

- A vehicle equipped with the wrong option package (e.g., options with premium sound, air, ABS or heavy-duty suspension).
- An engine oil/coolant leak.
- Squeaks, rattles or loose parts.
- Parts that become damaged during assembly.

Now that we have examined the difference between errors and defects, let us look into the distinction between *error-proofing* and *mistake-proofing*.

Error-proofing. Error-proofing is based on two essential attitudes about human error: mistakes are inevitable, and errors can be eliminated. Error-proofing is a process improvement that is designed to prevent a specific defect from occurring. It is generally associated with design, since it is a system that:

- Prevents personal injury.
- Prevents faulty products.
- Promotes job safety.
- Prevents machine damage.

Error-proofing can have different definitions, but they all have the same core elements that focus on elimination as follows:

- The application of tools and devices to a process to eliminate the possibility of errors occurring.
- The application of tools and devices to a process to eliminate the possibility of defects that have occurred continuing on to the customer.
- The use of functional design features to eliminate the possibility of parts being assembled incorrectly.

Mistake-proofing. Mistake-proofing, although often used interchangeably with error-proofing, focuses on reduction of the defect and is associated with manufacturing:

- The application of tools and devices to a process to reduce the possibility of errors occurring.
- The application of tools and devices to a process to reduce the possibility of defects that have occurred continuing on to the customer.
- The use of functional design features to reduce the possibility of parts being assembled incorrectly.

Another way of differentiating between the two variations of poka-yoke is to say that mistake-proofing focuses on reducing risk, while error-proofing focuses on eliminating the risk of errors occurring.

Generic five-step process for poka-yoke

The generic 5-step process shown in Table 4.8 is a proven method that can be applied to most error-proofing situations. It shares a similar framework with many other methodologies, including phases for problem definition and solution review and implementation.

Table 4.8 Generic five steps for poka-yoke

Step 1: Define the problem • What is the problem? • Whom does it affect? (Internal/external customer) • Where does the problem occur? • When does the problem occur? • How did the problem occur? • How many defects are produced? • Problem statement • What will determine that the problem has been solved?	**Tools** • Pareto diagrams • Run charts • Scatter diagrams • Floor plans • Brainstorming
Step 2: Implement interim solution • How can we keep the effects of this problem from affecting the internal/external customer? How do we contain the problem?)	**Tools** • Brainstorming, etc.
Step 3: Define root cause • People • Method • Machine • Material • Measurement • Environment	**Tools** • Fishbone diagrams • Brainstorming • Five whys • Performance checklist
Step 4: Define and select solution • Recommended action • Rationale • Pilot plan • Problem solved according to criteria stipulated in step 1?	**Tools** • Brainstorming • Pilot programs • Run charts • Scatter diagrams
Step 5: Implement solution • Solution • Necessary communication	

Generic mistake-proofing implementation process

Table 4.9 shows the generic mistake-proofing implementation process.

Table 4.9 Generic mistake-proofing implementation process

Task	Major steps	Specific individual characteristics
Preparation of application area	Step 1. Deliver mistake-proofing overview	1. Mistake-proofing definition 2. Approaches to mistake-proofing 3. Other definitions 4. Mistake-proofing preparation and deployment steps 5. Function of mistake-proofing devices 6. Examples of mistake-proofing devices 7. Benefits to mistake-proofing
	Step 2. Creating a mistake-proofing log	1. Establish format for collection, storage, maintenance of mistake-proofing information 2. Designate persons) to update mistake-proofing log
	Step 3. Prioritizing defects collection points in the application area	1. Identify all data 2. Collect existing quality data from plant sources 3. Collect current and historical data from all collection points 4. Categorize collected data according to defect type 5. Summarize data for each defect type using a Pareto chart 6. Select top 3 to 5 defects

Table 4.9 (*Continued*)

Task	Major steps	Specific individual characteristics
	Step 4. Choosing defects	1. Complete part description 2. Identify the defect 3. Identify the financial impact of the defect 4. Identify where the defect was found 5. Identify where the defect was originally made 6. Identify time and distance of defect 7. Select defect for which mistake-proofing is to be developed
	Step 5. Document rationale for defect selection	1. Define the reasons for the selecting the defect 2. Document the reasons for selecting defect in mistake-proofing log
Deploy mistake-proofing to application area	Step 1. Establish objectives for implementation of mistake-proofing	1. Review the current and historical data 2. Estimate and document improvement 3. Calculate the expected impact
	Step 2. Deliver mistake- and error-proofing implementation worksheet	1. Define and discuss the purpose of the mistake-proofing implementation worksheet (MPIW) 2. Discuss the key components of the MPIW
	Step 3. Define the source error	1. Complete the heading area on the error-proofing implementation worksheet (EPIW)

(*Continued on next page*)

Table 4.9 *(Continued)*

Task	Major steps	Specific individual characteristics
Deploy mistake-proofing to application area *(Cont.)*	Step 3. *(Cont.)*	2. Describe the defect on the EPIW 3. Document the defect rate on the EPIW 4. Identify where the defect was found on the EPIW 5. Identify where the defect was made on the EPIW 6. Describe the current process where the defect was made on the EPIW 7. Identify any errors or deviations from process standards on the EPIW 8. Investigate/analyze the causes for each error/deviation
	Step 4. Create and install selected mistake-proofing devices	1. Develop ideas for improving, eliminating and detecting errors on the EPIW 2. Create an error-proofing device and test for effectiveness
	Step 5. Measure, document and standardize results and benefits	1. Measure and document the improvement on the MPIW 2. Measure and document the impact on the MPIW 3. Compare the mistake-proofing results and objectives 4. Update standardized work sheets and other appropriate documents

Table 4.9 (*Continued*)

Task	Major steps	Specific individual characteristics
	Step 6. Notify other areas	1. Consider who may benefit from the improved process 2. Fill in the appropriate suggestion form 3. Consider ways to visually post improvement 4. Congratulate the team on their achievement

Examples of poka-yoke elements

In a typical mistake-proofing situation there are three elements for consideration: inspection systems (i.e., successive check, self check or source), setting functions (e.g., contact, fixed value and motion step) and regulatory functions (e.g., control and warning). Using three distinct examples, let us examine these elements:

Example 1. Some manual transmissions allow drivers to start the car while in gear, causing the car to lunge forward or backward unexpectedly. In some newer models with standard transmissions, the car cannot be started unless the clutch is depressed.

- Inspection system: self check.
- Setting function: contact.
- Regulatory function: control.

Example 2. Vehicle name plates are rotated 180 degrees, causing them to be installed upside down. A larger hole was created on the right-hand side of the install area and a smaller hole on the left-hand side. A large pin is placed on the right-hand side of the back of the name plate, with a smaller pin on the left.

- Inspection system: source.
- Setting function: contact.
- Regulatory function: control.

Example 3. During the assembly of a simple pushbutton switch that consists of an ON button and an OFF button, workers sometimes forget to install the small springs that go under the buttons. When this error is discovered during a subsequent inspection or by a customer, company inspectors are sent to examine every switch assembled over that same time period. Faulty switches are disassembled and correctly reassembled. At the beginning of the operation, workers take two springs out of a box and place them on a small dish. If any springs remain on the dish after switch assembly, the worker recognizes that a mistake has occurred and reassembles the switch correctly.

- Inspection system: self check.
- Setting function: fixed value.
- Regulatory function: warning.

Lean manufacturing process

The lean manufacturing error-proofing implementation process is another example of an error-proofing methodology at many corporations. This process is made up of two groups of tasks: preparation and deployment. Both tasks contain sequential steps to follow when implementing error-proofing; each is discussed in the following sections.

Preparation. This includes the start-up steps workers take when preparing to implement error-proofing. The goal is to create an understanding of the situation before rushing to implement a change. The steps for preparation are:

1. Deliver an error-proofing overview.
2. Create an error-proofing log.
3. Prioritize defects.
4. Choose defects.
5. Document the rationale for defect selection.

Deployment. This includes the steps to implement a standardized method of error-proofing. This is a proven process that, when followed correctly, will error-proof any given operation or piece of equipment. This phase should be started only after the preparation phase. The steps in deployment are:

1. Establish objectives for the implementation of error-proofing.
2. Complete error-proofing implementation worksheet.
3. Define the source error.
4. Create and install selected error-proofing devices.
5. Measure, document and standardize results and benefits.
6. Notify other areas.

Specific relationship of six sigma and lean

It appears that the lean methodology is running parallel to the six sigma philosophy. In fact, in some cases the six sigma methodology incorporates the concepts of lean manufacturing. That is because with lean, you have to know what your customers require and understand concepts such as mean time between failures with equipment in your process. You have to calculate takt times to know how much product you produce per second and match production to your customers' demands. In other words, in any lean environment, part of what you are trying to create is the atmosphere for people to look creatively at what they do on a daily basis and enable them to do it better and smarter. That is precisely what six sigma is trying to do, but in a slightly different way. The difference is that six sigma is focused on a systematic approach (via the DMAIC model) to eliminate variation, and the lean methodology is focused on eliminating waste through correction, overproduction, processing, conveyance, inventory motion and waiting by using the 5Ss (sorting, storage, shining, standardizing and sustaining). A sixth one, safety, has recently been added.) The goal is the same.

Womack's (1990, 1996) principles for lean manufacturing are quite similar to those associated with six sigma. They are:

- Specify the value desired by the customer.
- Identify the value stream for each product, providing the relevant values, and challenge all of the wasted steps (generally nine out of ten) currently necessary to provide those values, since these steps are value non-added. However, these non-value-added steps are part of the current value stream.
- Make the product flow continuously through the remaining value-creating steps.
- Introduce pull between all the steps where continuous flow is impossible.

- Aim for perfection, so that the number of steps and the amount of time and information needed to serve the customer is continually reduced.

Caution on lean manufacturing

Even at Toyota, home of lean, or at Omark Industries (now Blount International) and Harley-Davidson, which were both in the news in the 1980s as roaring JIT success stories (Schonberger, 2002), lean manufacturing hasn't always remained as successful over time. The numbers from their annual reports, and those of over 500 other companies in many countries, tell the tale. The analysis, tracking inventory turnover trends for up to 50 years, reveals that in its glory years—the late 1970s and into the 1980s—Toyota's inventories were turning an awesome 60, 70, and 80 times per year. A decade later its inventory turnover had fallen to the 20s, and has dropped steadily since then—all the way to 12.1 in 2001. Blount/Omark roared upward until 1987, but has been in a fluttering stall since then. Harley's top year was 1995. (Inventory turnover is cost of goods sold, from the income statement, divided by value of inventory, from the balance sheet.)

Inventory is the simplest marker of leanness, and it is not only of interest to those with lean aspirations (i.e., the makers, shippers, distributors and sellers). Inventories are tied to cash flow, which savvy analysts on Wall Street monitor even more carefully than they do earnings. However, focusing on just three companies, regardless of their reputations, does not make a story. Nor do the inventory turns of any one- or two-year period. What is interesting is the totality of long-term trend data from the 500-plus companies, which include almost every industry. For what they reveal about lean supply chains, some retailers and distributors are included. About 37 percent, nearly 200 of the database companies, are the success stories: their inventory improvement trend stretches over at least 10 years, and in some cases 25 or 50 years. That group includes such stalwarts in the machining and metalworking trades as Dana, Ingersoll Rand and Milacron in the United States, Lucas in the United Kingdom (a recent acquisition of Dana), SKF in Sweden, and Tata Engineering & Locomotive in India. The other 63 percent make up the bad reviews. Fully 28 percent have stalled or have been fattening up on inventories for at least 10 and up to 50 years. One of them is the world's most esteemed manufacturer: General

Electric. That maker of jet engines, electric power equipment, loco-motives and major appliances had its "leanest" year in 1973 and has lost ground, in a valley-peak-valley pattern, since then—its six sigma prowess notwithstanding. Twin Disc, a key player in making MRP (material requirements planning) famous in the 1970s, has seen its inventory situation worsen since 1985. A.O. Smith, Toro and Snap-on Tools have been on a downslope since 1985, 1986, and 1989 respectively (Schonberger, 2002).

Why, in the midst of lean, six sigma, 5S, total production management (TPM), and supply-chain management fervor, are so many companies backsliding or why are so many plateauing? In Japan the decade of 1990s was an economic downer. The fortunes of its manufacturers were the same. One reason for worsening inventory patterns in so many companies may relate to Japan's cherished, though fading, reluctance to reduce labor. In the face of declining sales, an excess labor force just keeps producing and producing and producing. Why, then, are some companies not getting lean? The following may give us a clue:

- *Complacency.* This is a fallout of the prosperity of the 1990s.

- *Stock-hyping deal making.* Executives are looking past the basics of good process management.

- *Growth and retention of unprofitable customers and product variations.* This is often the company's fault for not bringing sales and marketing into multifunctional teaming with finance and operations.

- *Legacies.* Mega-machines that produce fat inventories, outsized factories that require marathon flow distances, systems that bog down rather than link up manufacturing and supply chains, and job designs that instill mindless boredom rather than inspiring waste-chopping ideas contribute to this problem.

- *Retention of command-and-control management.* This stifles broad involvement. As control increases, involvement decreases. This is because individuals think or rather perceive their input as irrelevant and or useful when management is commanding and controlling both inputs and outputs of the decision process.

- *Job-hopping managers and engineers.* These people launch initiatives, but do not follow through; they favor what is hot while losing touch with what is still successful.

Corrective responses revolve around reversing these points. Complacency and job-hopping are already on a course of self-correction, and the basics are back in style, especially in the aftermath of the Enron financial manipulation debacle. Clearing out the unprofitable, attacking the legacies, tapping companywide human potential, and maintaining continuity, however, require upgraded awareness and commitment. Those of us in the engineering community bear much of the blame for past failures and must take much of the initiative in achieving truly lean results and making them stick.

Failure mode and effect analysis (FMEA)

A failure mode and effect analysis (FMEA) is a methodology to evaluate a system, a design or a process for possible ways in which failures can occur. For each bona fide or potential failure, an estimate is made of its effect on the total system and of its seriousness. In addition, a review is made of the action being taken (or planned) to minimize the probability of failure or to minimize the effect of failure.

This simple, but straightforward, approach can be very technical (quantitative) or very non-technical (qualitative), utilizing three main factors for the identification of the specific failure:

1. *Occurrence.* How often the failure occurs.

2. *Severity.* how serious the failure is.

3. *Detection.* How easy or difficult it is to detect the failure.

How complicated the approach is always depends on the complexity of the problem as defined by the following (Juran and Gryna, 1980):

- *Safety.* Injury is the most serious of all failure effects. In fact, in some cases, it is of unquestionable priority and of course, at this point it must be handled either with a hazard analysis and/or failure mode and critical analysis (FMCA).

- *Effects on downtime.* How are repairs made? Can repairs be made while the machine is off-duty or while the machine is operating?

- *Access.* What hardware items must be removed to get at the failed component? This area will be of great importance as environmental laws are changed to reflect world conditions for disassembly.

- *Repair planning.* Repair time, maintainability, repair tools, cost, recommendations for changes in design specifications all should be considered. Here, the Shingo approach, DOE or design for manufacturability may be considered.

To carry this methodology to its proper conclusion the following prerequisites in understanding are necessary.

- *You must understand that not all problems are important.* This is very fundamental to the entire concept of FMEA, because unless this concept is internalized, we are going to be "chasing fires" in the organization. We must recognize that some problems have a higher priority than others for whatever the reason. FMEA helps identify this priority.

- *You must know the customer.* The customer is usually thought of as the end user. However, a customer may also be defined as a subsequent or downstream operation, as well as a service operation. When using the term customer from a FMEA perspective, the definition plays a very major role in addressing problems. For example, as a general rule in the design FMEA, one views the customer as the end user, while in the process FMEA, the customer is viewed as the next operation in line. This next operation may indeed be the end user, but it does not have to be. Once you define your customer (internal, intermediate or external) you may not change it—at least, not for the problem at hand—unless you recognize that by changing it you may indeed have changed your problem and/or consequences.

- *You must know the function.* It is imperative to know the function, purpose and objective of what you are trying to accomplish. Otherwise you are going to waste time and effort in redefining your problem based on interpretations of specific problems or situations. If you have to, take extra time to make sure you understand the function or purpose of what you are trying to accomplish.

- *You must be prevention-oriented.* Unless you recognize that continual improvement is in your best interest, the FMEA is going to be a static document to satisfy your customer or market requirements. The push for this continual improvement makes the FMEA a dynamic document, changing as the design and/or process changes with the intent to always make a better design and/or process.

Why do we do FMEAs?

The propensity of our managers and engineers to minimize the risk in a particular design and/or process has forced us to look at reliability engineering to not only minimize, but also to define the risk. Perceived risk is driven by the following factors:

- Competition.
- Warranty and service costs.
- Evolving technical risks.
- Market pressure.
- Management emphasis.
- Customer requirements.
- Safety.
- Legal and statutory requirements.
- Public liability.

These risks can be measured through reliability engineering and/or statistical analyses. However, because of their complexity, the FMEA has extracted the basic principles without the technical mathematics and has provided us with a tool that anybody committed to continual improvement can utilize.

Statistical process control (SPC) is another tool that provides the impetus for the FMEA, especially for a process FMEA. SPC provides information about the process in regard to changes. These changes are called common and special causes. From an FMEA perspective we may look at the common causes as failures that are the result of inherent failure mechanisms, and as such, they can affect the entire population. In this case, this is a cause for examining the design (Denson 1992).

On the other hand, special causes are looked at as failures that result from part defects and/or manufacturing problems, and as such, they can affect a relatively small population. In this case, there is cause for examining the process.

Customer requisition is, of course, a very strong influence on why we may be doing a FMEA. For example, all major automobile companies in their supplier certification standards require a FMEA program from their suppliers.

Courts, through product liability, may require some substantiation as to how reliable the products and their performance are.

International standards such as the ISO-9000 series may define for you the program of documentation in your design. For example, the Product Liability Directive of the European Community in 1985 stipulates that manufacturers of a product will be held liable, regardless of fault or negligence, if a person is harmed or an object is damaged by a faulty or defective product (this includes exporters into the EC market). This liability directive essentially reverses the burden of proof of fault from the injured to the producer. Quality systems incorporating specific tools such as FMEA or fault tree analysis (FTA) or failure mode and critical analysis (FMCA) with safety prevention provisions, will be particularly important in protecting a company from unfounded liability claims. Furthermore, proposed safety directives would oblige manufacturers to monitor the safety of their products throughout their foreseeable life (Stamatis 1992).

Other benefits of the FMEA are:

- Improves the quality, reliability and safety of the products.
- Improves the company's image and competitiveness.
- Helps increase customer satisfaction.
- Reduces product development time and costs.
- Helps select the optimum system design.
- Helps determine the redundancy of the system.
- Helps identify diagnostic procedures.
- Establishes a priority for design improvement actions.
- Helps identify critical and/or significant characteristics.
- Helps in the analysis of new manufacturing and/or assembly processes.

Even though all of these reasons are legitimate, the most important reason for writing an FMEA is the need to improve. Unless this need is part of the culture of the organization, the FMEA program is not going to be successful.

Vocabulary of FMEA

To understand the FMEA one must understand its language. There are several terms that one must understand.

Function. The function is the task that a component, subsystem or system must perform. This function is very important in understanding the entire FMEA process. It has to be communicated in a way that is concise, exact and easy to understand—no jargon. To facilitate this, it is recommended that an active verb be found to best describe the function. The active verb, by definition, defines performance, and performance is what a function is—for example, position, support, retain, lubricate.

Failure. The failure is the problem—that is, the inability of a component, subsystem or system to perform to design intent. This inability can be defined as both a known failure and a potential failure. Typical failures are identified as no function; partial function, over function, degraded over time, intermittent function and unintended function. When potential failures in terms of functional defectives are identified, the FMEA is fulfilling its mission of prevention.

Functional defectives are failures that do not meet the customers' requirements, but we ship those products with the failures to them anyway because:

- The customer will never know the difference.

- The customer will never find out.

- The customer will find out, but the failed product that is delivered can still be used.

- The customer will find out, but the failed product that is delivered has to be used because there are no alternatives.

Examples of failures are: broken, worn, corrosion and noise.

Causes of failure. Next to the function, the cause of failure is perhaps the most important section of the FMEA. It is indeed here that we point the way toward preventive and/or corrective action. The more focused we are on the root cause, the more successful we are in eliminating failures. In this section, we must be careful not to be too eager for solutions, because we are going to fall victim to symptoms and short-term remedies, rather than completely eliminating the real problems. What is of supreme importance here is that we must be able to find an actionable root cause. Otherwise, we will fall victims of analysis paralysis. Examples of design causes of failure include wall thickness, vibration, torque specifications and shock loads. Examples of process causes of failure are voltage surge, dull tools, improper set-up and worn bearings.

Effects of failure. This is the outcome of the failure on the system and/or the product. In essence, the effects of the failure have to do with what happens when a failure occurs. We must understand, however, that the effects of the failure must be addressed from two viewpoints. The first is local, in which the failure is isolated and does not affect anything else. The second is global, in which the failure can and does affect other functions and/or components. This creates a domino effect. Generally speaking, the failure with a global effect is more serious than a failure of a local nature.

The effect of the failure will also define the severity of a particular failure. For example, a local failure might be a parking light bulb going out; a global failure would be if the power brakes went out. In the first case one can identify a nuisance; in the second case, a catastrophic event is likely to occur.

Product validation controls. These controls exist to prevent the causes of the failure from occurring and to validate repeatability for certain processes, especially with the FDA.

Current controls. These controls exist to prevent the causes of the failure from occurring in the process phase. Some examples are any of the SPC tools, capability and any testing including non-destructive testing.

Design verification controls. These controls exist to prevent causes of the failure from occurring in the design phase—for example, design guidelines and design review specifications.

Relationship between FMEA and other tools

Fault tree analysis (FTA). Fault tree analysis is a deductive analytical technique. It uses a "tree" to show the cause and effect relationships between a single undesired event (failure) and the various contributing causes. The tree shows the logical branches from the single failure at the top of the tree, to the root cause or causes at the bottom of the tree. Standard logic symbols are used.

After the tree has been constructed and the root causes identified, the corrective actions required to prevent or control the causes can be determined. The FTA always supplements the FMEA and not the other way around. In general, the FTA is used to identify the root factors that could cause a failure and their interdependent relationships. Other benefits of the FTA may be to:

- Determine the probability of occurrence for each of the root causes.

- Help visualize the analysis.

- Help identify the reliability of higher-level assemblies or the system.

Failure mode analysis (FMA). Failure mode analysis is a systematic approach to quantify the failure modes, failure rate, and root causes of known failures. Usually, the FMA is based on historical information such as warranty, service, field or process data.

The FMA is used to identify the operation, failure modes, rates and critical design parameters of existing hardware or processes. Because of its ability to utilize historical data and known failures, the FMA is used primarily on current production, as opposed to the FMEA, which is used on changed and new designs or processes.

Both the FMA and the FMEA deal with failure modes and causes. However, the FMA is usually done first, and the information gained is fed into the FMEA.

Failure mode and critical analysis (FMCA). The failure mode and critical analysis is a systematic approach to quantify the failure modes, rates and root causes from a criticality perspective. Criticality is the product of severity and occurrence. It is very similar to the FMEA in all other respects.

The FMCA is used primarily with government contracts based on the MIL-STD-1629A, where the identification of critical, major and minor characteristic is of importance.

Block diagrams and process flow diagrams. A block diagram illustrates the physical or functional relationships as well as the specific interfaces within a system or assembly under analysis.

The block diagrams used in FMEA are:

- *System*. This diagram is for identifying the relationships between major components and subsystems.

- *Detail*. This diagram is for identifying the relationships between each part within an assembly or subsystem.

- *Reliability.* This diagram is for identifying the series dependence or independence of major components, subsystems or detail parts in achieving required functions.

Block diagrams are not intended to illustrate all the functional relationships which must be considered in the FMEA. The diagrams should be made as simple and explicit as possible.

Whereas the block diagram assists in the definition of scope and the definition of interfaces in the system or design phase of development, the process flow diagram does the same thing, but in a given process.

P-diagrams, interface diagrams and FMEA. A P-diagram (parameter diagram) is a tool that helps the experimenter focus on robustness. It relates inputs (signals) to energy transformation to outcomes (responses). Also, it identifies the noise and control factors, as well as the error states. The error states are the failures.

The interface diagram is a visual tool that helps the FMEA team evaluate interactions between the following considerations: physical proximity, energy transfer, material differences and communication.

Design of experiments (DOE). DOE is a special way of conducting an experiment or a study by which certain independent variables are varied to a predefined plan, and the effects are determined on the dependent variable.

DOE is used in reliability testing and can identify the primary factors that are causing an undesired event. The optimum use for DOE in FMEA applications is when there is a concern about several independent variables or an interaction effect of the causal factors.

Control plan. A control plan is a written summary of the producer's quality planning actions for a specific process and/or product. The control plan lists all process parameters and design characteristics considered important to customer satisfaction and which require specific quality planning actions. The control plan describes the actions and reactions required to ensure the process is maintained in a state of statistical control (as agreed between customer and supplier).

It is the FMEA that identifies the critical and significant characteristics and is, therefore, the starting point for initiating a control plan—it is never the other way around.

Mechanics of FMEA

Team. To do a complete job with the best results, an FMEA must be written by a team. The reason for this is that the FMEA should be a catalyst to stimulate the interchange of ideas between the functions affected. A single engineer or any other single person cannot do it.

The team should be made up of five to nine persons (preferably closer to five). All team members must have some knowledge of group behavior, the task at hand, some knowledge about the problem to be discussed, and some kind of either direct or indirect ownership of the problem. Above all, they must all be willing to contribute. Team members, must be cross-functional and multidisciplined. Furthermore, whenever possible or neccessary, the customer or the supplier should actively participate.

Design FMEA. A design FMEA is a systematic method to identify and correct any known or potential failure modes before the first production run. A first production run is viewed as the run where you produce a product or service for a specific customer with the intent of getting paid. This definition is important because it excludes part submission warrant (PSW), initial sample runs (ISR), trial runs, sometimes the prototype runs, etc. The threshold of the first production run is important, because, up to that point, to decide to modify or change the design is not a major thing. After that point, however, the customer gets involved through the letter of deviation, waiver of change or some other kind of formal notification.

Once these failures have been identified, we rank them and prioritize them.

The leader (the person responsible for a design FMEA) should be the design engineer, primarily because he or she is the most knowledgeable about the design and can best anticipate design failures. To facilitate the meeting, the quality engineer may be designated as the facilitator.

The minimum make-up of the team for the design is the design engineer and the process or manufacturing engineer. Anyone else that can contribute, or whom the design engineer feels would be appropriate, may also participate. A typical design team consists of:

- A design engineer.
- A manufacturing engineer.

- A test/development engineer.
- A reliability engineer.
- A material engineer.
- A field service engineer.

Of great importance in the make-up of the team is that the team must be cross-functional and multidisciplined. There is no such thing as the perfect team for all situations. Each team is unique. Each organization must define its optimum team participation, recognizing that some individuals may indeed hold two or more different positions at the same time.

The focus of the design is to minimize failure effects on the system by identifying the key characteristics of the design. These key characteristics may be found as part of the customer requirements, engineering specifications, industrial standards, government regulations and courts—through product liability.

The objective of the design FMEA is to maximize the system quality, reliability, cost and maintainability. It is important here to recognize that in design we have only three possibilities to look at defects, which are:

- Components—the individual unit of the design.
- Subsystem or subassembly—two or more combined components.
- System or assembly—a combination of components and subsystems for a particular function.

Regardless of what level we are in the design, the intent is the same: no failures on the system. To focus on these objectives, the design team must use consensus for their decision, but more important they must have the commitment of their management. The timing of the design FMEA is initiated during the early planning stages of the design and is continually updated as the program develops. As a team, you must do the best you can with what you have, rather than wait until all the information is in. By then, it may be too late.

Process FMEA. A process FMEA is a systematic method to identify and correct any known potential failure modes before the first production run, which, as discussed in the previous section, is the run where you produce a product or service for a specific customer with the intent of getting paid. Once these failures have been identified, we rank them and prioritize them.

For the process FMEA, the leader should be the process or manufacturing engineer, primarily because he or she is the most knowledgeable about the process structure and can best anticipate process failures. As with the design FMEA team, the quality engineer may be designated as the meeting facilitator.

The minimum make-up of the team for the process is the process or manufacturing engineer, the design engineer and operators. Anyone else that can contribute, or the process engineer feels appropriate, may also participate. A typical process team is:

- Process or manufacturing engineer.

- Design engineer.

- Quality engineer.
  - Reliability engineer.
  - Tooling engineer.
  - Operators.

As with the design FMEA, the team must be cross-functional and multidisciplined. Each organization must define its optimum team participation, recognizing that some individuals may indeed hold two or more different positions at the same time.

The focus of the process FMEA is to minimize production failure effects on the system by identifying the key variables. These key variables are the key characteristics of the design, but now in the process, they have to be measured, controlled, monitored, and so on. This is where SPC comes in.

The objective of the process FMEA is to maximize the system quality, reliability and productivity. The objective is a continuation of the design FMEA—more or less—since the process FMEA assumes the objective to be as designed. Because of this, potential failures that can occur because of a design weakness are not included in a process FMEA. They are only mentioned if those weaknesses affect the process, and they appear under the root cause column.

The process FMEA does not rely on product design changes to overcome weaknesses in the process, but it does take into consideration a product's design characteristics relative to the planned manufacturing or assembly process to ensure that, to the extent possible, the resultant product meets customer needs, wants and expectations.

A process FMEA is much more difficult and time-consuming than a design FMEA. The reason for this is that in a design FMEA we have three possibilities of analysis, (i.e. system, subsystem, and component) and in the process we have six, and each one of them may have even more subpossibilities. The six major possibilities for process are:

- Manpower.
- Machine.
- Method.
- Material.
- Measurement.
- Environment.

To show the complexity of each one of these possibilities let us take the machine, for example. To assess a machine failure, a team may have to examine some or all of the following contributing factors, and this list is by no means complete:

- Tools.
- Workstations.
- The production line.
- The process itself.
- Gauges.
- Operators.

Again, just like in the design FMEA, the process team must use consensus for their decision but more important they must have the commitment of their management.

To facilitate this consensus and gain the commitment of their management, the team in both design and process FMEAs must set specific improvement goals. To do that, the leader of the team must use the following specific behaviors:

- *Focus the team on result areas.* The leader should stress the importance of goal-setting for focusing team efforts and discuss possible result areas the team may choose.

- *Review existing trends, problem areas and goals.* The leader should share with the team data that could shed light on the team's performance and indicate possible areas for improvement.

- *Ask the group to identify possible areas for investigation.* The leader should actively and constantly encourage complete participation from all team members. The more the participation, the more ideas will surface. Brainstorming, affinity charts and force-field analysis are some of the tools that can be used by the leader to facilitate an open discussion by all.

- *If possible, ask the team to identify the goal.* The leader, after a thorough discussion and perhaps ranking, should have the team agree on the selected goal. This will enhance the decision and will ensure commitment.

- *Specify the goal.* It is the leader's responsibility, once the goal has been set, to identify the appropriate measures, time and amount of improvement. As a general rule, cost is not considered at this stage. The cost is usually addressed as part of another analysis called value engineering.

In the final analysis, regardless at what level the FMEA is being performed, the intent is always the same: no failures on the system.

The timing of the process FMEA is initiated during the early planning stages of the process before machines, tooling, facilities, etc. are purchased. The process FMEA, just like the design FMEA is continually updated as the process becomes more clearly defined.

Forms

In this section the forms will not be discussed primarily because there are no standards available. Each organization has their own forms, except the automotive industry, which uses the Automotive Industry Action Group approved form. A typical FMEA form is shown in Figure 4.7.

FMEA Guidelines

Because most organizations use their own individualized guidelines for FMEA, a discussion of specific guidelines is impossible. In general, however, the guidelines are numerical values based on certain statistical distributions that allow us to prioritize the failures. They are usually in two forms: the qualitative and the quantitative. In the qualitative form, one bases the meaning on theoretical distributions such as normal, norm-log (skewed to the left) and discrete distributions for the occurrence, severity and detection respectively.

In the quantitative form, one uses actual statistical and/or reliability data from the processes. This actual data may be historical and/or current. In both cases, the numerical values are from 1 to 10 and they denote set probabilities from low to high.

Description	Failure Mode Analysis							Action Plan				
Part name or process step & function	Potential Failure Mode	Potential Effect of Failure Mode	S	C L A S S	Potential Cause of Failure Mode	O	RPN	Recommended Action & Responsibility	Target Finish Date	Actual Finish Date	Actions Taken	Remarks

Figure 4.7 Typical FMEA Body

Occurrence. Under occurrence we look at the frequency of the failure as a result of a specific cause. The ranking that we give to this occurrence has a meaning rather than a value. The higher the number, the more frequent the failure.

Severity. In severity we assess the seriousness of the effect of the potential failure mode to the customer. Severity applies to the effect and to the effect only. The ranking that we give is typically 1 to 10, with 1 usually representing a nuisance and 10 representing a very major non-compliance to government regulations or safety item.

Detection. In detection we assess the probability of a failure reaching the customer. The numbers 1 to 10 again represent meaning rather than value. The higher the number the more likely your current controls or design verification were unsuccessful in containing the failure within your organization. Therefore, the likelihood of your customer receiving a failure is increased.

A general complaint about these guidelines is frequently heard in relation to consensus. For example, how can a group of people agree on everything? The answer is that they cannot, but you can still use consensus to decide the issue at hand. For example, if the decision falls in an adjacent category, the decision should be averaged out. If, on the other hand, it falls in more than an adjacent category, you should stick to the consensus. A problem at this point may be that someone in the team may not understand the problem, or some of the assumptions may have been overlooked, or maybe the focus of the group has drifted.

If let us say one person says that the severity is 7 and someone else says it is 8 or 6. These numbers are adjacent to each other therefore the average of the numbers is sufficient. (7 + 8 = 15, 15/2 = 7.5 or rounded off to 8; 7 + 6 = 13. 13/2 = 6.5 or 7). On the other hand, if one person says that the severity is 7 and another 3, there is a major problem in understanding and/or assumptions. The difference cannot be averaged out. It must be discussed and agreed upon before moving on to a different item.

If no consensus can be reached with a reasonable discussion with all the team members, then traditional organizational development processes (group dynamic techniques) must be used to resolve the conflict. Under no circumstances should a mere agreement or majority be pushed through, so that an early completion may take place. All FMEAs are time-consuming and the participants, as well as their management, must be patient for the proper results.

Risk priority number (RPN)

This number is the product of the occurrence, severity and detection. The value should be used to rank order the concerns of the design and/or process. In themselves, all RPNs have no other value or meaning.

A threshold of pursuing failures is a RPN equal to, or greater than, 50 based on a 95 percent confidence. (Although there is nothing magical about 50, by convention many companies use 50 as a threshold, only because it is the traditional statistical confidence of choice.) We can identify this threshold by any statistical confidence. For example, say 99 percent of all failures must be addressed for a very critical design, what is our threshold? There are 1,000 points available ($10 \times 10 \times 10$) from occurrence, severity and detection, 99 percent of 1,000 is 990. So, anything equal to, or over, 10 as a RPN must be addressed. On the other hand, if we want a confidence of only 90 percent then, 90 percent of 1,000 is 900. So, anything equal to, or greater than 100 as a RPN must be addressed. This threshold is therefore organizationally dependent and can change, not only with the organization, but with the product and/or the customer.

If there are more than two failures with the same RPN, then we use severity, then detection, and finally occurrence as the order of priority. Severity is used first because it deals with the effects of the failure. Detection is used over the occurrence because it is customer dependent, which is more important than just the frequencies of the failure.

A very important exception to this rule is in the automotive industry, which does not accept any threshold. Rather, the risk is identified through severity first, criticality (severity $\times$ occurrence) second and last through the RPN.

Recommended action

When the failure modes have been rank ordered by RPN, corrective action should be first directed at the highest ranked concerns and critical items. The intent of any recommended action is to reduce the occurrence, detection and/or severity rankings. Severity will change only with changes in design, otherwise, more often than not, the reductions are expected in either occurrence and/or detection. If no actions are recommended for a specific cause, then this should be indicated. On the other hand, if causes are not mutually exclusive, a DOE recommendation is in order.

In all cases where the effect of an identified potential failure mode could be a hazard to manufacturing and assembly personnel, corrective actions should be taken to prevent the failure mode by eliminating or controlling the causes. Otherwise appropriate operator protection should be specified.

The need for taking specific, positive corrective actions with quantifiable benefits, recommending actions to other activities and following-up all recommendations cannot be overemphasized. A thoroughly thought-out and well-developed FMEA will be of limited value without positive and effective corrective actions. It is the responsibility of all affected activities to implement effective follow-up programs to address all recommendations.

Completing an FMEA

To complete an FMEA effectively, one must follow a systematic approach. The recommended approach is an eight-step method that facilitates the system, the design and process FMEAs (Stamatis, 1995).

1. *Brainstorm.* Try to identify in what direction you want to go. Is it design or process? What kind of problems are you having with a particular situation? Is the customer involved or are you pursuing continual improvement on your own? If the customer has identified specific failures, then your job is much easier, because you already have a direction. On the other hand, if you are trying on your own to brainstorm and/or to define the cause and effect of a problem, you may have a difficult time, since what you will end up with is your opinion and nothing else. It is therefore important when you brainstorm to have a team that has ownership of the problem.

2. *Develop a process flow chart.* Make sure everyone in the team is on the same wavelength. Does everyone understand the same problem? The process flowchart will focus the discussion. If nothing else, it will create a baseline of understanding for the problem at hand.

3. *Prioritize.* Once you understand the problem, the team must begin the analysis of the flowchart. What part is important? Where do we begin?

4. *Begin data collection.* Begin to collect data of the failures and start filling out the appropriate form.

5. *Perform analysis.* Focus on the data and perform the appropriate and applicable analysis. Here, you may want to use QFD, DOE, another FMEA, SPC and anything else that you, as a group, may think suitable.

6. *Obtain results.* Based on the analysis, you derive the results. Make sure the results are data driven!

7. *Confirm, evaluate and measure.* Once the results have been recorded, it is time to confirm, evaluate and measure success or failure. This evaluation takes the form of three basic questions:
   - Are we better off than before?
   - Are we worse off than before?
   - Are we the same as before?

8. *Do it all over again.* Regardless of how you answer step 7, you must pursue improvement all over again, because of the continual improvement philosophy. Your long-term goal is to completely eliminate all failures, and your short-term goal is to minimize your failures, if not eliminate them entirely. Of course, perseverance for those goals have to be taken into consideration in relation to the needs of the organization, cost, customer and competition.

Conclusion

As we have seen, the FMEA is a tool to identify the priority of failures in both design and process. It demands that a team be utilized to identify several points of view and a corrective action. Furthermore, it utilizes some qualitative and quantitative approaches to prioritize these failures.

Finally, it always focuses on the corrective action with the intent of eliminating failures from the design, system or the process. This focus is prioritized through an evaluation of the failure in terms of severity, occurrence and detection. Therefore, to have the best results, the FMEA is positioned very early in the quality planning agenda to prevent failures from occurring downstream in the system, design or process. The interrelationships are quite obvious.

Project management

Project management is the application of functional (and other) management skills under time-limited, goal-directed conditions. The success of the six sigma methodology depends on the selection of the appropriate and applicable project and its completion. Therefore all concerned should be at least familiar with some basic concepts of project management. In the six sigma methodology the key project manager is the black belt. As such, to ensure effectiveness in their projects they must avoid pitfalls, although that is not enough. To be truly effective, the black belt must guide the project forward in the best possible manner. Guiding the project has to do with leadership and entrepreneurial skills. Black belts must be able to influence people.

But what is a project? It involves effective utilization of human and non-human (i.e., technological, financial, informational and material) resources to achieve a specific purpose, such as:

- To establish a set of well defined, related and controllable tasks.
- To establish goals that are consistent over extended period of time.
- To establish goals that may be defined for longer or shorter duration.
- To establish a convergence (a culmination point) in a major output.

In the six sigma methodology, by a project we mean elimination of a problem in a process or preventing the problem from entering the process. In other words, there are unique aspects of project management as we try to implement it within the six sigma methodology. That uniqueness can especially be seen under the following circumstances:

- When something is new, or never been done quite like this before.
- When there is a need to deal with diverse people in a team setting.

- When strict time deadlines and performance expectations are highly visible.
- When there is a need to manage interface problems—especially in cross-functional departments.

When uniqueness is present in a project, the implication is that we cannot count on past experience risk and uncertainty. When inter-relatedness is present in a project, the implication is that we need a broader perspective (e.g., a system view, schedule adherence, or a need for replanning flexibility). When goal orientation is present in a project, the implications are that we deal with a set of interrelated goals. This is very important, because it implies that we must zero in on the goal definition and operational definitions that we are dealing with that we need to control group processes—and in fact preferably isolate each one as much as possible—and that we understand our success or failure is highly visible. When resources are present in a project, the implications are that we need some form of negotiation and strong leadership for support. Under this condition the champion's contribution is of paramount importance.

Project management depends, therefore, on three items:

- *People*. The person in charge should be very familiar with the concepts of team, conflict management, project organization and managing for task accomplishment.
- *Planning*. The person in charge should be very familiar with statement of work, project planning, work breakdown structures, project risk analysis and responsibility charts.
- *Control*. The person in charge should have at least a basic knowledge of the critical path of the project, costs and budgets, project scheduling, project control and replanning.

Why project management principles are essential to the six sigma methodology

The single most important characteristic of project management is the consistent ability to get things done. It is a results or goal-oriented approach, where other considerations are secondary, so the single-minded concentration of resources greatly enhances prospects for success. This also implies that the results, success or failure, are quite visible.

Integrative and executive functions of the project manager provide another inherent advantage in the project management approach that improves the likelihood for success because of the single point of responsibility for those functions. Specific advantages of the single-point integrative characteristic include:

- Placing accountability on one person for the overall results of the project.
- Assurance that decisions are made on the basis of the overall good of the project, rather than the good of one or another contributing functional department.
- Coordination of all functional contributors to the project.
- Proper utilization of integrated planning and control methods and the information they produce.

Advantages of integrated planning and control of projects include:

- Assurance that the activities of each functional area are planned and carried out to meet the overall needs of the project.
- Assurance that the effects of favoring one project over another are known.
- Early identification of problems that may jeopardize successful project completion, which enables effective corrective action to prevent or resolve the problem.

Project management is a specialized management form. It is an effective management tool that is used because something is gained by departing from the normal functional way of doing things. This departure from the norm requires changes in three areas: people, organizations and methods. Conflict, confusion and additional costs are often associated with significant changes of this nature. Poorly conceived or poorly executed project management can be worse than no project management at all. Project management should be used well or not at all. Executives should not permit a haphazard, misunderstood use of project management principles.

Although simple in its concepts, project management can be complex in its application. Project management is not a cure-all intended for all projects. Before project management can succeed, the application must be correct. Executives should not use project management unless it appears to be the best solution. The use of project management techniques seems most appropriate when:

- A well-defined goal exists.
- The goal is significant to the organization.
- The undertaking is out of the ordinary.
- Plans are subject to change and require a degree of flexibility.
- The achievement of the goal requires the integration of two or more functional elements and/or independent organizations.

Even though project management may not be feasible, good project management principles have contributed to the success of thousands of small and medium-size projects. Many managers of such projects have never heard of project management, but have used the principles successfully.

Executives play a key role in the successful application of project management. A commitment from top management to ensure it is done right must be combined with the decision to use this approach. Top management must realize that establishing a project creates special problems for the people on the project, for the rest of the organization and for top managers themselves. If executives decide to use this technique, they should expend the time, decision-making responsibility and executive skills necessary to ensure that it is planned and executed properly. Before it can be executed properly, sincere and constructive support must be obtained from all functional managers. Directives or memos are not enough. It takes personal signals from top management to members of the team and functional managers to convey that the project will succeed, and team members will be rewarded by its success. In addition, necessary and desirable changes in personnel policies and procedures must be recognized and established at the onset of the project.

The human aspect of project management is both one of its greatest strengths and most serious drawbacks. Only capable staff can make a project successful. However, good people alone cannot guarantee project success; a poorly conceived, badly planned, or inadequately resourced project has little hope for success. The project leader, more than any other single variable, seems to make the difference between success and failure. Large projects require one person to be assigned the full-time role of project manager. If a number of projects exist and there are not enough project managers available for full-time assignment to each of them, several projects can be assigned to one full-time project manager. This approach has the advantages that the individual is continually acting in the same role, that of a project manager, and is not distracted or encumbered by functional responsibilities.

To conclude, project management is an effective management tool used by business, industry and government, but it must be used skillfully and carefully. In review, the following major items are necessary for successful six sigma results from project management:

- Wholehearted executive support and commitment when the decision is made to use this approach.
- Project management is known to be the best solution or right application for the project.
- Emphasis is placed on selecting the best people for staff, especially the project leader.
- Proven principles of project planning and controlling are applied.

Effective use of project management reduces costs and improves efficiency. However, the main reason for its widespread growth is its ability to complete a job on schedule and in accordance with original plans and budget.

Factors leading to project failure

Applying project management as part of a six sigma initiative does not guarantee that the project will be a success. It may still fail! The following are some reasons:

- Management is not involved:
  - Does not support the project for any reason.
  - Ignores, or does not act, on reports.
  - Is too too broad.
- Management is too involved:
  - Fails to delegate.
  - Is too restrictive.
  - Floods the project with demands.
- Improper planning:
  - Planning is incomplete or indefinite.
  - Planning is done in isolation, without usufructuary (to hold property for use by usufruct, as a tenant) or other contributors.
  - Pressure exists for unstructured change in budgets or schedules.

- Ineffective operations:
    - Lack of a formal change system.
    - Inadequate reporting structure.
    - Lack of priorities.
    - Project leader lacks authority.
- Incompetent project leader.
- Unwilling team members.
- Uncooperative functional departments.
- Poor controls.
- Failure to assure key relationships and cooperation.
- Lack of sanctions.

How can we overcome these problems? Some suggestions follow depending on the specific issue:

Management is either not involved or too involved. In this case, the champion is in the supportive mode and the black belt is the primary mode. To avoid these pitfalls:
- Create a formal project charter and project plan, including reporting requirements, structure, change procedures and approval mechanisms.
- Disseminate the document.
- Have a formal project plan acceptance meeting.

Incomplete plans, completed in isolation, unstructured changes in budgets and schedules. The black belt here is the primary mode and project team is the supportive mode. To avoid these pitfalls:
- Create a project schedule, work breakdown structures and budgets. Stress formalism in the planning process. Use a team approach. Get approvals and disseminate information.
- Ensure that changes in budgets and schedule are carried out according to established procedures only. Apply discipline! Benefits go beyond the project.

Incompetent project leader, poor team interaction, uncooperative functional managers/departments. The black belt is primary, and the champion plays a supportive role. To overcome these obstacles:

- Understand the requirements of a project manager; pick the right individual and train if necessary.
- Involve the project team early to create a sense of ownership, project mission and scope.
- Communicate freely and frequently with functional managers regarding such matters as project goals, charter, need for replanning and so on.
- Tell people not only what but also why.
- Use a project plan acceptance meeting as a forum to get commitment.
- Take on a synergistic attitude. Tie the project plan to the business plan and goals.
- Set up a reward system.
- Create an obligation to perform.

Factors determining the success of a project

In the six sigma methodology, the project is the focus in any improvement initiative. Therefore, how one goes about specifying the project requirements becomes very important. Six items are fundamental in the process of specifying these guidelines:

1. State requirements explicitly and have project staff and users sign off on them.
2. Be realistic. If a requirement can be misinterpreted, it will be misinterpreted.
3. Recognize that changes are inherent in projects.
4. To as great an extent as possible, include nonverbal depictions of requirements. For example, when you purchase a car you do not ask the salesperson if the vehicle comes with battery, or brakes, etc. You expect those items to be part of the vehicle. This is an example of a non-verbal requirement.
5. Establish a system to monitor changes in requirements.
6. Educate project staff and users on the importance of accurately specifying requirements.

Specifically, these fundamentals may be expanded on a project basis into the following factors that will improve the chances of success:

- Promulgation by higher management of the project and the black belt.
- Choosing a competent black belt.
- Charter and authority for black belt.
- Well-chosen, well-staffed, goal-oriented team.
- Sound planning.
  - ◆ Project definition:
    - – Phases.
    - – Work breakdown structures.
    - – Resource designation and allocation.
  - ◆ Budgeting of adequate time and resources.
  - ◆ Detail, schedules.
  - ◆ Promulgation.
  - ◆ Participation of management and usufructuary.
- Administrative and technical means and support.
- Operating systems:
  - ◆ Direction and launch mechanisms.
  - ◆ Congruent with plan and organizational goals.
  - ◆ Obligation to perform.
  - ◆ Change procedures.
  - ◆ Reports and information flow.
  - ◆ Control mechanisms.
- Participation and involvement of management.
- Sanctions.

Cost of quality

Six sigma methodology demands quantification of improvement. In order for that quantification to materialize there must exist in the organization a system for identifying the cost associated with problems, inefficiencies and, in general, customer dissatisfaction. As it turns out, the system most often responsible for such tracking is called cost of quality (COQ). With COQ in any organization (manufacturing and non-manufacturing alike) quality and improvement may be measured at the same time. However, within the COQ, there are two categories that define the structure and reporting of that cost. They are:

- Avoidance costs.
- Total failure costs.

These two categories comprise the two operating curves used for achieving the break-even point of the quality costs break-even chart. Avoidance costs and total failure costs are broken down further into two categories:

- Avoidance costs:
  - *Appraisal costs.* These are the expenditures that an organization makes to examine the levels of quality at which products are being produced. If the product quality levels are satisfactory, production is allowed to continue. If the quality levels are unsatisfactory, production is suspended until effective corrective action has been implemented to return levels to satisfactory product quality levels. Examples are: all inspection and associated expenses; inspector's wages and fringe benefits; laboratory test technicians' wages, salaries and fringe benefits; test samples for destructive testing; laboratory materials consumed in the process testing; laboratory tooling expenses; the portion of direct labor wages devoted to performing statistical process control (SPC); inspections and tests within the process; and process capability studies.
  - *Prevention costs.* These are the expenditures a company makes to keep from producing defective or unacceptable product. Examples are all training; quality assurance wages, salaries and fringe benefits; cost of design changes incurred prior to releases for production; the portion of product design engineering devoted to quality assurance; and cost of processing changes incurred prior to releases for production.

These avoidance cost categories are, in the case of appraisal costs, expected to discover and correct problems after the problems surface. On the other hand, prevention costs are intended to be applied before the fact of producing defective product, to prevent the defective product from being produced.

- Total failure costs:
  - *Internal failure costs.* These are the costs incurred by an organization while it still has ownership of the product. Examples are: scrap; waste in process; rework charges; and repair charges.

- *External failure costs*. These are the costs incurred by an organization after it has transferred ownership of the product to its customer, the customer has received and originally accepted the product. Examples are: warranty costs; returned goods; design error; and marketing error.

It is beyond the scope of this book to address the details for constructing a quality cost reporting system. However, a simple and practical approach is to start with a review of the company's "Chart of Accounts" to determine which of those accounts should be selected and to which quality cost category those selected accounts should be assigned. Table 4.10 gives a cursory view of the

Table 4.10 A typical cost of quality report

	Time period A	Time period B	Difference
Appraisal costs			
Account 1			
Account 2			
Account 3			
Account n			
Prevention costs			
Account 1			
Account 2			
Account 3			
Account n			
Internal failure costs			
Account 1			
Account 2			
Account 3			
Account n			
External failure costs			
Account 1			
Account 2			
Account 3			
Account n			

most standard form based on a typical chart of accounts. By identifying each of the accounts, the reader of the report can see the influence of these costs to the total cost of the organization and, as a result, an appropriate management decision will be made to reduce the out-of-line cost. What is important about the form is the fact that it has two time periods for comparison purposes. The reason for the two periods is to evaluate progress. It is the performance difference (variance, in the language of cost of quality) of the two periods that establishes the improvement trend.

Teams

An old Yiddish proverb states that "the girl who can't dance says the band can't play." In the work environment we find quite often that we blame failures on anything that makes sense at the time. For some reason, we go to great lengths to find justification of failures rather than look no further than the individuals involved in the process and their behavior as a team.

Six sigma methodology depends on the team concept. Without a team effort, nothing will be accomplished. Therefore, a team-building effort must be initiated before the six sigma initiative takes hold of any specific project. But what is team-building? Team-building is the process of taking a collection of individuals with different needs, backgrounds and expertise, and transforming them by various methods into an integrated, effective work unit. This implies that developing a cohesive team requires developing a set of norms or standards for behavior that might be different from the standards the team members are accustomed to using. That means that the team must work together to develop an initial project plan. The usual process for this development is: initiation, idealization, iteration and implementation. While this development is taking place, we must also recognize that the team itself is going through a transformation in the following stages: forming, storming, norming (standardizing) and performing.

Team structure

Project teams are transitory. That means that team members may move in and out when their assigned tasks are completed. Project teams also have structure. Team structure determines patterns of interaction among team members, with a client, with the black belt, with the product being developed, and so on. Finally, how a team is structured determines a project's success. This is why the team formation must be designed in such a way that the team efficiency is enhanced. Efficiency, of course, is the ratio of output to input. (Teams should be cross-functional and multidisciplined, so that there are many variations, making the ratio always larger than 1.)

In a project environment, input consists of team members and other resources. Output consists of work performed and goals accomplished. Inefficiency in teams is attributable to many factors. However, two of the major factors are:

- *Poor team structure.* Projects that are organized based on the matrix structure, while offering many advantages, have built-in inefficiencies. Team membership is temporary. Time is lost in learning the work done by others. (Recommendation: Keep team membership stable.) A second issue is the fact that sometimes the black belt may not control resources directly. When that happens, more time is spent in acquiring human and material resources. (Recommendation: Make it a practice to engage in pre-planning.)

- *Team friction.* By definition a team is a system comprised of many interrelated parts. Therefore, the pieces have to be brought together. If team effort is not properly integrated, team inefficiencies will occur. To avoid this situation, make sure that the team's configuration closely reflects the structure of the deliverable, i.e. what is the deliverable; who is responsible for the deliverable; when it is to be delivered; in what shape, form, or even packaging; what will constitute success and so on.

In both cases, poor communication is a major component of the failure. After all, information is the lifeblood of projects and communicating this information is essential to project success. There are various communication-based frictions that contribute to team inefficiency, for example, communication as an end rather than a means. In other words, in the process of communicating we use too many channels or use up too much time and effort at the expense of actual action. This, of course, is indicative of a bureaucratic system—the failure to separate important from routine information and/or garbled messages.

Effective team-building

To understand the effectiveness of a team, we must understand what prevents a team from being effective. There are four major barriers to effective team-building. They are:

- *Differing outlooks of team members.* The strategy to eliminate, or at least to minimize, this barrier may be based on getting to know your people early in the project, blending individual interests with team and organizational objectives, defining responsibilities clearly and without any ambivalence and stressing the team concept.

- *Role conflicts.* The strategy to eliminate, or at least to minimize this barrier, may be based on asking team members where they see themselves fitting into the project, conducting regular status meetings and handling any conflicts directly.

- *Unclear project objectives.* The strategy to eliminate, or at least to minimize this barrier, may be based on developing and publicizing a clear set of project objectives, communicating frequently with team members and checking for understanding

- *Lack of management support.* The strategy to eliminate, or at least to minimize this barrier, may be based on involving management in project reviews, keeping management well informed, and telling management what you need.

So, how may we go about building effective teams? The following practical guidelines may be of help:

- Eliminate "back home" behavior by establishing group norms.

- Develop a "group mind" phenomenon—that is, a common set of objectives and motives shared by the group.

- Recognize implicit contract (i.e., establish mutual experiences).

- Avoid neglected resource syndrome (e.g., a retiring expert whose views are never heard or never noticed because participation is low—create ways to make participation mandatory).

- Beware of hidden agendas of team members.

- Build trust. In evolving a realistic plan, ask each person to make trade-offs, state contributions, and so on. If they stay true to these aims, it will build trust.

Conflict resolution

As already mentioned, every time there is a change, there is bound to be a conflict. Let us then identify some typical situations that foster an environment for conflict.

- The greater the diversity of disciplinary expertise among the participants of a project team, the greater the potential for conflict to develop among members of the team.

- The lower the black belt's degree of authority, reward, and punishment power over those individuals and organizational units supporting his project, the greater the potential for conflict to develop.

- The less the specific objectives of a project (cost, schedule, and technical performance) are understood by the project team members, the more likely it is that conflict will develop.

- The greater the ambiguity of roles among the participants of a project team, the more likely it is that conflict will develop.

- The greater the agreement on superordinate goals (the big picture goals as they relate to the business strategy of the organization) by project team participants, the lower the potential for detrimental conflict.

- The more the members of functional areas perceive that the implementation of a project management system will adversely usurp their traditional roles, the greater the potential for conflict.

- The lower the need for interdependence among organizational units supporting a project, the greater the potential for dysfunctional conflict.

- The higher the managerial level within a project, the more likely it is that conflicts will be based upon deep-seated parochial resentments. By contrast, at the project or task level, it is more likely that cooperation will be facilitated by the task orientation and professionalism that a project requires for completion.

Typical conflict handling modes are:

- *Withdrawal.* Retreating or withdrawing from an actual or potential disagreement.

- *Smoothing.* De-emphasizing, or avoiding areas of difference, and emphasizing areas of agreement.

- *Compromising.* Bargaining and searching for solutions that bring some degree of satisfaction to the parties in a dispute. Characterized by a give and-take attitude.

- *Forcing.* Exerting one's viewpoint at the potential expense of another. Often characterized by competitiveness and a win/lose situation.

- *Confrontation.* Facing the conflict directly, which involves a problem-solving approach whereby affected parties work through their disagreements.

In any team environment conflicts will arise. The issue is not why the conflict exists, but how should it be handled? Typical conflicts in the life of a black belt using the six sigma methodology may involve the following:

- People resources.
- Equipment and/or facilities.
- Capital expenditures.
- Costs.
- Technical opinions and trade-offs.
- Priorities.
- Procedures.
- Scheduling.
- Responsibilities.
- Personality clashes.

In the traditional world we try to avoid conflicts. We will not let go of our ego and we view conflict as bad. In the six sigma methodology conflicts are viewed as possibly beneficial. They are understood to be part of change and therefore inevitable, and they are seen as naturally occurring issues arising from relationships among components (i.e., system structure). Therefore, a black belt must confront conflict, not try to avoid or prevent it. While a number of alternatives for dealing with conflict are available, only three are considered to be suitable for resolving conflict in the six sigma methodology. These approaches are win/lose, negotiation and problem-solving. In order to select the best approach to resolve conflict, the black belt should know the uses as well as the dangers and difficulties of each alternative.

Win/lose. This is usually a poor choice, but it is useful when:

- It is clarifying and educational. Many people will not examine assumptions they make until they are called on to clarify and support them by someone with an opposing view.
- Quick, decisive action is vital to company welfare.
- Other alternatives have been genuinely tried and failed.

The difficulties and dangers of win/lose conflict resolution are:

- A poor choice when there is a dependence relationship.
- Can be very costly.
- May irreparably destroy participant's future.
- Destroys all trust.

Negotiating. Negotiating a conflict resolution is useful in the following situations:

- When two opponents with equal power are strongly committed to mutually exclusive goals.
- To achieve a temporary settlement to complex issues.
- To arrive at expedient solutions under time pressure.
- To move opponents toward problem-solving by learning each other's thinking patterns and priorities, increasing trust and providing a mutually rewarding experience.
- To establish a precedent.

The difficulties and dangers associated with negotiation include:

- One party may not see that it is in his or her own best interest to compromise.
- If conflicting personalities are involved, conflict can be heightened.
- A temporary solution does not resolve the underlying problem.

Problem-solving. The use of problem-solving to resolve conflicts are:

- To find an integrative solution when both sets of concerns are too important to be compromised.
- To gain commitment by incorporating others' concerns into a consensual decision.

- To work through hard feelings which have been interfering with an inter-personal relationship.

- To merge insights of people with different perspectives.

- When your object is to learn (e.g., testing your own assumptions, understanding the views of others).

The difficulties and dangers of using problem-solving to resolve conflicts are that:

- It depends on an open atmosphere, requiring a high level of trust.

- It requires considerable time and stress to establish trust between parties at odds.

Statistics

The word *statistics* came into the English language from Greek, Latin and German and ultimately is understood to mean standing, status, state and even understand. In the minds of most people, the meaning of statistics has a lot in common with these related words, meaning roughly a description of how things are. It is, of course, true that a part of the theory of statistics concerns effective ways of summarizing and communicating masses of information that describe a situation. This part of the overall theory and set of methods is usually known as descriptive statistics.

Although descriptive statistics form an important basis for dealing with data, a major part of the theory of statistics is concerned with another question: How does one go beyond a given set of data, and make general statements about the large body of potential observations, of which the data collected represents only a sample? This is the theory of inferential statistics, with which six sigma methodology is mainly concerned.

Applications of inferential statistics occur in virtually all fields of research endeavor—the physical sciences, the biological sciences, the social sciences, engineering, market and consumer research, quality control in industry, and so on, almost without end. Although the actual methods differ somewhat in the different fields, the applications all rest on the same general theory of statistics. By examining what the fields have in common in their applications of statistics, we can gain a picture of the basic problem studied in mathematical statistics. The major applications of statistics in any field all rest on the possibility of repeated observations or experiments made under essentially the same conditions. That is, either the researcher actually can observe the same process repeated many times, as in industrial quality control, or there is the conceptual possibility of repeated observation, as in a scientific experiment that might, in principle, be repeated under identical conditions. However, in any circumstance where repeated observations are made, even though every precaution is taken to make conditions exactly the same, the results of observations will vary, or tend to be different, from trial to trial. The experimenter or researcher has control over some, but not all, of the factors that make outcomes of observations differ from each other.

When observations are made under the same conditions in one or more respects, but they give outcomes differing in other ways, then there is some uncertainty connected with the observation of any given object or phenomenon. Even though some things are known to be true about an object in advance of the observation, the experimenter cannot predict with complete certainty what its other characteristics will be. Given enough repeated observations of the same object, or kind of object, a good bet may be formulated about what the other characteristics are likely to be, but one cannot be completely sure of the status of any given object.

This fact leads us to the central problem of inferential statistics: a theory about uncertainty, the tendency of outcomes to vary when repeated observations are made under identical conditions. Granted that certain conditions are fulfilled, theoretical statistics permits deductions about the likelihood of the various possible outcomes of observation. The essential concepts in statistics derive from the theory of probability, and the deductions made within the theory of statistics are, by and large, statements about the probability of particular kinds of outcomes, given that initial, mathematical conditions are met.

Mathematical statistics is a formal mathematical system. Any mathematical system consists of these basic parts:

- A collection of undefined things or elements, considered only as abstract entities.

- A set of undefined operations or possible relations among the abstract elements.

- A set of postulates and definitions, each asserting that some specific relation holds among the various elements, the various operations, or both.

In any mathematical system, the application of logic to combinations of hypotheses and definitions leads to new statements, or theorems, about the undefined elements of the system. Given that the original hypotheses and definitions are true, then the new statements must be true. Mathematical systems are purely abstract, and essentially undefined, deductive structures. In other words, they are not really about anything in particular. They are systems of statements about things having the formal properties given by the hypotheses. No one may know what the original mathematician really had in mind with regard to these abstract elements. Indeed, they may represent absolutely nothing that exists in real world experience, and the sole concern may be what one can derive about the other necessary relations among abstract elements given particular sets of hypotheses. To clarify—statistics make sense only when defined from particular sets of hypotheses and not all hypotheses are derived from real world experience. It is perfectly true, of course, that many mathematical systems originated from attempts to describe real objects or phenomena and their interrelationships: historically, the abstract systems of geometry, school algebra and calculus grew out of problems where something very practical and concrete was in the back of the mathematician's mind. However, these systems deal with completely abstract entities.

When a mathematical system is interpreted in terms of real objects or events, then the system is said to be a mathematical model for those objects or events. Somewhat more precisely, the undefined terms in the mathematical system are identified with particular, relevant properties of objects or events. Thus, in applications of arithmetic, the number symbols are identified with magnitudes or amounts of some particular property that objects possess, such as weight, or extent, or numerousness. The system of arithmetic need not apply to other characteristics of the same objects, for example, to their colors. Once this identification can be made between the mathematical system and the relevant properties of objects, then anything that is a logical consequence in the system is a true statement about objects in the model, provided, of course, that the formal characteristics of the system actually parallel the real characteristics of objects in terms of the particular properties considered. In short, to be useful as a mathematical model, a mathematical system must have a formal structure that fits at least one aspect of a real situation. This is a very important characteristic and useful in predicting behavior and/or results in a given situation.

Probability theory and statistics are each both mathematical systems and mathematical models. Probability theory deals with elements called events, which are completely abstract. Furthermore, these abstract elements are paired with numbers called probabilities. The theory itself is the system of logical relations among these essentially undefined things. The experimenter uses this abstract system as a mathematical model: the experiment produces a real outcome, which is called an event, and the model of probability theory provides a value, which is interpreted as the relative frequency of occurrence for that outcome. If the requirements of the model are met, this is a true, and perhaps useful, result. If the experiment really does not fit the requirements of probability theory as a system, then the statement made about the actual result need not be true. This point must not be overstressed, however. We will find that often a statistical method can yield practical, useful results, even when its requirements are not fully satisfied. Much of the art in applying statistical methods lies in understanding when and how this is true.

Mathematical systems, such as probability theory and the theory of statistics are, by their very nature, deductive. Formal assertions are postulated as true, and then by logical argument true conclusions are reached. All well-developed theories have this formal, logic-deductive character.

On the other hand, the problem of the empirical scientist is essentially different from that of the logician or mathematician. Scientists search for general relations among events; these general relations are those that can be expected to hold whenever the appropriate set of circumstances exists. The very name *empirical science* asserts that these laws shall be discovered and verified by the actual observation of what happens in the real world of experience. However, no mortal scientist ever observes all the phenomena about which a generalization must be made. Scientific conclusions about what would happen for all of a certain class of phenomena always come from observations of only a very few particular cases of that phenomenon.

The reader acquainted with logic will recognize that this is a problem of induction. The rules of logical deduction are rules for arriving at true consequences from true premises. Scientific theories are, for the most part, systems of deductions from basic principles held to be true. If the basic principles are true, then the deductions must be true. However, how does one go about arriving at and checking the truth of the initial propositions? The answer is, for an empirical science, observation and inductive generalization—going from what is true of some observations to a statement that this is true for all possible observations made under the same conditions. Any empirical science begins with observation and generalization.

Furthermore, even after deductive theories exist in science, experimentation is used to check on the truth of these theories. Observations that contradict deductions made within the theory are prima facie evidence against the truth of the theory itself. Yet, how does the experimenter or scientist know that the results are not an accident, the product of some chance variation in procedure or conditions over which there is no control? Would the result be the same in the long run if the experiment could be repeated many times?

It takes only a little imagination to see that this process of going from the specific to the general is a very risky one. Each observation the experimenter or scientist makes is different in some way from the next. Innumerable influences are at work altering—sometimes minutely, sometimes radically—the similarities and differences the experimenter or scientist observes among events. Controlled experimentation in any science is an attempt to minimize at least part of the accidental variation or error in observation. Precise techniques of measurement are aids to scientists in sharpening their own rather dull powers of observation and comparison among events. So-called exact sciences, such as physics and chemistry, have thus been able to remove a substantial amount of the unwanted variation among observations from time to time, place to place and observer to observer, and hence are often able to make general statements about physical phenomena with great assurance from the observation of quite limited numbers of events. Observations in these sciences can often be made in such a way that the generality of conclusions is not a major point at issue. Here, there is relatively little reliance on probability and statistics. However, as even these scientists delve into the molecular, atomic and subatomic domain, negligible differences turn into enormous, unpredictable occurrences and statistical theories become an important adjunct to their work.

In the biological, behavioral, and social sciences, however, the situation is radically different. In these sciences the variations between observations are not subject to the precise experimental controls that are possible in the physical sciences. Refined measurement techniques have not reached the stage of development that they have attained in physics and chemistry.

Consequently, the drawing of general conclusions is a much more dangerous business in these fields, where the sources of variability among living things are extremely difficulty to identify, measure and control. Yet the aim of the social or biological scientist is precisely the same as that of the physical scientist—to arrive at general statements about the phenomena under study. Faced with only a limited number of observations or with an experiment that can be conducted only once, the scientist can reach general conclusions only in the form of a "bet" about what the true, long-run situation actually is like. Given only sample evidence, the experimenter or scientist is always unsure of the accuracy of any assertion made about the true state of affairs. The theory of statistics provides ways to assess this uncertainty and to calculate the probability of being wrong through deciding in a particular way. Provided that the experimenter can make some assumptions about what is true, then the deductive theory of statistics tells us how likely particular results should be. Armed with this information, the experimenter is in a better position to decide what to say about the true situation. Regardless of what one decides from evidence, it could be wrong; but deductive statistical theory can at least determine the probabilities of error in a particular decision.

In recent years, a branch of mathematics has been developed around this problem of decision-making under uncertain conditions. This is sometimes called statistical decision theory. One of the main problems treated in decision theory is the choice of a decision rule, or deciding how to decide from evidence. Decision theory evaluates rules for deciding from evidence in the light of what the decision-maker wants to accomplish. While it is true that mathematics can tell us wise ways to decide how to decide under some circumstances, mathematics can never tell the experimenter how a decision must be reached in any particular situation. The theory of statistics supplies one very important piece of information to the experimenter: the probability of sample results given certain conditions. Decision theory can supply another: optimal ways of using this and other information to accomplish certain ends. Nevertheless, neither theory tells the experimenter exactly how to decide—how to make the inductive leap from observation to what is true in general. This is the experimenter's problem, and the answer must be sought outside of deductive mathematics, and in the light of what the experimenter is trying to do.

Furthermore, a true revolution has occurred in the past two decades, deeply affecting the application and the teaching of statistical methodology. This has been brought about by the new generations of computers, which are faster, more flexible and cheaper to use than anyone would have dreamed only a few years back. Large-scale statistical analysis is now done by computer in almost all research settings.

There is hardly any area in which the impact of statistics has been felt more strongly than in both research and business activities. Indeed, it would be hard to overestimate the contributions statistical methods have made to the effective planning and control of all types of business activities. In the past 25 to 30 years the application of statistical methods has brought about drastic changes in all the major areas of business management: general management, research and development, finance, production, sales, advertising, etc. Of course, not all problems in these areas are of a statistical nature, but the list of those that can be treated either partly or entirely by statistical methods, is very long. To illustrate, let us mention but a few which might face a large manufacturer.

In the general management area, for example, where long-range planning is of great concern, population trends must be forecast and their effects on consumer markets must be analyzed. In research and engineering, costs must be estimated for various projects, and manpower, skill, equipment and time requirements must be anticipated. In the area of finance, the profit potential of capital investments must be determined, overall financial requirements must be projected and capital markets must be studied so that sound long-range financing and investment plans can be developed. Although we cannot illustrate in this book how specific statistical tools are actually used in these areas of application, let us point out that they are all excellent candidates for six sigma application.

In production, problems of a statistical nature arise in connection with plant layout and structure, size and location, inventory, production scheduling and control, maintenance, traffic and materials handling, quality assurance, etc. Enormous strides have been made in recent years in the application of statistics to sampling inspection and quality assurance and control. In the area of sales, many problems require statistical solutions. For instance, sales must be forecast for both present and new products for existing as well as new markets, channels of distribution must be determined and requirements for sales forces must be estimated. Building a successful advertising campaign is also a troublesome task; budgets must be determined, allocations must be made to various media and the effectiveness of the campaign must be measured (or predicted) by means of survey samples of public response and other statistical techniques.

So far we have been speaking of problems of a statistical nature that might typically be encountered by a large manufacturer. However, similar problems are faced, say, by a large railroad trying to make the best use of its thousands of freight cars, by a large rancher trying to decide how to feed his cattle so that nutritional needs will be met at the lowest possible cost or by an investment company trying to decide which stocks and bonds to include in its portfolio.

It is not at all necessary to refer to large organizations to find business applications of statistics. For smaller businesses, problems usually differ more in degree than in kind from those of their large competitors. Neither the largest supermarket nor the smallest neighborhood grocery store, for example, has unlimited capital or shelf space, and neither can afford to tie these two assets up in the wrong goods. The problem of utilizing capital and shelf space most effectively is as real for the small store as for the large, and it is extremely shortsighted to think that modern management tools (including modern statistical techniques) are of value only to big business. In fact, they could hardly be needed more anywhere else than in small business, where each year thousands of operating units fail and many of the thousands of new units entering the field are destined to fail because of inadequate capital, overextended credit, overloading with the wrong stock, and generally speaking, no knowledge of the market or the competition.

The intention of this book is not to introduce the reader to specific tools of statistical analysis. It is, however, to acquaint and sensitize the reader to the concepts and opportunities that statistical methods may provide to solve real business problems. Furthermore, it is the intention of this section to make sure that the reader understands that the formal notions of statistics as a way of making rational decisions ought to be part of any thoughtful person's equipment. After all, business managers are not the only ones who must make decisions involving uncertainties and risks; everyone has to make decisions of this sort professionally or as part of everyday life. It is true that many of the choices we have to make entail only matters of taste and personal preference, in which case there is, of course, no question of a decision being right or wrong. On the other hand, many choices we have to make between alternatives can be wrong in the sense that there is the possibility of an actual loss or penalty of some sort involved—possibly only a minor annoyance, perhaps something as serious as loss of life, or anything in between these two extremes. The methods of modern statistics deal with problems of this kind and they do so not only in business, industry, and in the world of everyday life, but also in such fields as medicine, physics, chemistry, agriculture, economics, psychology, government and education, to name a few.

There are many kinds of statistical analyses and presentations are beyond the scope of this book. However, although specialized techniques exist for handling particular kinds of problems, the underlying principles and ideas are identical, regardless of the field of application. The next section, however, reviews some of the most simple and common tools that the practitioner of the six sigma methodology may want to use.

Tools

There are many individual tools that one may use to pursue the six sigma methodology. Here, however, we present the tools on a table format along with the individual stage of the DMAIC model. There is not much discussion with each tool since its availability is quite abundant and may be found in many textbooks, training materials, and so on. Some of the most common tools used in the process of implementing six sigma are shown in Table 4.11.

These tools help the experimenter with the following items in the process of a legitimate and authorized program or project:

- Giving appropriate and applicable feedback (vertical and horizontal).
- Dealing with change.
- Working smarter.
- Being a team player.
- Listening to understand clearly.

Table 4.11 Typical tools used in the six sigma methodology

Tool	Define	Measure	Analyze	Improve	Control
Flowcharts	X			X	
Brainstorming	X		X	X	
Cause and effect diagrams	X	X	X		
Data collection	X			X	X
Graphs and charts (box plots, histograms, control charts, and so on)	X	X		X	X
Pareto analysis	X	X			X
Measurement		X			X
Problem criteria selection	X				
Employee involvement	X				
Auditing			X		
Benchmarking			X		
Central limit theorem		X	X		
Checksheets			X		
Cleanliness (visual factory)		X	X		
Continual improvement techniques (lean manufacturing)			X	X	
Customer feedback techniques (surveys, warranty, etc.)			X	X	X
Control plan	X				X
Design of experiment				X	
FMEA			X	X	X
Gage control				X	
Geometric dimensioning and tolerancing (GD&T)		X	X		X
Preventive maintenance			X		
Process capability	X				
Project planning	X				X
Sampling plans			X	X	
Self-directed teams		X	X	X	X
Standard operating procedures	X	X			X

- Taking a new assignment.
- Requesting help (as needed).
- Getting your point across (two-way communicating).
- Resolving issues with others (conflict resolution).
- Actively participating in any meeting.
- Keeping management informed.
- Responding positively to negative people/situations.

References

Automotive Industry Action Group. *Measurement System Assessment Analysis*. 3rd ed. Southfield, MI: AIAG, 2002.

Bothe, D. R. *Measuring Process Capability*. New York: McGraw-Hill, 1997.

Juran, J. M. and F. M. Gryna, Jr. *Quality Planning and Analysis*. New York: McGraw-Hill, 1980.

Denson, D. "The Use of Failure Mode Distributions in Reliability Analysis." *RAC Newsletter* (Spring 1992), pp. 9-10.

Schonberger, R. J. "Lean Is as Lean Does." *Manufacturing Engineering* (June 2002), p. 104.

Stamatis, D. "ISO 9000 Series: Are They Real?" *Technology* (August 1992), pp. 13-16.

Stamatis, D. *Failure Mode and Effect Analysis: FMEA from Theory to Execution*. Milwaukee, WI: Quality Press, 1995.

Stamatis, D. H. *Six Sigma and Beyond: Statistical Process Control*. Boca Raton, FL: St. Lucie Press, 2003.

Womack, J. P., D. T. Jones, and D. Roos. *The Machine That Changed the World*. New York: Harper Collins, 1990.

Selected bibliography

Daimler Chrysler, Ford Motor Company, and General Motors. *Failure Mode and Effect Analysis*. 3rd ed. Distributed by Automotive Industry Action Group (AIAG). Southfield, MI: AIAG, 2001

Daimler Chrysler, Ford Motor Company, and General Motors. *Measurement System Analysis*. 3rd ed. Distributed by Automotive Industry Action Group (AIAG). Southfield, MI: AIAG, 2001

Hays, R., and S. C. Wheelwright. *Restoring Competitive Edge*. New York: John Wiley & Sons, 1984.

Olexa, R. "SME: Leading Manufacturers with Lean Information." *Manufacturing Engineering Journal–Lean Manufacturing Insert* (October 2002), pp. L19-20.

Schonberger, R. J. Let Us Fix It. New York: Free Press, 2001.

Stamatis, D. H. *Six Sigma and Beyond: Statistical Process Control*. Boca Raton, FL: St. Lucie Press, 2003.

Stamatis, D. H. *Failure Mode and Effect Analysis: FMEA from Theory to Execution*. Milwaukee, WI: Quality Press, 1985.

Stamatis, D. H. *TQM Engineering Handbook*. New York: Marcel Dekker, 1997.

Stamatis, D. H. *Failure Mode and Effect Analysis: FMEA from Theory to Execution*. 2nd ed. Milwaukee, WI: Quality Press, 2003.

Womack, J. P., and D. T. Jones. *Lean Thinking*. New York: Simon & Schuster, 1996.

Chapter 5

Design for Six Sigma: the DCOV Model

In chapter 3, we introduced the DMAIC model. However, as we mentioned, there is another way of improving—through design for six sigma (DFSS). Preventing defects by completing projects in the design process aimed at improving functional performance over time, with a quantified reduction in product or manufacturing or service process variability. The approach is both systematic and dynamic. In its entirety, the approach or model is to define, characterize, optimize and verify. This chapter focuses on both these models and summarizes some of the key events that make the model effective.

The DCOV model

One of the most predominant ideas for design for six sigma is the notion of historical perspective and paradigm change. Our commitment to solving our problems must be based on the precept that we want to avoid problems rather than fix them. To do that we must recognize that old Einstein saying paraphrased here: You cannot solve problems with the same level of knowledge that created them. In other words, we have to look elsewhere for our answers. We cannot always depend on history. We have to look beyond our current status and capability if we are indeed committed to continual improvement.

To fix problems before they happen is an issue of planning and design. It certainly goes beyond the current knowledge and quite often beyond the current modus operandi of a given organization. It forces one to think of future designs. Design for six sigma (DFSS) is a proactive approach to preventing problems from occurring. That is a design issue. Therefore, the power of the six sigma methodology is in the design for six sigma.

As powerful as DFSS is to problem resolution and avoidance, it must also be recognized that there are some problems that do not need to be fixed. Simply stated: some problems are not worth solving. Some issues may seem like they should be problems, but are not problems at all. A problem may be an inherited part of the way you do business and you may not want to change. Or the problem may be part of everyday variability. Trying to solve it is like trying to stop the tides. Trying to fix it wastes effort, and your misguided efforts might make things worse.

Some problems are not worth solving because their consequences are too small to worry about. Your focus should instead be to attack the problems that cumulatively cause enough loss to worry about. Also, some problems are blessings in disguise—problems that, if solved, would allow an even bigger problem to cause a real disaster.

On the other hand, for problems that really need to be fixed, design for six sigma is the only way. For the problems that should be investigated, a rigorous approach is recommended, such as the design for six sigma process, using the define, characterize, optimize and verify (DCOV) model. The minimum effort required to solve problems using the DCOV model is as follows:

- Completely understand what happened.
- Identify the causal factors that led to the problem.
- Systematically find the root causes of each causal factor.
- Develop and implement solutions to eliminate the root causes.

To be sure, design for six sigma is very demanding, and yet the opportunity for true improvement and real customer satisfaction lies only with a systematic study up front (in the design). The goal is to improve customer functionality through customer satisfaction and customer loyalty. The process of improvement then is to:

- Establish a functional relationship between customer satisfaction drivers (dependent variables) and specific design parameters,

CTQ characteristics (independent variables). By reducing the sensitivity of the associated system to noise factors and then manufacturing the independent variables at the 6 (six standard deviations) level, the performance that drives customer satisfaction and ultimately loyalty will be more consistently achieved over time.

- While the DFSS process steps are presented in a sequential flow, process execution is not necessarily sequential. For example, the capturing of the voice of the customer, system design and functional mapping are typically iterative processes. On the other hand, design for robustness and for productivity are both simultaneous and iterative.

- The DFSS process may become generic and can also be applied during any of the following phases (i.e., advanced project, forward product and ongoing).

To apply these principles to a successful design, these items must be followed:

- Understand the fundamental ideas underlying the notion of manufacturability.

- Understand how statistically designed experiments can be used to identify leverage variables, establish sensitivities, and define tolerances.

- Understand how product and process complexity impacts design performance.

- Explain the concept of error propagation (both linear and non-linear) and what role product/process complexity plays.

- Describe how reverse error propagation can be employed during system design.

- Explain why process shift and drift must be considered in the analysis of a design and how it can be factored into design optimization.

- Describe how six sigma tools and methods can be applied to the design process in and of itself.

- Discuss the pros and cons of the classical approach to product/process design relative to that of the six sigma approach.

The following sections discuss the four stages of the DCOV model: define, characterize, optimize and verify.

The define stage

In the first phase of the DCOV model, the define stage is first explored. The purpose of this stage is to identify the critical to satisfaction (CTS) drivers, Y_i and to establish an operating window for chosen Ys for new and aged conditions. The define stage is divided into three areas:

- *Inputs*. These are the activities that are the initiators for further evaluation. Typical activities are: researching the quality and customer satisfaction history; evaluating warranty data; benchmarking; checking functional, serviceability, corporate and regulatory requirements; evaluating the process in integrating targets; conducting surveys; auditing the current design or process; profiling the brand; performing a Kano analysis; undergoing quality function deployment (QFD); and defining design specifications.

- *Action*. These are the activities that actually help in the selection of the Ys. Typical activities are definition of customer and/or product requirements, relating requirements to customer satisfaction, and conducting peer review.

- *Output*. These are the results of the action. Typical results are projected targets and a preliminary model of understanding.

The characterize stage

In the second phase of the DCOV model, the characterize stage is explored. This stage is generally completed through a two-step approach. The first is the system design and the second is the functional mapping. In both cases, the goal is to characterize the robustness of the design. Therefore, the purpose of the first step is to flow CTS Ys down to lower y's ($Y = f(y_1, y_2, y_3, \ldots y_n)$) and to characterize robustness opportunities ($Y = f(x_i n)$). The purpose of the second step is to relate CTS ys to CTQ design parameters (xs) and to optimize the strategy to deliver this robustness.

System design. The process for exploring the first step of the characterize stage is divided into three areas:

- *Inputs*. These are the activities that will generate the action of this step. Typical actions are creating functional boundaries and interface matrices as applicable, function trees ($Y \rightarrow y$), a P-diagram; and robustness and/or reliability checklists.

- *Action.* These are the activities that help the decomposition of Y into contributing elements, y_i; obtain ($Y = f(y_1, y_2, y_3, \ldots y_n)$) through modeling, such as DOE, using CAE or hardware (if applicable), experience or prior knowledge and peer review.
- *Output.* This is the result of the action. Typical results are Pareto diagrams, benchmarked CTS factors and the target range of y.

Functional mapping. The process for exploring the second step of the characterize stage is divided into three areas:

- *Inputs.* These are the activities that will generate the activity of this step. Typical activities are creating functional boundaries and interfaces of system design specification (SDS), a functional tree ($y \rightarrow x$), P-diagrams and a robustness and/or reliability checklist.
- *Action.* These are the activities that actually help the decomposition of y_i into contributing elements, x_i. Typical activities are: relate independent ys to xs (modeling) or relate correlated ys to xs (modeling, axiomatic design); choose robustness strategy; innovate using structured inventive thinking (SIT) or the theory of inventive problem-solving (TRIZ), understand manufacturing capability and conduct peer review.
- *Output.* This is the result of the action. Typical results are results of screening experiments and prior engineering knowledge, a Pareto diagram, preliminary target and/or range estimates of x_i and internal and/or external benchmark of manufacturing capability of xs.

The optimize stage

In the third phase of the DCOV model, the optimize stage is explored. This stage is also generally completed through a two-step approach. The first is the design for robust performance and the second is the design for productivity. In both cases, the goal is to improve robustness. Therefore, the purpose of the first step is to characterize the present long time in service robustness for the product, and improve robustness by further minimizing product sensitivity to manufacturing and usage conditions, as required. The purpose of the second step is to characterize capability and stability of the present process. This is done simultaneously with the first step. Furthermore, in this step we are also interested in minimizing process sensitivity to product and manufacturing variations, as required.

Design for robust performance. The process for exploring the first step of the optimize stage is divided into three areas:

- *Inputs.* These are the activities that will generate the activity of this step. Typical activities are completing a P-diagram (important y_is);, determining what to measure, control factors (xs), noise factors and error states; conducting an experimental plan (two-step optimization with confirmation run); devising a robustness and reliability checklist; perform a design FMEA (including noise factor analysis) and determining process capability.

- *Action.* These are the activities that actually help find nominals (targets) for xs that minimize variability. In other words, specify tolerances. Typical activities are reducing sensitivity to noise (parameter design, robustness assessment, reliability and robustness), determining tolerances (tolerance design, statistical tolerance, reliability and robustness), eliminating specific failure modes using strategies such as redundancy, eliminating noise and compensating.

- *Output.* These are the results of the action. Typical results are variability metric for CTS or related function (i.e., range, standard deviation, signal to noise (S/N) ratio improvement) and target and tolerances specified for specific characteristics.

Design for productivity. The process for exploring the second step of the optimize stage is divided into three areas:

- *Inputs.* These are the activities that will generate the activity of this step. Typical activities are to present process capability, historical process data (model, surrogate), assembly and manufacturing process flow diagrams (process mapping), reference gauge R&R capability studies and a process FMEA, including noise factor analysis.

- *Action.* These are the activities that actually help the optimization process to produce x_i's nominal with 6σ capability by applying robustness methods to the process (using two-step optimization: reduce variability and then shift to target); using appropriate error-proofing such as DFA, DFM, assembly sequence, poka-yoke, etc.; update the control plan; conduct peer review.

- *Output.* This is the results of the action. Typical results are short-term capability, long-term capability and an updated control plan.

The verify stage

In the fourth phase of the DCOV model, the verify stage is explored. This stage is also typically completed through a two-step approach. The first is the overall DFSS assessment and the second is the test and verify. In both cases the goal is to verify that the capability and product integrity over time is as it was designed and as the customer is expecting it to be. Therefore, the purpose of the first step is to estimate for process capability and product function over time. The purpose of the second step is to assess actual performance, reliability and manufacturing capability, as well as to demonstrate customer correlated (real world) performance over time. If the results of design for robust performance, design for productivity, assessment and testing are not satisfactory, the model action may revert back to the previous stage, or even as far back as the functional mapping stage. Furthermore, in every one of these stages, a trade-off analysis will be performed to ensure all CTSs factors are met.

Overall DFSS assessment. The process for exploring the first step of the verify stage is divided into three areas:

- *Inputs.* These are the activities that will generate the activity of this step. Typical activity is evaluating data from previous steps.

- *Action.* These are the activities that actually help the DFSS overall assessment. Four predominant activities are conducted here: a) determine the CTS/CTQ characteristic/measure and conduct a comparison between the $Z_{estimate}$ and Z_{actual}, b) conduct sub-assessments, as needed, c) perform tests and simulation as well as a comparison between the $Z_{estimate}$ and Z_{actual}, and d) conduct a variability study over time for both product and process.

- *Output.* This is the results of the action. Typical results are an overall review of assessments for previous steps with the champion or appropriate management.

Test and verify. The process for exploring the second step of the verify stage is divided into three areas:

- *Inputs.* The activities that will generate the activity of this step. Typical activities are developing a reliability and/or robustness plan and designing a verification plan with key noises.
- *Action.* These are the activities that actually help to conduct physical, analytical performance tests enhanced with appropriate noise factors. Typical activities are correlating tests to customer usage; improving ability of tests to discriminate good/bad parts, subsystems and systems; and conducting peer review.
- *Output.* This is the results of the action. Typical results are testing results such as key life testing; accelerated tests; long-term process capabilities; product performance over time (e.g., Weibull test and survival plot); and a reliability/robustness demonstration matrix.

Typical tools/methodologies and deliverables for each stage of the DCOV model are shown in Table 5.1.

Table 5.1 Typical tools/methodologies and deliverables for the DCOV model

Stage	Tools/methodology	Deliverables
Define	• Kano model • Quality function deployment • Regression • Conjoint analysis	• Kano diagram • CTS scorecard • *Y* relationship to customer satisfaction • Benchmarked CTSs • Target and ranges for CTS *Y*s

Characterize	• Functional structures
	• Axiomatic designs
	• TRIZ
	• P-diagram
	• R&R checklist
	• DOE
		• Function diagrams
		• Mapping of Y→ critical function → ys
		• P-diagram, including critical
		  ♦ Technical metrics, *ys*
		  ♦ Control factors, *xs*
		  ♦ Noise factors, *ns*
		• Transfer function
		• Scorecard with target and range for *ys* and *xs*
		• Plan for optimization and verification
		  ♦ R&R checklist

Table 5.1 (*Continued*)

Stage	Tools/methodology	Deliverables
Optimize	• Design FMEA • Process FMEA • Experimental design—response surface • Parameter design—two step optimization • Tolerance design • Simulation tools • Error prevention—compensation, estimate noise, mistake-proofing • Gage R&R • Control plan	• Transfer function • Scorecard with estimate of σ_y • Target nominal values identified for xs • Variability metric for CTS Y or related function (e.g., range, standard deviation, S/N ratio improvement) • Tolerance specified for important characteristics • Short-term capability, "z" score • Long-term capability • Updated verification plans: robustness and reliability checklist (if available) • Updated control plan
Verify	• Reliability methods • Design reviews • Customer requirements, including governmental requirements	• Reliability testing • Specific testing based on requirements • Customer functionality • Product and/or service as designed

Test and verify. The process for exploring the second step of the verify stage is divided into three areas:

- *Inputs.* The activities that will generate the activity of this step. Typical activities are developing a reliability and/or robustness plan and designing a verification plan with key noises.

- *Action.* These are the activities that actually help to conduct physical, analytical performance tests enhanced with appropriate noise factors. Typical activities are correlating tests to customer usage; improving ability of tests to discriminate good/bad parts, subsystems and systems; and conducting peer review.

- *Output.* This is the results of the action. Typical results are testing results such as key life testing; accelerated tests; long-term process capabilities; product performance over time (e.g., Weibull test and survival plot); and a reliability/robustness demonstration matrix.

Typical tools/methodologies and deliverables for each stage of the DCOV model are shown in Table 5.1.

Special comments on the verify stage

The verify stage for most practitioners is the most difficult to use. Because of that perceived difficulty, we present an overview of some of its key elements with the assumption that the verify stage—more than any other stage—is a team activity.

Design verification process (DVP) team roles and responsibilities:

- Interface with other teams to meet requirements.
- Review generic requirements.
- Identify, add, or modify requirements not included with the generic requirement.
- Classify requirements assigned to the DVP team.
- Develop minimum feature configurations.
- Record program-specific targets.
- Develop design verification methods (DVMs) to verify requirements.
- Plan when and how to best verify requirements-driven design.
- Complete DVP for the requirements-driven designs.
- Monitor progress of design.
- Prepare sign-off documentation.

The application process of design verification:

1. Review generic requirements, either online or as paper reports.
2. Classify each requirement based on applicability to your program. Record and document the classification in appropriate and applicable log.
3. Modify or add requirements based on assumptions and targets. Record and document the classification in appropriate and applicable log.
4. Determine the minimum feature configurations that your DVP team will need to verify its requirements.

5. Establish targets for each requirement and configuration. Record the targets on the target matrix.

Tool requirements

To facilitate a DVP and be able to update and communicate the results, a good software package is recommended. Such software requirements may be met through the use of Microsoft Windows™ (Win 95 or above).

Security

To ensure security, every user should be assigned one of the following levels of access by the program administrator:

- *Engineer.* This level allows the user to view data of all programs using the DVS. Users at this level are permitted to only manipulate data assigned to their DVP team.
- *Program manager.* This level allows the user to have the same authority as an engineer. Users at this level can also change frozen data.
- *Program administrator.* This level allows the user to have the same authority as an engineer. Users at this level also have access to administrative functions.
- *Full service supplier.* This level allows the user to view and manipulate data assigned to their DVP team.

  What is in it for me?
- Improved test time utilization.
- Consistent standardized reporting.
- Improved DVP tracking and reporting.
- Disciplined adherence to program quality operating system (QOS).
- Multiple users allowed access to a central database.
- Effort reduced to create and report on DVP.
- Connectivity to other systems and databases.
- Ensures that you get a verifiable full-product understanding of the requirements (in both functionality and performance).

Defining program requirements

Any design verification must begin with the definition of the requirements. This is to make sure that the design meets the expected requirements. This review should follow a very structured approach. Some of the issues, concerns, questions and discussions should focus in the following items:

- Are all requirements accounted for? Requirements come from a variety of sources (customer requirements, corporate requirements, government requirements, system design specifications, safety regulations, and so on).

- Is there a possibility of adapting surrogate requirements? Generic requirements can be a source of information that can then be adapted.

- Are all requirements have been accounted? The DVS should treat all requirements the same, regardless of level or priority; within DVS, each requirement has an owning DVP team.

- Do all requirements have a level of specificity? Requirements capture program-specific targets.

- Are appropriate releases defined? Released requirements are available for all programs to use.

- Are requirements sufficient for a prototype? Requirements are needed by anyone who needs to schedule a prototype.

- Is the design on time? Requirements are frozen according to the timing of your program.

Classification and categories of requirements

Classification is an arrangement according to some systematic division into classes or groups. On the other hand, category is a class of division in a scheme of clasification. When classifying requirements, the following typical codes are used:

- *Unclassified*. Initial classification of all requirements.
- *Does not apply*. DVP team determined that the requirement is not applicable to the program.
- *Meet*. DVP team intends to meet this requirement.

- Deviate from requirement. DVP team intends to meet this requirement, but there is a potential to deviate. Deviation process is handled outside the design verification specification (DVS).

- *Support.* DVP team is aware of the requirement, but does not own it and will not write a DVP. Can only be used with a cascaded requirement.

- *Open.* DVP team is still investigating the impact of this requirement on the program.

There are six common categories of requirements:

- *New requirement.* A new requirement is a requirement that never has been in existence—at least for the organization. The mandatory items of concern regarding a new requirement are:
  - Program.
  - Title.
  - DVP team.
  - Unit of measure.
  - Owning attribute or SDS information.

- *Modifying requirements.* Generic and program-specific requirements can be modified to reflect program needs and assumptions. Modified requirements have the following typical characteristics:
  - A modified requirement is an in-process copy of a requirement.
  - In-process requirements can only be viewed and modified by the owning DVP team.
  - Up to only a certain number of in-process copies of the same requirement can exist at one time. This limit should depend on the project.
  - When an in-process requirement is released, other in-process copies are deleted.
  - In-process requirements must be released before they become part of the DVP team's set of requirements.
  - All released requirements must be classified using the classifications listed above.
  - Modified requirements retain the ID number of the original requirement.

- *Adding requirements.* New requirements can be added to reflect the program's needs and assumptions:

- ♦ New requirements can be based on existing requirements or can be created from scratch.
- ♦ Once the mandatory fields are entered and saved, the new requirement is in process.
- ♦ New requirements are given an ID number based on the owning SDS and are numbered beginning with a serial number.
- ♦ All in-process requirements must be released and classified.
- *Deleting requirements.* As the review progresses, it may be necessary to delete some requirements. The delition may be because of obsolescence, irrelevancy or some other reason. The following are some rules to follow when evaluation the design for deleting requirements.
  - ♦ Only in-process requirements can be deleted. (Caution: Once a requirement is deleted, it cannot be retrieved.)
  - ♦ Generic requirements can never be deleted. If they are not needed, they are classified as "does not apply."
  - ♦ Released information cannot be deleted.
- *Releasing requirements.* Once the requirements have been agreed by the team, then they must be released. Typical rules for releasing the requirements are:
  - ♦ In-process requirements can be updated as necessary.
  - ♦ Released requirements allow changes to accomondate robustness. If not, then the design should identify these items with specific identification marks.
  - ♦ Unit of measure field on the requirements text and target/assessments milestones.
  - ♦ Classification code, classification comments, cascade relationship fields on the classification tab.
  - ♦ Engineer, DVP team, sequence number, part number and DVP comments fields on the DVP information tab.
- ♦ Only released requirements can be classified.

Special note: It should be emphasized here that the engineer can only create and/or edit a requirement, whereas the manager has authority to release and classify a requirement or transfer ownership of a requirement to another DVP team.

Cascading requirements. At this stage of the review process the team is ready to pass on the design to the appropriate person(s) or department or process. It is imperative, then, that it follow the following typical rules for making sure that the requirements as defined will be passed on correctly and effectively:

- *Cascade to existing.* This option is used when the owner of a *from* requirement knows that a *to* requirement exists and wants to cascade or link to an existing lower-level *to* requirement. However, there is a caution here: Using the cascade *to* same option causes the requirement to appear on two DVP teams. This is not recommended, it can cause a great deal of confusion as to who is responsible for verification.

- *Cascade to same.* This option is used when the owner of a *from* requirement wants to cascade the same requirement to a *to* or lower-level DVP team. The cascaded requirement will be a released copy of the *from* requirement. The new requirement's ID number should be prefixed by the ID of the assigned SDS and be numbered as a program-specific requirement for less confusion if needed to be traced.

- *Cascade to new.* This option is used when the owner of a *from* requirement wants to create a new requirement and cascade it *to* a DVP team. The cascaded requirement will be an in-process requirement. The new requirement's ID number should be prefixed by the ID of the assigned SDS and be numbered as a program-specific requirement to avoid confusion if needed to be traced.

Requirement reports. Once the category has been identified and the classification has been defined, then the appropriate requirements for reports should be produced. The following reports can be generated, as required by the program:

- *Ad hoc classifications.* Reports on requirements. Details, graphics, and DVMs.

- *DVP team classifications.* Prints paper version of requirements for review and classification purposes.

- *Requirement classification.* Reports number of requirements and totals for each classification.

- *Classification issues.* Lists the requirements that are open, unclassified, or deviate.

- *Engineering verification report.* Prints your design verification plan at specific milestones as the plan is being developed.

- *Program metrics*. Downloads to Excel used to track the program's progress in recording a design verification plan.
- *DVP&R*. Provides two separate reports:
  - ◆ Plan. Provides a snapshot of the current status of all applicable requirements (per DVP team or ad hoc search) for incomplete DVPs and focus on the detail of the plan.
  - ◆ Report. Provides a snapshot of the current status of all applicable requirements (per DVP team or ad hoc search) for assessment issues and focus on the detail of the status.

Minimum feature configurations. A minimum feature configuration is a set of codes that define minimum features or systems required to verify requirements. This configuration is company- or project-dependent. These configurations are representative of different combinations of features that will be offered to the customer. The configurations are owned by the DVP that created it and are used to determine the prototypes needed to complete the program's design verification. On the other hand, a minimum feature configuration is not:

- Used to identify specific CAE models or products.
- An order for a physical build.
- A parts list.

How then do we proceed to generate these configurations? The following are some typical guidelines:

- Identify the target configuration by:
  - ◆ Representing program-specific build features.
  - ◆ Allowing for the entry of target values.
  - ◆ Linking to requirements for DVP planning purposes.
- Conduct a benchmark configuration by:
  - ◆ representing your competitors' build features.
  - ◆ allowing for entry of target values.
  - ◆ not linking to DVMs for DVP planning purposes.
- Ask perhaps the most important question,
  - ◆ Who defines a minimum feature configuration? There are two options:
    - a) The project action team/project management team (PAT/PMT) engineers, and

b) Anyone on a program who needs to schedule a prototype. In discussing the issue of minimum configuration, at least the following should be specified: a) a default value, and b) ad hoc (temporary) search results.

Creating a minimum feature configuration. A minimum feature configuration consists of two parts.

A header-record that contains identification information. A new minimum feature configuration record requires:

- Program.
- DVP team.
- Prototype class.
- Model year.
- Product type.
- Product line.
- Description.

Minimum feature configurations content uses predefined codes or manually entered features. Minimum feature configurations can be copied by the owning DVP team and transferred to the requesting DVP team within the same program. This allows DVP teams to share configurations with common predefined codes. The requesting team can modify its copy of the configurations without affecting the original. Finally, if a specific configuration is not going to be used by a DVP team, it can be deleted. A deleted configuration:

- Will not show up on the target matrix.
- Will not be reported.
- Must not have a target recorded against it.
- Cannot be retrieved.

Entering target values. For any design verification system to work effectively, there are several prerequisites dealing with targets that need to be addressed. Therefore, before working with the target matrix, the generic requirements must be classified. These are requirements at appropriate levels that need to be identified, added, or modified and classified in the overall DVS. In addition, target and benchmark minimum feature configurations need to be developed and entered—they must be set at the system level and be able to be cascaded on other systems or subsystem levels. By entering the appropriate and applicable target values, we are, in effect, planning for the effectiveness of our design. Therefore,

- Target values must be linked to requirements.
- A minimum feature configuration must be selected.
- Target values must be either be numeric or pass/fail.
- Values may be changed until the targets are frozen, according to your program's timing.

Alignment of requirements and configurations may be used when assessments are made. (Special note: only enter targets for requirement and minimum feature configuration combinations that are absolutely necessary to sign-off the specific requirement.) Appropriate and applicable risk assessment analysis must be performed. Typical risk status are: a) unassessed, b) comply, c) minor, d) major, e) major not evaluated, f) not acceptable, and g) not certified.

Reviewing the application process

Any system for any product is not going to be effective unless there is continual feedback on that process. The verification process is not an exception. An ongoing review is recommended to include at least the following actions:

Review your generic requirements either online or on-paper reports.

- Classify each requirement based on applicability to your program. Record the classification in the appropriate documentation log.
- Modify or add requirements based on assumptions and targets. Record the changes in the appropriate documentation log.
- Determine the minimum feature configurations that your DVP team will need to verify its requirements.
- Establish targets for each of the requirements and configurations. Record the targets on the target matrix.

As the review progresses, the team should be able to consider the next steps. These are:

- Contact your program administrator about the following:

- ♦ Have you been set up with a user ID and password? (if you are working with a computer, this is very important step).
- ♦ Has your DVP team been established?
- ♦ have the generic requirements been assigned to your DVP team?
- ♦ Print the ad hoc classification report for your DVP team. (The content in DVS may continue to change. Use updated ad hoc classification reports as necessary.)

When these things have been completed, you need to start the application process.After the target recording process is completed, register for DVS.

Whereas the process evaluation is ongoing activity throughout the verification, at the very end there should be an overall review of the verification process that should allow the following activities to take place:

- • Review generic DVMs.
- • Develop DVMs to verify requirements.
- • Plan when and how to best verify requirement-driven design.
- • Complete design verification plan for the requirement-driven designs.
- • Monitor progress of design.
- • Prepare sign-off documentation.

When everything has been reviewed and agreed upon, the team should consider the next steps to complete the design verification plan. Typical steps are:

- • Review requirement details for linked DVMs.
- • Review the generic DVMs.
- • Create and release new DVMs, if the appropriate generic does not exist.
- • Record a DVP request.
- • Maintain assessment records.
- • Generate sign-off documents.
- • Record risk assessments.

The typical tools used are:
- • A reliability and/or robustness plan.
- • A design verification plan with key noises.

- Correlation tests with customer usage.
- A reliability/robustness demonstration matrix.The typical deliverables of any complete design review should include at least the following:
- Test results, including:
    - Product performance over time.
    - Weibull test, hazard plot and so on.
    - Long-term process capabilities.
- Completed robustness and reliability checklist (if available) with demonstration matrix.
- Scorecard with actual values of y, σ_y.
- Lessons learned, captured and documented.

Chapter 6

Common Methodologies and Tools Used in the DCOV Model

Just as the DMAIC model has several methodologies and specific tools that are used in the analysis of the problems for each of the phases, so does the DCOV model. These typical methodologies and tools are:

- Systems thinking.
- Advanced product quality planning (APQP).
- Production part approval process (PPAP).
- Kano model.
- Ideation.
- Quality function deployment (QFD).
- Statistics/modeling/simulation.
- Reliability.
- Function structures.
- Axiomatic designs.
- Statistical tolerancing.
- Survey.
- Audit.

Each of these is discussed in the following sections.

Systems thinking

Dealing with design for six sigma (DFSS) one must be able to think in a system approach. A system may be considered to be a nucleus of elements structured to accomplish a function and satisfy an identified need. A system may also vary in form, fit and function. For example, a world communication network, a group of aircraft accomplishing a mission at a designated geographical location, or a small ship transporting cargo from one location to another are all considered systems. On the other hand, examples of a functional system are a financial system, a quality system, a purchasing system and a design system. The elements of a system include all equipment, related facilities, material, software, data, services and personnel required for its operation and support, to the degree that it can be considered a self-sufficient entity in its intended operational environment, throughout its planned life cycle.

DFSS relates to the support of a system and includes the elements of test and support equipment, supply support, personnel and training, transportation and material handling, special facilities, computer resources, data and so on, necessary for the accomplishment of breakthrough innovations in design of process, product and/or service. It is imperative that the experimenter or engineer, when pursuing improvements with six sigma, take a holistic approach, so that all interactions and interfaces are accounted for. The more aware the experimenter or engineer is of the parameters, interactions and the interfaces of the undertaken study, the greater the chance of success.

Advanced product quality planning (APQP)

Before we address the "why" of planning, we must assume that things do go wrong.Obviously, there are many specific answers that address the question of why they go wrong. Often the answer falls into one of these four categories:

- We do not have enough time, so some things do not get done.
- We have done something in a particular way, so we minimize our effort.
- We assume that we know what has been requested, so we do not listen carefully.

- We assume that, because we finish a project, improvement will automatically follow, so we bypass the improvement steps.

In essence, the customer appears satisfied, but a product, service or process is not improved at all. This is precisely why it is imperative for organizations to look at quality planning as a totally integrated activity that involves the entire organization. The organization must expect changes in its operations by employing cross-functional and multidisciplinary teams to exceed customer desires—not just to meet requirements. A quality plan includes but is not limited to:

- A team to manage the plan.
- Time to monitor progress.
- Procedures to define operating policies.
- Standards to clarify requirements.
- Controls to stay on course.
- Data and feedback to verify and to provide direction.
- An action plan to initiate change.

Advanced quality planning (AQP), then, is a methodology that yields a quality plan for the creation of a process, product or service consistent with customer requirements. It allows for maximum quality in the workplace by planning and documenting the process of improvement. AQP is the essential discipline that offers both the customer and the supplier a systematic approach to quality planning, to defect prevention and to continual improvement. Some specific uses are:

- In the auto industry, demand is so high that DaimlerChrysler, Ford and General Motors have developed a standardized approach to AQP. That standardized approach is a requirement for the QS-9000 certification as well as the ISO/TS 16949. In addition, each company has its own way of measuring success in the implementation and reporting phase of AQP tasks.
- Automobile suppliers are expected to demonstrate the ability to participate in early design activities from concept through to prototype and on to production.
- Quality planning is initiated as early as possible, well before blueprint release.
- When a company's management establishes a policy of prevention, as opposed to detection.

- To provide the resources needed to accomplish the quality improvement task.
- To prevent waste (scrap, rework and repair), identify required engineering changes, improve timing for new product introduction and reduce costs.
- To facilitate communication with all individuals involved in a program and ensure that all required steps are completed on time at acceptable cost and quality levels.
- To provide a structured tool for management that enforces the inclusion of quality principles in program planning.

When do we use AQP?

Design for six sigma is a true breakthrough approach for satisfying the customer with something better than the status quo. AQP is the vehicle for measuring this breakthrough approach from very early on (concept stage) all the way through production. Therefore, we use AQP when we need to meet, or exceed, expectations in the following situations:

- During the development of new processes and products.
- Prior to changes in processes and products.
- When reacting to processes or products with reported quality concerns.
- Before tooling is transferred to new producers or new plants.
- Prior to process or product changes affecting product safety or compliance to regulations.

The supplier—as in the case of certification programs such as ISO 9000, QS-9000—has to maintain evidence of the use of defect-prevention techniques prior to production launch. The defect-prevention methods used are to be implemented as soon as possible in the new product development cycle. It follows, then, that the basic requirements for appropriate and complete AQP are:

- A team approach.
  - ◆ A systematic development of products/services and processes.
  - ◆ A reduction in variation (this must be done, even before the customer requests improvement of any kind).
  - ◆ Development of a control plan.

As AQP is continuously used, the obvious need for its implementation becomes stronger and stronger. That need may be demonstrated through:

- Minimizing the current level of problems and errors.
- Yielding a methodology that integrates customer—and supplier—development activities, as well as concerns.
- Exceeding current reliability and durability levels to surpass the expectations of the competition and the customer.
- Reinforcing the integration of quality tools with the latest management techniques for total improvement.
- Exceeding the limits set for cycle time and delivery time.
- Developing new, and improving existing, methods of communicating the results of quality processes for a positive impact throughout the organization.

What is the difference between AQP and APQP?

AQP is the generic methodology for all quality planning activities in all industries, so APQP is AQP. However, APQP emphasizes the product orientation of quality. APQP is used specifically in the automotive industry. In this book, both terms are interchangeable.

How do we make AQP work?

There are no guarantees for making AQP work. However, there are three basic characteristics that are essential and must be adhered to for AQP to work. They are:

- Activities must be measured based on who, what, where, and when.
- Activities must be tracked based on shared information (how and why), as well as work schedules and objectives.
- Activities must be focused on the goal of quality-cost-delivery, using information and consensus to improve quality.

As long as our focus is on the triad of quality-cost-delivery, AQP can produce positive results. After all, we all need to reduce costs while we increase quality and reduce lead time. That is the focus of an AQP program, and the better we understand this, the more likely we are to have a workable plan.

The qualitative methodology in an AQP setting. Since this book focuses on the applicability of tools rather than on the details of the tools themselves, the methodology is summarized in seven steps:

1. *Begin with the result in mind.* This may be obvious, but it is how most goals are achieved. This is the stage where the experimenter determines how the study results will be implemented: what course of action can the customer take and how will that action be influenced by the study results? Clearly understanding the goal defines the study problem and report structure. To ensure implementation, determine what the report should look like and what it should contain.

2. *Determine what is important.* All resources are limited and, therefore, we cannot do everything. However, we can do the most important things. We must learn to use the Pareto principle (i.e., vital few, as opposed to the trivial many). To identify what is important, we have many methods, including asking about advantages and disadvantages, desired benefits, likes and dislikes, importance ratings, preference regression, key driver analysis, conjoint and discrete choice analysis, force-field analysis, value analysis, and many others. The focus of these approaches is to improve performance in areas in which a competitor is ahead or in areas where your organization is determined to hold the lead in a particular product or service.

3. *Use segmentation strategies.* Not everyone wants the same thing. Learn to segment markets for specific products and/or services that deliver value to your customer. By segmenting based on wants, the engineering and product development groups can develop action-oriented recommendations for specific markets, and therefore contribute to customer satisfaction.

4. *Use action standards.* To be successful, standards must be defined at the outset—with diagnostics. They are always considered as the minimum requirements. When the results come in, there will be an identified action to be taken, even if it is to do nothing. List the possible results and the corresponding actions that could be taken for each. Diagnostics, on the other hand, provide the "what if" questions that one considers in pursuing the standards. Usually, they provide alternatives through a set of questions, specific to the stan-

dard. If you cannot list actions, then you have not designed an actionable study and will have to redesign.

5. *Develop optimals.* Everyone wants to be the best. The problem with this statement is that there is only one best. All other choices are second best. When an organization focuses on being the best in everything, that organization is heading for failure. No one can be the best in everything and sustain it. What we can do is focus on the best combination of choices. By doing so, we usually have a usable recommendation based on a course of action that is reasonable and within the constraints of the organization.

6. *Give grasp-at-a-glance results.* The focus of any study is to turn people into numbers (wants into requirements), numbers into a story (requirements into specifications) and that story into action (specifications into products and/or services). However, the story must be easy to understand. The results must be clear and well-organized so that they and their implications can be grasped at a glance.

7. *Recommend clearly.* Once you have a basis for an action, recommend that action clearly. You do not want a doctor to order tests and then hand you the laboratory report. You want to be told what is wrong and how to fix it. From an advanced quality planning perspective, we want the same response. That is, we want to know where the bottlenecks are, what kind of problems we will encounter and how we will overcome them for a successful delivery.

APQP initiative and its relationship to DFSS. The APQP initiative in any organization is important because it demonstrates our continuing effort to achieve the goal of becoming a quality leader in the given industry. Inherent in the structure of APQP are the following underlying value-added goals:

- It reinforces the company's focus on continuous improvement in quality, cost and delivery.
- It provides the ability to look at an entirely new program as a single unit:
  - Preparing for every step in the creation.
  - Identifying where the most amount of effort must be centered.
  - Creating a new product with efficiency and quality.

- It provides a better method for balancing the targets for quality, cost and timing.
- It deploys targets with detailed practical deliverables and specific timing schedule requirements.
- It provides a tool for program management to follow-up all program planning processes.

The APQP initiative explicitly focuses on basic engineering activities to avoid concerns, rather than focusing on the results in the product throughout all phases. Based on the fact that the deliverables are clearly defined between departments (supplier-customer relationships), program concerns and issues can be solved efficiently.

The APQP initiative views waiting until the end of the entire planning cycle to conduct a review as unacceptable. Instead, it requires conducting a review at the end of each planning step. This provides a critical step-by-step review of how the organizations are following best possible practices. Also, this APQP initiative has a serious impact on stabilizing the program timing and content. Stabilization results in cost improvement opportunities, including reduction of special samples test trials. Understanding the program requirements for each APQP element from the beginning provides the following advantages:

- It clarifies the program content.
- It controls the sourcing decision dates.
- It identifies customer related significant or critical characteristics.
- It evaluates and avoids quality, cost and timing risks.
- It clarifies for all organizations product specifications using a common control plan concept.

Application of APQP in the DFSS process provides a company with the opportunity to achieve the following benefits:

- Program management has a value-added tool to track and follow-up on all the program planning processes, focusing on engineering method and quality results.
- It provides a critical review of how each organization is following best possible practices by focusing on each planning step.
- It identifies the complete program content upon program initiation, viewing all elements of concern for the organization and project as a whole.

Once program content has been clarified, the following steps can be taken:

- Sourcing decision dates are identified.
- Customer-related significant/critical characteristics are specified.
- Quality, cost and timing risks are evaluated and avoided.
- Product specifications are established for all organizations using a common control plan concept.

Using the APQP process to stabilize program timing and content, the opportunities for cost improvement are dramatically increased. When we are aware of the timing and concerns that may occur during the course of a program, it provides us the opportunity to reduce costs in the following areas:

- Product changes during the program development phase.
- Engineering tests.
- Special samples.
- Number of verification units to be built (prototypes, first preproduction units, etc.).
- Number of concerns identified and reduced.
- Fixture and tooling modification costs.
- Fixture and tooling trials.
- Number of meetings for concern resolution.
- Overtime.
- Program development time and deliverables (an essential aspect of both APQP and DFSS).

(Note: for a very detailed discussion on APQP see Stamatis 1998.)

Production part approval process (PPAP)

The PPAP is discussed here to support the topic of the voice of the process or statistical process control or the process behavior. Its use in the DFSS process may be significant, as can be shown from its application in the automotive industry (see the third edition of the A.I.A.G. publication by the same name). Fundamentally the PPAP system is an automotive system that ensures the quality of the product by focusing on the approval process from the supplier to the customer. (However, it may be applied in other industries with appropriate and applicable modifications.) This approval process is based on:

- Customer requirements.
- Measurement system analysis.
- Statistical process control.
- Potential failure modes and effects analysis.
- Assurance of quality consistency at the time of delivery.

  The fundamental purpose of PPAP is to:

- Determine if all customer requirements are really understood by the supplier.
- Determine if the supplier's process can really produce acceptable product during production runs at the quoted production rate.
- Fine-tune original equipment manufacturers (OEM) assembly and subassembly processes.

  For the actual and specific requirements the reader is advised to consult the PPAP publication, distributed by the A.I.A.G.

Kano model

Kano is a simple model that forces the experimenter or engineer to take into account the basic performance and excitement characteristics of the customer. It is an essential early step of understanding the customer and how the functionality of the particular design may affect the customer satisfaction. Ultimately the understanding gained by the Kano model is used in the QFD analysis to define and redefine customer requirements.

In the most simplistic understanding of the Kano model one has to understand the two variables that effect the clarity of the customer functionality. They are closeness, which refers to how direct the communication with the customer actually is; and effectiveness, which refers to the accuracy of the information collected from the customer.

The process for collecting the information usually falls into the following typical categories: 1) customer complaint(s); 2) survey(s); 3) marketing research (data mining, conjoint analysis, focus group(s)and so on); and 4) interview(s). Of these, the interview is the most powerful since it closes the "gap" in the customer requirement perspective in the most direct way. All of them are used with good results. In fact, quite often a combination of these may be the best approach, so that leverage of their strengths can be optimized. However, we believe that by interviewing someone the experimenter acknowledges that he or she cares about the customer, acknowledges the use of the product and/or service, and acknowledges the fact that perhaps the product or service is not what the customer wants. Therefore, in essence the experimenter is asking the customer for his or her help to understand what is really wanted. The personal interaction for this is very important and quite often not emphasized. The drawback of the interview, of course, is time and money.

Ideation

DFSS by definition (almost) demands out-of-the-box thinking. A longstanding tool to inspire creativity in the world of quality, in fact in all team activities, has been the use of the brainstorming technique. In the last couple years, however, a new twist on the brainstorming methodology has been used and it is called ideation.

The brainstorming activity focuses on the process. However, that focus sometimes created a problem in the creativity process. Ideation, on the other hand, focuses on the results and, as a consequence, eliminates the confusion of the process. Whereas brainstorming breaks down barriers and allows participation from all the involved participants, based on a ritualistic approach, ideation goes a step further in the sense that it comes up with ideas without worrying about the process. In fact, because ideation does not worry about the process, participants are more likely to push the development of ideas into concepts.

Ideation is very flexible, and uses fewer rubrics in deciding on a particular result. It is more efficient than brainstorming and thus may be used in a variety of activities. The actual application of ideation is the same as brainstorming, but without the rules. While brainstorming involves only a facilitator and the employees, in a typical ideation approach, outsiders may be involved. These outsiders may be from cross-functional and multidisciplined areas. Their function is to give their perspective and to break as many barriers as possible.

To have excellent results in any ideation process, the make-up of the participants should have at least the following profile characteristics:

- *Those who envision.* These people add direction, inspiration and momentum to the discussion. They focus on the end result and present a vision of what they want to create. They are very good for strategic planning activities, since they are capable of describing their vision of the ideal future and how to achieve it in 5 to 10 years.

- *Those who modify.* These people examine the components of problems and bring stability and thoroughness to the process. They prefer to take things one step at a time and build on what they already know.

- *Those who experiment.* These people like to test carefully and receive input to confirm ideas. They like to troubleshoot and answer questions on how to use products within their intended markets and how to find other possible uses.

- *Those who explore.* These people excel in taking a product and incorporating new ideas for improvement or enhancement of the product. They thrive on the unknown and have a sense of adventure.

A typical creative usage analysis using ideation may be the TRIZ (the theory for inventive problem-solving).

Quality function deployment (QFD)

QFD is a systematic way of ensuring that the development of the features, characteristics and specifications, as well as the selection and development of process equipment, the methods and controls of a product or service are driven by the demands of the customer or marketplace. The term *development of a product* includes several things: applying new technology, combining existing and new technology and improving quality of performance.

From a QFD perspective, planning is determining what to make and designing is deciding how to make it. Both are important and both depend on the level and the degree of understanding the customer's wants and needs and the product in question. Whereas the traditional approach of transferring the customer's wants into engineering requirements is using the house of quality approach, in this section of the methodology we are going to present a somewhat more detailed, yet systematic, approach based on the work of Clausing and Hauser (1988), as well as the work of Akao (1990). The idea here is to demonstrate that QFD can actually be used, not only in the appraisal mode of quality, but also in the planning mode of quality. (We make the differentiation of the traditional QFD methodology in the DMAIC model and the QFD approach as used in the DCOV model. The first is very common, whereas the second is not used extensively.)

The foundation of any QFD study is the usage of several quality charts. Of course, these charts may be defined broadly or narrowly. Broadly, we can say that a quality chart is a matrix or series of matrices used to correlate everything from product design plan through the quality control process chart, including what we have called the house of quality chart. In a more narrow definition we can define it as a two dimensional matrix consisting of a demanded quality chart combined with a quality characteristics deployment chart. The traditional approach of QFD is shown in Figure 6.1.

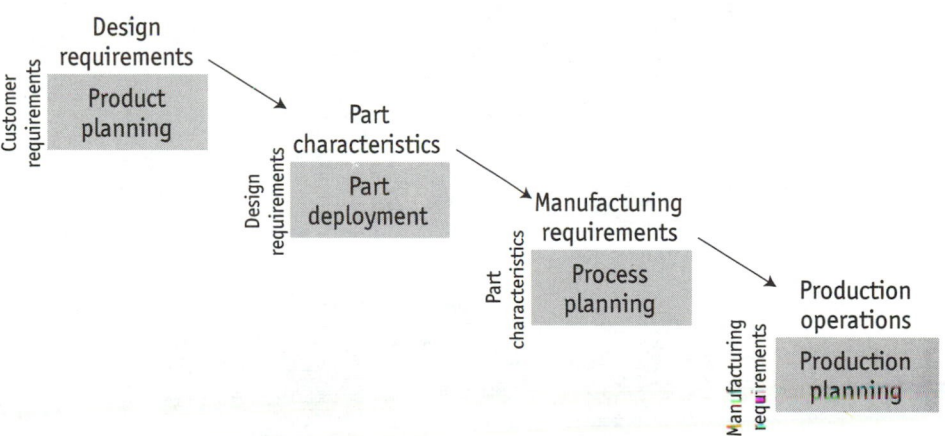

Figure 6.1 The traditional approach of QFD

The value of this approach is its ability to trace the wants of the customer all the way to manufacturing. This approach is very effective for certain parts and components, but awkward for computers, automobiles and other complex systems. It is good for minor improvements in existing technology, but is not well suited for cost-effective innovation.

A more generic approach was developed by Yoji Akao in the mid 1980s and refined in 1990. Its value was that it included linkages with value engineering and reliability charts such as FMEA and FTA. This was adapted by Clausing and Hauser (1988) to include new concept selection and other enhancements. Their interpretation was based on a matrix of matrices (see Figure 6.2). This matrix, though very versatile, does provide a significant level of difficulty in the implementation process. The practical sequence of the matrices is based on the purpose to be achieved. As a consequence, a typical flow is shown in Table 6.1.

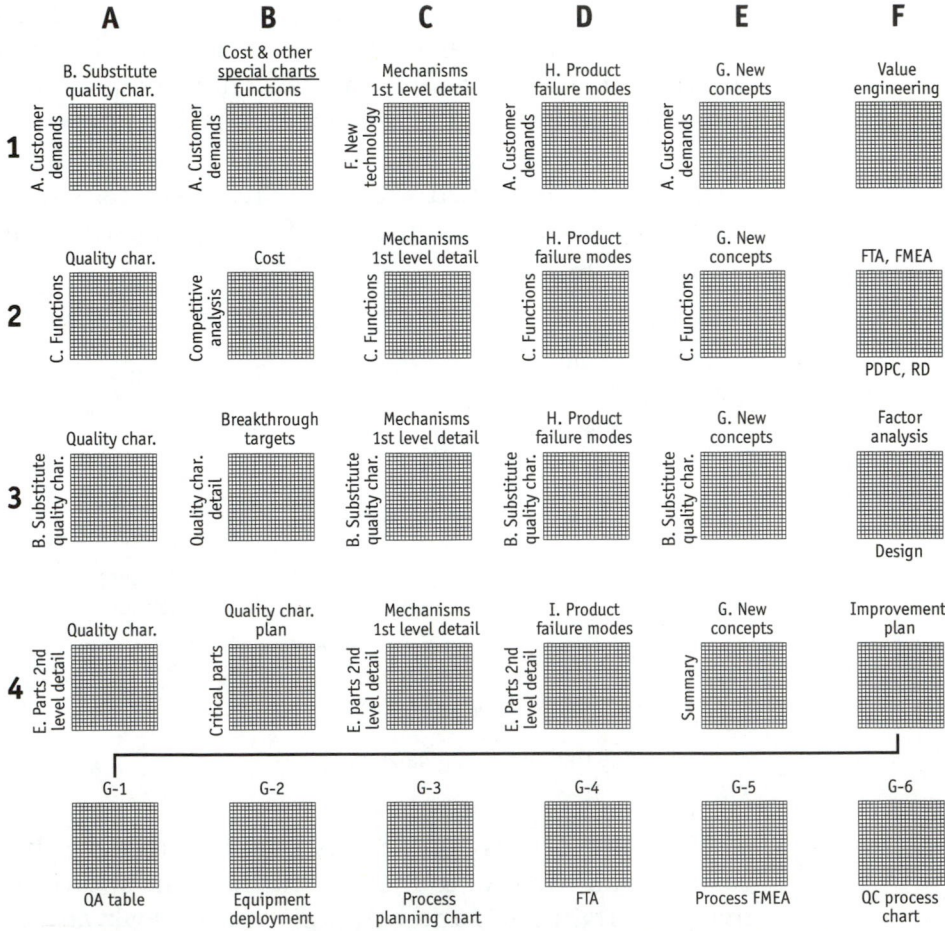

Figure 6.2　The generic approach of QFD with the adaptation of individual matrices

Table 6.1 The flow of the matrices

Purpose to be achieved	Chart to use
Analyze customer demands	A1, B1, D1, E1
Critique functions	A2, C2, D2, E2
Set quality characteristics	A1, A2, A3, A4
	B3, B4, C3, D3, E3
Identify critical parts	A4, B4, C4, E4
Set breakthrough targets	C1, B2, B3, B4
Set cost targets	B1, C2, C3, C4
Set reliability targets	D1, D2, D3, D4
Select new concepts	E1, E2, E3, E4
Identify breakthrough methods	D4, F1, F2, F3, F4
Identify manufacturing methods	G1, G2, G3, G4, G5, G6

An alternate visualization of the sequence is shown in Table 6.2.

Table 6.2 An alternate sequence of the quality charts.

Tables 6.1 and 6.2 and Figure 6.2 show not only which charts must be completed first, but also, in conjunction with the legend, identify the general purpose of each chart, thus encouraging the reader to be problem-focused rather than tool-focused. The disadvantage of these charts is that they suggest that the charts are static where, in effect, they are interactive.

In the six sigma methodology these matrices may be helpful because each of the charts focuses on a particular target of the five-phase innovation process. The five phases are:

- System innovations. Identify the two or three most important system breakthroughs.
- Subsystem innovations. Identify the two or three most important subsystem breakthroughs.
- Part and component innovations. Identify the two or three most important part or component breakthroughs.
- Manufacturing innovations. Finalize manufacturing controls for critical components, parts, subsystems and systems.
- Part and component innovations. After job 1 (the first day of production) identify target annual breakthroughs for subsystems, parts and components.

Within these five phases of innovation, the process of actually carrying out the QFD may be summarized in four stages; each is discussed in the following sections.

Stage 1. During this stage the team should establish targets. This is when the first quality management meeting is held to critique the design concept and to set the targets for whatever the team wants to accomplish. The two major steps are:

1. Develop a planning matrix (multiple functions) in which you:
   - Recognize the voice of the customer.
   - Analyze major product features.
   - Perform market and technical evaluation of competitive products and/or services.
   - Establish targets for major features.
2. Evaluate the strengths and weaknesses of your product or service offering in terms of:
   - Design, technology, reliability and cost.
   - Major selling features, critical targets, and necessary breakthroughs.

Stage 2. During this stage you finalize design timetables and proto-type plans. The major step here is to:

1. Discuss and evaluate all possible means of achieving impor-tant characteristics. This should include:
   - A decision on the technology to be used.
   - Targets and tolerances for critical components.
   - Fault tree analysis, design FMEA, and Taguchi optimization methods to be used.
   - A final characteristic deployment matrix.

Stage 3. This stage establishes the conditions of production. A thorough discussion of the process of targeting and mass-production planning takes place at this point. The two major steps here are:

1. Determine process design:
   - Relate critical component targets and tolerances to proto-type processing conditions.
   - Perform optimization experiments as needed.

2. Transfer leadership of the QFD process from engineering to manufacturing when the decision to go ahead with mass production is made. At this point:
   - Significant control items and means of control are established.
   - Process FMEA, FTA and poka-yoke methods are established.
   - Further need for breakthroughs is defined.
   - Trial runs are used to verify forecasted process stability, capability, adequacy of control points and product quality.
   - The minimum factory effort needed to provide excellent results should be determined.
   - Process quality planning matrices are generated.

Stage 4. This stage is the mass production start-up—where the final quality management meeting is held, approximately three to six months after start-up of production. The discussion is led by manufacturing and engineering is an active participant. Items of discussion may be issues of actual performance and data to be inte-grated in current and/or future QFDs and whether or not additional study is needed for more detailed information and whether or not additional or clarified commitments must be made. The major steps in the overall discussion are to:

1. Develop a database on actual mass production capabilities versus the plan.
2. Identify problems and areas for further improvement.
3. Integrate operator suggested efficiency or effectiveness improvements into the plan.
4. Identify additional customer valued inputs.

Statistics, modeling and simulation

In chapter 4 we talked about the significance and the role of statistics in the DMAIC model of the six sigma methodology. In this chapter we are focusing on the statistical role in the DCOV model. The reader will notice that statistics, modeling, and simulation play a much more important role in the design for six sigma as applied through the DCOV model.

Especially in DFSS we must be cognizant of parametric and non-parametric statistics and their application. The term *parameter* is generally employed to connote a characteristic of the population. A parameter is often an unspecified constant appearing in a family of probability distributions, but the word can also be interpreted in a broader sense to include almost all descriptions of population characteristics within a family. In other words, they are distribution dependent.

The term non-parameter, on the other hand, is a distribution-free inference, and the methods used are based on functions of the sample observations whose corresponding random variable has a distribution that does not depend on the specific distribution function of the population from which the sample was drawn. In other words, assumptions regarding the underlying population are not necessary for testing or estimation.

DFSS by definition is a planning activity, to plan in advance, as much as possible, "flawless" designs that meet or exceed customer expectations. Toward that end robustness is utilized in the form of $Y = f(x, n)$, and modeling is used to predict outcomes. Typical modeling techniques are parameter design, regression, MANOVA (multiple analysis of variance), structural modeling and tolerance design.

Furthermore, we must also consider how a system in the design phase will perform once it is built. Questions include: Will it be stable? Is the control system adequate? How can the performance of an existing system be improved? These are the kinds of tough questions faced every day by engineers working with complex dynamic systems in a broad range of industries—automotive, off-highway equipment, transportation, aerospace, defense, health care, education and so on. Traditionally, solutions to these questions have been found by building costly prototypes and pilots, as well as performing extensive laboratory tests.

Today, especially organizations with a DFSS commitment may reduce their time to market and their development costs using simulation. Simulation is a tool that allows the experimenter to see "what happens if...". For simulation to be effective, the experimenter must have technical expertise and must know the simulated process. Conducting any simulation, however, is just a means to an end, not an end in itself. Common simulations are based on Monte Carlo and numerical approximation methods such as finite element analysis, root sum of squares (RSS) method, successive linear approximation method (SLAM), Taguchi's tolerance design and others.

An effective simulation starts with a model—that is, a set of equations that accurately characterizes system dynamics—and it is here that the big problems begin. Deriving system equations is difficult and confounds even the best engineers. (Sometimes it is so difficult that many companies give up on simulation altogether.) When there is a real difficulty in deriving equations, we can still use simulations with either surrogate data or similar designs and historical experiences. To be sure, the results will be approximations and must be adjusted accordingly as more information is gained through our experimentation.

Reliability

Reliability is valued by the organization and is a primary consideration in all decision-making. Reliability techniques and disciplines are integrated into system- and component-planning, design, development, manufacturing, supply, delivery and service processes. The reliability process is tailored to fit individual business unit requirements and is based on common concepts that are focused on producing reliable products or services and systems, not just components.

In pursuing DFSS, an organization should have a broad statement that frames the overall task and is deployed within the organization. The reliability process must include robustness concepts and methods that are integrated into the organizational design culture and are in tandem with the customer's needs, wants and expectations.

Reliability can be defined simply as the probability that a system or product will perform in a satisfactory manner, for a given period of time, when used under specified operating conditions. This definition stresses the elements of probability, satisfactory performance, time and specified operating conditions. These four elements are extremely important, since each plays a significant role in determining system or product reliability.

Probability. Probability, the first element in the reliability definition, is usually stated as a quantitative expression representing a fraction or a percent signifying the number of times that an event occurs (successes), divided by the total number of trials.

Satisfactory performance. Satisfactory performance, the second element in the reliability definition, indicates that specific criteria must be established that describe what is considered to be satisfactory system operation. A combination of qualitative and quantitative factors defining the functions that the system or product is to accomplish, usually presented in the context of a system specification, is required.

Time. The third element, time, is one of the most important, since it represents a measure against which the degree of system performance can be related. One must know the time parameter in order to assess the probability of completing a mission, or a given function, as scheduled. Of particular interest is being able to predict the probability of an item surviving (without failure) for a designated period of time (sometimes designated as "R"). Also, reliability is frequently defined in terms of mean time between failure (MTBF), mean time to failure (MTTF), or mean time between maintenance (MTBM); thus, the aspect of time is critical in reliability measurement.

Specified operating conditions. The specified operating conditions, under which we expect a system or product to function, constitute the fourth significant element of the basic reliability definition. These conditions include environmental factors such as geographical location where the system is expected to operate, the operational profile, the transportation profile, temperature cycles, humidity, vibration, shock and so on. Such factors must not only address the conditions for the period when the system or product is operating, but the conditions for the periods when the system (or a portion thereof) is in a storage mode or being transported from one location to the next. Experience has indicated that the transportation, handling and storage modes are sometimes more critical from a reliability standpoint than the conditions experienced during actual system operational use.

These four elements are critical in determining the reliability of a system or product. System reliability (or unreliability) is a key factor in the frequency of maintenance, and the maintenance frequency obviously has a significant impact on logistical support requirements. Therefore, reliability predictions and analyses are required as an input to the logistic support analysis.

Reliability is an inherent characteristic of design. As such, it is essential that reliability be adequately considered at program inception, as part of the DFSS process and be addressed throughout the system life cycle.

Robustness and reliability

The traditional six sigma methodology focuses on the DMAIC model which, of course, is based on the notion of $Y = f(x)$. The DFSS methodology is based on the DCOV model and is focused on the notion of $Y = f(x, n)$. Mathematically these two distinct approaches can be shown as:

$$\sigma_y = \left[\left(\frac{\partial y}{\partial x_1} \right)^2 \sigma_{x_1}^2 + \left(\frac{\partial y}{\partial x_2} \right)^2 \sigma_{x_2}^2 + \ldots \right]^{1/2}$$

Whereas the focus of the DMAIC model is to reduce $\sigma^2_{x_x}$ (variability),

the focus of the DCOV is to reduce the $\left(\dfrac{\partial y}{\partial x} \right)$ (sensitivity).

This is very important and that is why we use the partial derivatives of the xs to define the Ys. Of course, if the transformation function is a linear one, then the only thing we can do is to control variability. Needless to say, in most cases we deal with polynomials, and that is why DOE and especially parameter design are very important in any DFSS endeavor. The fact that we introduce the noise in the $f(x, n)$ makes the equation quite powerful, because we are focusing on satisfying the customer regardless of the present noise. In fact, that is what robustness is.

In a more descriptive manner, this robustness may be explained as a 15-step process (shown in Figure 6.3) that reduces complexity, and therefore, variation. The steps are grouped into six sections. The reader will notice that robust, reliable products may be generated from a seed—a vision of unprecedented customer satisfaction, which is the iteration of the 15 simple steps.

Program input

1. Work as a program team with a shared vision.
   Purpose: establish and maintain a program development team for both product and process that has a shared vision.
   Idea and vision: high-performance teams emerge and grow through the systematic application of learning organization and team disciplines to foster synergy, shared direction, interrelationships and a balance between intrinsic and extrinsic motivational factors. A rapid, focused, simultaneous start-up enables teams to develop a high-quality product on schedule.
2. Create a program information center.
   Purpose: establish and maintain a program information center to understand program, social and institutional knowledge.
   Idea and vision: create an information environment with networks to foster program and/or product knowledge via prior lessons learned, best practices, inter- and intradisciplinary communication and collaboration.

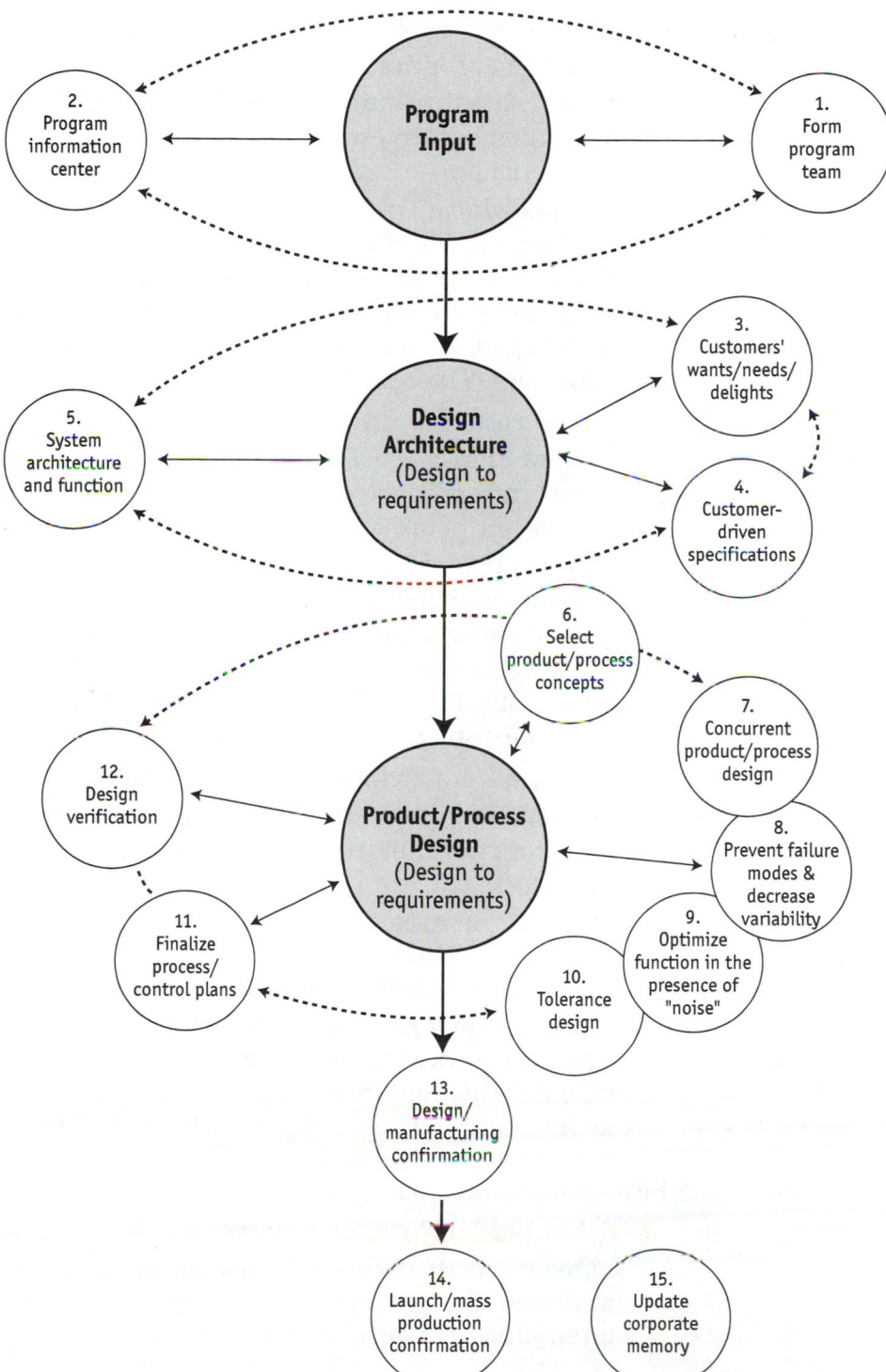

Figure 6.3 The flow of a typical robustness approach to reduce complexity

Design architecture

3. Establish and prioritize customer wants, needs and delights.

   Purpose: Identify customers and create opportunities for team members to establish and/or prioritize customer wants, needs, delights, usage profiles and demographics.

   Idea and vision: Foster intense customer engagement to identify base expectations, as well as distinctive opportunities that differentiate and characterize a winning product. Conditions are set that allow the team to get a deep understanding of what is a desirable product from a customer viewpoint. The result is products customers will want to buy.

4. Derive customer-driven specifications.

   Purpose: Translate customer, corporate and regulatory requirements into product/process specifications and engineering and/or test plans.

   Idea and vision: Establish the foundation (maximum potential) for customer satisfaction by systematically translating the customer definition of a "good" product into engineering language and competitive targets. Customer-driven specifications describe a final product that satisfies the real world customer.

5. Define system architecture and function.

   Purpose: Define system architecture, inputs/outputs and ideal function for each of the system elements and identify interfaces.

   Idea and vision: Lay the foundation for analytical optimization of function, cost, quality and performance by gaining understanding of how the system and system elements function ideally, and by gaining understanding of the interfaces and interactions between functional system elements. The engineer has the opportunity to create and innovate high-level architecture to make a significant competitive difference.

Product/process design

6. Select product/process concept.

   Purpose: Create and/or establish alternative product design and manufacturing process concepts and derive enhanced alternatives for development.

Idea and vision: Derive a concept to meet or exceed customer expectations through systematic exploration of many alternatives. Creative thinking is crucial here. At this point in the process, with only 10 percent of the total product development time committed, 80 percent of the future success is determined.

7. Conduct product and process design.

   Purpose: Design and model product and process concurrently, using low-cost tolerances and inexpensive materials.

   Idea and vision: Achieve superior performance through simultaneous integration of engineering, manufacturing and delivery functions.

8. Prevent failure modes and decrease variability.

   Purpose: Improve product and process through reduction of failure modes and variability.

   Idea and vision: Improve product and process by asking: "what can go wrong?" and "where can variation come from?" Revise design and process to prevent occurrence and reduce variation.

9. Optimize function in the presence of noise.

   Purpose: Optimize product and manufacturing/assembly process functions by testing them in the presence of anticipated sources of variation and/or noise.

   Idea and vision: Improve performance against customer targets, during the development process, by adjusting controllable parameters to minimize deviations from the intended or ideal function.

10. Perform tolerance design.

    Purpose: Selectively tighten tolerances and upgrade materials to achieve desired performance (with cost/benefit trade-offs). Identify key characteristics for manufacturing control and variability reduction.

    Idea and vision: Achieve functional targets at lowest cost by selectively tightening tolerances and upgrading materials only where necessary. Demonstrated customer sensitive characteristics are chosen for ongoing variation reduction. By applying preventive and robust methods early in the design process (steps 7–10), you simultaneously greatly enhance ideal function performance, create a superior product and increase investment and resource efficiency.

11. Finalize process and control plans.

    Purpose: Finalize process and establish tooling, gages and control plans.

    Idea and vision: The manufacturing and assembly processes, tooling, gages and control plans are appropriately designed to control and reduce variation in characteristics that influence customer satisfaction.

12. Verify the design.

    Purpose: Integrate and verify design and manufacturing process functions with production-like hardware and software.

    Idea and vision: Improve quality and reduce time to market by enabling a single prototype build/test/fix cycle. A high-quality, cost-efficient manufacturing process or product is ensured.

Design/manufacturing confirmation

13. Confirm manufacturing capability.

    Purpose: Confirm manufacturing and assembly process capability to achieve design intent.

    Idea and vision: Enable rapid, smooth confirmation of production and assembly operations with minimal refinements. Unanticipated trial concerns are identified and corrected to ensure a low-risk launch.

Launch and mass production confirmation

14. Launch product and ramp-up production.

    Purpose: Launch the product, ramp-up and confirm that mass production delivers function, cost, quality and performance objectives.

    Idea and vision: Implementation of robust processes and up-front launch planning, with just-in-time training, will promote a smooth launch and rapid ramp-up to production speed. Final confirmation of deliverables enables team learning with improved understanding of cause-effect relationships. All the time and effort spent at the beginning of the process now starts to pay off.

For all activities

15. Update corporate memory.

    Purpose: Update the corporate knowledge database with technical, institutional and social lessons learned (both TGR and TGW should be evaluated and logged).

    Idea and vision: Retain what has been learned. Create and maintain capability for locating, collecting and synthesizing data and information into profound knowledge. Communicate, in a timely and user-friendly manner, all technical, institutional and social lessons learned. As we increase our knowledge, we increase our power to become the best.

Maintainability

Maintainability, like reliability, is an inherent characteristic of system, or product, design. It pertains to the ease, accuracy, safety and economy in the performance of maintenance actions. A system should be designed so that it can be maintained without large investments of time, cost or other resources (e.g., personnel, materials, facilities and test equipment) and without adversely affecting the mission of that system. Maintainability is the ability of an item to be maintained, whereas maintenance constitutes a series of actions to be taken to restore or retain an item in an effective operational state. Maintainability is a design parameter. Maintenance is a result of design.

Maintainability can also be defined as a characteristic in design that can be expressed in terms of maintenance frequency factors, maintenance times (i.e., elapsed times and labor hours) and maintenance cost. These terms may be presented as different figures of merit. Therefore, maintainability may be defined on the basis of a combination of factors involving all aspects of the system. The measures of maintainability often include a combination of the following:

- MTBM. Mean time between maintenance includes both preventive (scheduled) and corrective (unscheduled) maintenance requirements. It includes consideration of reliability MTBF and MTBR (see next item). MTBM may also be considered as a reliability parameter.

- MTBR. Mean time between replacement of an item due to a maintenance action (usually generates a spare-part requirement). Items and their symbols associated with MTBR are:

  1. $\bar{M}$—mean active maintenance time (a function of and).
  2. $\bar{M}ct$—mean corrective maintenance time. Equivalent to mean time to repair (MTTR).
  3. $\bar{M}pt$—mean preventive maintenance time.
  4. $\tilde{M}ct$—median active corrective maintenance time. Equivalent to equipment repair time (ERT).
  5. $\tilde{M}pt$—median active preventive maintenance time.
  6. $MTTR_g$—geometric mean time to repair.
  7. M_{ax}—maximum active corrective maintenance time (usually specified at the 90% and 95% confidence levels).
  8. MDT—maintenance downtime (total time during which a system/equipment is not in condition to perform its intended (function). MDT includes active maintenance time ($\bar{M}$), logistics delay time (LDT), and administrative delay time (ADT).
  9. MMH/OH—maintenance man-hours; per equipment operating hour.
  10. Cost/OH—maintenance cost per equipment operating hour.
  11. Cost/MA—maintenance cost per maintenance action.
  12. Turnaround time (TAT)—that element of maintenance time needed to service, repair, and/or check out an item for recommitment. This constitutes the time that it takes an item to go through the complete cycle from operational installation through a maintenance shop and into the spares inventory ready for use.
  13. Self-test thoroughness—the scope, depth, and accuracy of testing.
  14. Fault isolation accuracy—accuracy of equipment diagnostic routines in percent.

Maintainability, as an inherent characteristic of design, must be properly considered in the early phases of system development, and maintainability activities are applicable throughout the life cycle.

Supportability

Supportability relates to the degree to which the system can be Supported, both in terms of the inherent characteristics of prime equipment design and the effectiveness of the overall support capability (i.e., elements of logistic support). This term is commonly used in a rather general sense, and its use often implies some degree of overlap with reliability and maintainability.

Serviceability

Serviceability relates to how fast an incapacitated system can be fixed or brought back to service. Serviceability is closely related to human factors—sometimes referred to as ergonomics. Human factors pertain to the human element of the system and the interfaces between the human being, the machine and associated software. The objective is to ensure complete compatibility between the system's physical and functional design features and the human element in the operation, maintenance and support of the system. Considerations in design must be given to anthropometric factors (e.g., the physical dimensions of the human being), human sensory factors (e.g., vision and hearing capabilities), physiological factors (e.g., impacts from environmental forces), psychological factors (e.g., human needs, expectations, attitude, motivation) and their interrelationships. Just as with reliability and maintainability, human factors must be considered early in system development through the accomplishment of functional analysis, operator and maintenance task analysis, error analysis, safety analysis and related design support activities. Operator and maintenance personnel requirements (i.e., personnel quantities and skill levels) and training program needs evolve from the task analysis effort. Maintenance personnel requirements are also identified in the logistic support analysis (LSA).

Maintenance

Maintenance includes all actions necessary for retaining a system or product in, or restoring it to, a serviceable condition. Maintenance may be categorized as corrective maintenance or preventive maintenance:

- *Corrective maintenance.* This includes all unscheduled maintenance actions performed as a result of system or product failure to restore the system to a specified condition. The corrective maintenance cycle includes failure localization and isolation, disassembly, item removal and replacement or repair, reassembly, and checkout and condition verification. Also, unscheduled maintenance may occur as a result of a suspected failure, even if further investigation indicates that no actual failure occurred.

- *Preventive maintenance.* This includes all scheduled maintenance actions performed to retain a system or product in a specified condition. Scheduled maintenance includes the accomplishment of periodic inspections, condition monitoring, critical item replacements and calibration. In addition, servicing requirements (e.g., lubrication and fueling) may be included under the general category of scheduled maintenance.

Maintenance level. Corrective and preventive maintenance may be accomplished on the system itself (or an element thereof) at the site where the system is used by the consumer, in an intermediate shop near the consumer, and/or at a depot or manufacturer's plant facility. Maintenance level pertains to the division of functions and tasks for each area where maintenance is performed. Task complexity, personnel-skill-level requirements, special facility needs, and so on, dictate to a great extent the specific functions to be accomplished at each level.

Maintenance concept. The maintenance concept constitutes a series of statements and/or illustrations defining criteria covering maintenance levels. The maintenance concept is defined at program inception and is a prerequisite to system or product design and development. The maintenance concept is also a required input to logistic support analysis (LSA).

Maintenance plan. The maintenance plan (as compared to the maintenance concept) is a detailed plan specifying the methods and procedures to be followed for system support throughout the life cycle during the consumer use period. The plan includes the identification and use of the required elements of logistics necessary for the sustaining support of the system. The maintenance plan is developed from logistic support analysis (LSA) data and is usually prepared during the detail design phase.

System effectiveness

System effectiveness is one or more figures of merit representing the extent to which the system is able to perform the intended function. The figures of merit used may vary considerably depending on the type of system and its mission requirements, and should consider the following:

- *System performance parameters.* These might include the capacity of a power plant, range or weight of an airplane, destructive capability of a weapon, quantity of letters processed through a postal system, amount of cargo delivered by a transportation system and the accuracy of a radar capability.

- *Availability.* This is the measure of the degree a system is in the operable and committable state at the start of a mission when the mission is called for at an unknown random point in time. This is often called operational readiness. Availability is a function of operating time (reliability) and downtime (maintainability/supportability).

- *Dependability.* This is the measure of the system operating condition at one or more points during the mission, given the system condition at the start of the mission (i.e., availability). Dependability is a function of operating time (reliability) and downtime (maintainability/supportability).

A combination of the foregoing considerations (measures) represents the system effectiveness aspect of total cost-effectiveness. By inspection, one can see that logistics impacts the various elements of system effectiveness to a significant degree, particularly in the areas of availability and dependability. System operation is highly dependent on support equipment (handling equipment), operating personnel, data and facilities. Maintenance and system downtime are based on the availability of test and support equipment, spare or repair parts, maintenance personnel, data and facilities. The effect of the type and quantity of logistic support is measured through the parameters of system effectiveness.

Life cycle cost (LCC)

LCC involves all costs associated with the system life cycle, and includes:

- *Research and development (R&D) cost.* These include the cost of feasibility studies; system analyses; detail design and development, fabrication, assembly, and test of engineering models; initial system test and evaluation; and associated documentation.

- *Production and construction cost.* These include the cost of fabrication, assembly, and test of operational systems (production models); operation and maintenance of the production capability; and associated initial logistic support requirements (e.g., test and support equipment development, spare/repair parts provisioning, technical data development, training, entry of items into the inventory and facility construction).

- *Operation and maintenance cost.* This is the cost of sustaining operation, personnel and maintenance support, spare/repair parts and related inventories, test and support equipment maintenance, transportation and handling, facilities, modifications and technical data changes and so on.

- *System retirement and phase-out cost.* This is the cost of phasing the system out of the inventory due to obsolescence or wear-out, and subsequent equipment item recycling and reclamation as appropriate.

Life cycle costs may be categorized many different ways, depending on the type of system and the sensitivities desired in cost-effectiveness measurement.

Cost-effectiveness. The development of a system or product that is cost-effective, within the constraints specified by operational and maintenance requirements, is a prime objective. Cost-effectiveness relates to the measure of a system in terms of mission fulfillment (system effectiveness) and total life cycle cost. Cost-effectiveness, which is similar to the standard cost-benefit analysis factor employed for decision-making purposes in many industrial and business applications, can be expressed in various terms (i.e., one or more figures of merit), depending on the specific mission or system parameters that one wishes to measure.

Reliability factors

In determining system support requirements, frequency of maintenance becomes a significant parameter. Maintenance frequency for a given item is highly dependent on the reliability of that item. In general, as the reliability of a system increases, the frequency of maintenance will decrease, and conversely maintenance frequency will increase as system reliability is degraded. Unreliable systems will usually require extensive maintenance. In any event, logistic support requirements are highly influenced by reliability factors. Thus, a basic understanding of reliability terms and concepts is required. Some of the key reliability quantitative factors used in the system design process, and for the determination of logistic support requirements, are briefly defined here.

The reliability function

Reliability can be defined simply as the probability that a system or product will perform in a satisfactory manner for a given period of time when used under specified operating conditions. The reliability function, $R(t)$, may be expressed as:

$$R(t) = 1 - F(t)$$

where $F(t)$ is the probability that the system will fail by time t. $F(t)$, showing the failure distribution function, or the "unreliability" function. If the random variable t has a density function of $f(t)$, then the expression for reliability is:

$$R(t) = 1 - F(t) \int_t^\infty f(t) dt$$

Assuming that the time to failure is described by an exponential density function, then:

$$f(t) = \frac{1}{\theta} e^{-t/\theta}$$

where theta (θ) is the mean life, t is the time period of interest, and e is the natural logarithm base (2.7183). The reliability at time t is:

$$R(t) = \int_t^\infty \frac{1}{\theta} e^{-t/\theta} dt = e^{-t/\theta}$$

Mean life theta (θ) is the arithmetic average of the lifetimes of all items considered. The mean life theta for the exponential function is equivalent to mean time between failure (MTBF). Thus:

$$R\,(t) = ee^{-t/M} = e^{-\lambda t}$$

where lambda (λ) is the instantaneous failure rate and M is the MTBF. If an item has a constant failure rate, the reliability of that item at its mean life is approximately 0.37. In other words, there is a 37 percent probability that a system will survive its mean life without failure, Mean life and failure rates are related in the following equation:

$$\lambda = \frac{1}{\theta}$$

We must emphasize here that the failure characteristics of different items are not necessarily the same. There are a number of well-known probability density functions which, in practice, have been found to describe the failure characteristics of different equipments. These include the binomial, exponential, normal, Poisson, gamma and Weibull distributions. Therefore, one should take care not to assume that the exponential distribution is applicable in all instances, or the Weibull distribution is the best, and so on.

Function structures

In the DMAIC model, the process flowchart is an indispensable tool in identifying the "as is" process, as well as the "should be" process. Of course, the idea is to identify the value added steps and eliminate the hidden factory. In the DFSS approach we are still interested in function structures for the same reason. However, the structures in the DFSS are process mapping and datum flow chain.

Process mapping

Process mapping in the DFSS methodology is used as a process flow indicator and as a project status indicator. In the case of the first application, no special consideration is given. In fact, it is the traditional process flowchart. In the case of the project status, however, it attempts to provide a uniform, well-defined measure of the project activity currently underway. Using the activity underway—as opposed to the most recent activity completed or the next activity to be undertaken—as the project status reference point seems appropriate for most projects we have had experience with thus far.

The values in the diagram can help to identify bottlenecks in the flow of work through the organization and may validate project flows that are working well. (It is imperative for the black belt to note that if none of the status values is appropriate, to describe the project status in the comments section of the project. Of course, the status "on hold" may be set at any point in a project.) A typical sample of project status values is shown in Table 6.3.

Table 6.3 Typical project status values

Project status	Description
Potential	An idea for a project has shown merit, but no resources have been allocated.
Preplanning (1)	An initial project description is being created.
Business case preparation	Preliminary investigation is going on as to whether there is a valid business case for the project.
Conceptual design (2)	The basic idea of what the project will do, including what technology might be appropriate, is being fleshed out.
Seeking commitment	The business case and conceptual design are being presented to sponsors—in an effort to seek sponsor commitment to go forward.
Pending	Sponsor has committed to implementing the project, but the project has not yet gotten underway.
Requirements analysis	Project team is gathering and reviewing customer requirements.
Prototype	Project team is building and reviewing a prototype. For example, a low-fidelity prototype may be built to validate customer expectations.
Design	Team is figuring out how to accomplish the implementation.
Buy (5)	Implementation by purchase is underway. This stage may include related development, documentation, training, and other activities. Some projects involve both buy and build activities, with the "build" usually depending on the "buy" activity.
Build (3), (5)	Building the implementation is underway. This stage may include related development, documentation, training, and other activities. Some projects involve both buy and build activities, with the "build" usually depending on the "buy" activity. "Build" includes

(Continued on next page)

Table 6.3 (*Continued*)

Project status	Description
Build (3), (5), continued	development, documentation, training preparation, and other activities.
Internal test	Implementation is functionally complete and is being tested internally by the project team.
External test	After passing the internal testing stage and correcting all the show-stopper bugs, the implementation has been given to testers outside the project team.
Handoff/service review	People with expertise in service and support processes are working with the project team to determine whether the implementation is serviceable and supportable. This review may begin during internal testing—to permit service and support perspectives to influence the modifications undertaken as a result of testing. An alternative view of this stage, appropriate for some projects, is to make this a final gate, which is imposed after testing and rework is complete.
Ready (or operational)	Internal and external testing and handoff/service review are complete. All necessary modifications have been made. The implementation is ready for production use and has been accepted as such by the service and support teams. Its release may depend on scheduling and timing, as determined by the service and support teams.
Completed on hold	Project ended after successfully meeting its objectives. Work on the project has been suspended either temporarily or indefinitely. This status may be set at any point in the process.
Terminated (4)	The project was abandoned with significant objectives incomplete.
Comments	1. If none of the current status values apply, describe project status in the comments section for the project. 2. "On hold" status may be set at any point in the process. 3. "Build" includes development, documentation, training preparation, and other activities. 4. "Terminated" indicates that the project has ended with significant objectives incomplete. 5. The red line from "buy" to "build" represents those projects that involve both activities. For these projects, the "build" generally depends on the "buy" activity.

Datum flow chain

The datum flow chain (DFC) is a directed acyclic graph (a graph with no cycles) representation of assembly with nodes representing parts, as well as assembly fixtures and arc representing mates. The direction of the arc represents the direction of the content. Every arc constrains certain degrees of freedom depending upon the mating conditions. The sum of the degrees of freedom constrained by all incoming arcs to a node should be equal to six, unless motion is part of the function. That is, each part must be fully constrained; in each DFC there is only one root node with only outgoing arcs; every joint where the DFC passes is a mate.

The significance of the DFC to DFSS is that DFC directly controls the delivery of significant and critical to quality (STQ and CTQ) characteristic. For example, in a nominal analysis of assembly we may begin the process by:

- Identifying CTQ characteristics.
- Identifying the types of assembly (part-defined or assembly-defined).
- Identifying constraints and fixtures.
- Defining DFC, features, mates and contacts for each CTQ characteristic.
- Checking for proper constraint (six degrees of freedom, unless motion is required by function).
- Finding feasible assembly sequence with shorter CTQ chain of delivery.
- For multiple CTQ characteristics, checking if there is conflict in delivering CTQs. If there is, revise the assembly sequence, parameters or product architecture to remove the conflict.

Axiomatic designs

An approach that seeks to establish a scientific basis for design and create a theoretical foundation and associated tools, is the methodology developed by the MIT professor Nam Suh. Although his technique, known as axiomatic design, is not usually considered a quality methodology, proper application of its tools will result in robust products capable of exceeding customer expectations. It is also well suited to software engineering. The fundamental concepts of this technique are summarized in two axioms:

- Maintain the independence of functional requirements (independence axiom).
- Minimize the information content of the design (information axiom).

There are four domains within axiomatic design:

- Customer domain (attributes).
- Functional domain (functional requirements and constraints).
- Physical domain (design parameters).
- Process domain (process variables).

Items identified within one domain are mapped to the next. This facilitates the development of a design matrix that relates the functional requirements to the design parameters. Once the matrix is developed, successful application of the two fundamental axioms and related corollaries and theorems guides engineers to produce designs that avoid coupling.

In coupled designs, one design parameter influences multiple functional requirements. Therefore, those parameters cannot be optimized for one requirement without compromising another. For example, a water faucet with separate hot and cold valves is a coupled design—adjusting one valve changes both the water flow rate and its temperature. A faucet with one control lever is uncoupled—flow and temperature are controlled independently.

Successful execution of axiomatic design's algorithmic approach enables engineers to avoid the pitfalls of coupled designs and develop robust products.

In conjunction with the axiomatic design, we also may want to use signal flow graphs. These are graphs that represent relationships among a number of variables. A special condition exists when these relationships are linear. When that happens, the graph represents a system of simultaneous linear algebraic equations. For more on these topics see Eppinger, Nukala and Whitney (1997); Stamatis (2003), and Suh (1990).

Statistical tolerancing

Statistical tolerancing is an analysis of the tolerance accumulation, in an assembly or system, based on process capability through assembly stack-up, performance variation and cycle time stack-up. It is also the process to identify significant and non-significant effects of subsystems or component variation. The process of tolerancing analysis is based on four steps:

1. Identify the significant characteristic.
2. Develop a model.
3. Acquire process capability data.
4. Perform tolerance analysis.

Developing model for tolerancing

Typically, there are two types of models: a) linear (such that the coefficient of xs are constants (e.g., $Y = X1 + X2 + X3 - X4$, 1-D stack-up tolerance; $Y = X1 - X2$, cost model) and nonlinear (so that the coefficient of Xs are functions of Xs (e.g., $Y = X_1^2 + X_2^2$, geometric function; P = L/A, performance function; $Y = X_1 \exp(0.5 X_2 X_3)$). To develop a tolerancing model, we follow five steps. They are:

1. Developed from mechanical assembly tolerance model the parameters and the tolerances (using tolerance chain vector loop and/or assembly kinematics. Perhaps the most common technique to develop a tolerance chain for a one or two dimensional case is the "vector loop technique.")
2. Derived from physical principles parameters and the tolerances (engineering science, using models from surrogate data, and/or obtaining help from an expert).
3. Use computer-aided engineering (CAE) tools such as Abacus, ADAMS, Easy5, Nastran and Simulink.
4. Conduct computer experimentation and response surface using CAE.
5. Conduct hardware DOE and fit response model.

Survey

Survey research studies large and small populations by selecting and studying samples chosen from the interested populations to discover the relative incidence, distribution and interrelations of the selected variables. This type of survey is called a sample survey.

Surveys are not new. They have been around since the eighteenth century (Campbell and Katona 1953, Chap. 1). However, surveys in the scientific sense are a twentieth-century development. To be sure, surveys are considered to be a branch of social scientific research, which distinguishes survey research from the status survey (survey research is generally a systematic study of the relationship among items belonging to a greater domain or different domains with the intent to follow with another survey at a later time, whereas status survey is a survey that studies an item without any plan for repetition). The procedures and methods of survey research have been developed mostly by psychologists, sociologists, anthropologists, economists, political scientists and statisticians. All of them have a tremendous influence on how we perceive the social sciences.

In the quality profession, on the other hand, even though we use survey instruments, the process of surveying is not quite clear. To be sure, a survey, by definition, links populations and samples. Therefore, the experimenter is interested in the accurate assessment of the characteristics of whole populations. For example, a typical survey study may be conducted to investigate how many suppliers of type A material qualify for the approved supplier list, given characteristics such as delivery, price, quality, capability and so on. Another example of the use of a survey by the quality professional is in the area of identifying and/or measuring the current culture, attitude and general perception of quality in a given organization.

In using a survey, it must be understood that the experimenter uses samples—very rarely, if ever, will they use populations—by which they will infer the characteristics of the defined universe. To be successful, such undertaking must depend on random samples and unbiased questions. (For the mechanics on how to construct a questionnaire, see Stamatis 1996 and Kerlinger 1973).

Types of surveys

Surveys can be classified by the following methods of obtaining information:

- *Interviews.* Although they are very expensive, they do provide for individualized responses to questions as well as the opportunity to learn the reasons for doing, or even believing, something.

- *Panel technique.* A sample of respondents is selected and interviewed, and then reinterviewed and studied at later times. This technique is used primarily when one wants to study changes in behavior and/or attitudes over time.

- *Telephone survey.* At least from a quality application, they have little to offer other than speed and low cost.

- *Mail questionnaire.* These are quite popular in the quality field. They are used to self-evaluate your own quality system, culture of the organization and so on. Their drawback, unless used in conjunction with other techniques, is the lack of response, inappropriate questions (e.g., leading, biased or ambiguous) and the inability to verify the responses given.

The methodology for a valid survey

It is beyond the scope of this book to address the details of survey methodology (for details see Kerlinger 1973, and his references). However, the most fundamental steps are:

1. *Specify and clarify the problem.* To do this, the experimenter should not just expect to simply ask direct questions and be done. It is imperative that the experimenter should also have specific questions to ask, aimed at various facets of the problem. In other words, plan the survey.

2. *Determine the sample plan.* Remember, the sample must be representative of the population in order to be effective. For a good source of how to do this see Kish (1965).

3. *Determine the schedule and, if appropriate and applicable, what other measuring instruments are to be used.* This is a very difficult task and it must not be taken lightly. Here the experimenter is to translate the research question into an interview instrument and into any other instruments constructed for the survey. For example, one of the problems in a quality

survey may be how permissive and restrictive attitudes toward the new quality vision of our organization are related to perceptions of both employees and management. An example of the questions to be written to assess permissive and restrictive attitudes would be, "How do you feel about quality?"

4. *Determine the data collection method.* The experimenter's concern is how the information is going to be gathered. What method is to be used and to what extent should appropriate precaution be designed into the survey to help eliminate spurious answers and responses?

5. *Conduct analysis.* In this step of the survey, there are two issues that concern the experimenter: coding—the term used to describe the translation of question responses to specific categories for purposes of analysis—and tabulation—the recording of the numbers of types of responses in the appropriate categories, after which statistical analysis (i.e., percentages, averages, rational indices and appropriate tests of significance) follows. The analysis of the data is studied, collated, assimilated and interpreted. Never should the experimenter give the results without the rationale, assumptions and interpretation of the data and results.

6. *Report the results.* At this step, the results of the survey are reported to all concerned parties.

Audit

In this section, our intent is to give the reader a useful overview of the audit, rather than an exhaustive discussion. The reader is strongly encouraged to read Mills (1989); Arter (1994); Keeney (1995, 1995a); Russell (1995); Stamatis (1996a); and Parsowith (1995) for more detailed information.

Where the survey is a methodology to find and project the results of a sample to a population, an audit is a methodology that uses samples to verify the existence of whatever is defined as a characteristic of importance. That characteristic may be defined in terms of quality, finance and so on.

An audit from a quality perspective based on ISO 8402 and ISO 9000:2000 is a systematic and independent examination to determine whether quality activities and related results comply with planned arrangements, and whether these arrangements are implemental effectively and are suitable to achieve objectives (ANSI/ISO/ ASQC A8402–1994 and/or ISO 9000:2000). This definition implies, in no uncertain terms, that an audit is a human evaluation process to determine the degree of adherence to prescribed norms and results in a judgment. The norms, of course, are always predefined in terms of criteria, standards, or both.

The norms are defined by the management of the organization about to be audited. On the other hand, it is the responsibility of the auditor conducting the audit in any organization to evaluate the compliance of the organization to those norms. For this reason, the audit is usually performed as a pass/fail evaluation rather than a point system evaluation.

Any quality audit may be internal or external and take one of three forms:

- *First party audit.* This audit is conducted by an organization on itself and may be carried out on the entire organization or just a part. It is usually called an internal audit.

- *Second party audit.* This audit is conducted by one organization on another. It is usually an audit on a supplier by a customer, and it is considered an external audit.

- *Third party audit.* This audit is conducted by an independent organization (the third party) on another organization. It can only be performed at the request, or the initiative, of the organization seeking an impartial evaluation of the effectiveness of their own programs. This audit is mandatory for those organizations that seek ISO 9001, ISO 14000, ISO/TS 16949 and/or a QS-9000 certification. It is always an external audit.

The requirements to start any audit, fall into three categories. They are:

- *Starting.* Before starting the physical audit, an auditor must gain some knowledge about the organization and the audit environment.

- *Documenting.* Because documentation relies on the auditor to write the information down, he or she has the responsibility to be prepared, fair, impartial, inquisitive, honest and observant.

- *Evaluating.* An auditor's ultimate responsibility is to evaluate the quality system of a given organization based on the organization's appropriate standards and documentation (e.g., its quality manual, procedures and instructions). (If it is a registration or a surveillance audit, then the responsibility is to evaluate the compliance of the quality system to the standards and the documentation. If it is an internal audit, the responsibility is to find the gaps and nonconformities of the quality system against the standards and documentation, and to improve the quality system based on the findings. In either case, both activities of auditing are evaluating measures to improvement and compliance.)

On the other hand, the actual audit process follows a sequential path that has four phases. They are:

1. *Prepare (pre-audit).* This phase includes selecting the team, planning the audit and gathering pertinent information.

2. *Perform (on-site visit).* This phase begins with the opening meeting and finishes with the actual audit.

3. *Report (post-audit).* This phase includes the exit meeting and the audit report.

4. *Close.* This phase includes the actions resulting from the report and the documentation information.

Process auditing is an audit that looks at the inputs, energy transformation, output and their interfaces. It is much more time-consuming than a traditional audit, but it is much more value added. In the old way of conducting an audit, the questions had to do with a style of "do you...?" or "can you show me...?" Now the style has changed to "how do you...?" or "why is...?" or "is the process effective?" and so on. A typical process audit is shown in Figure 6.4.

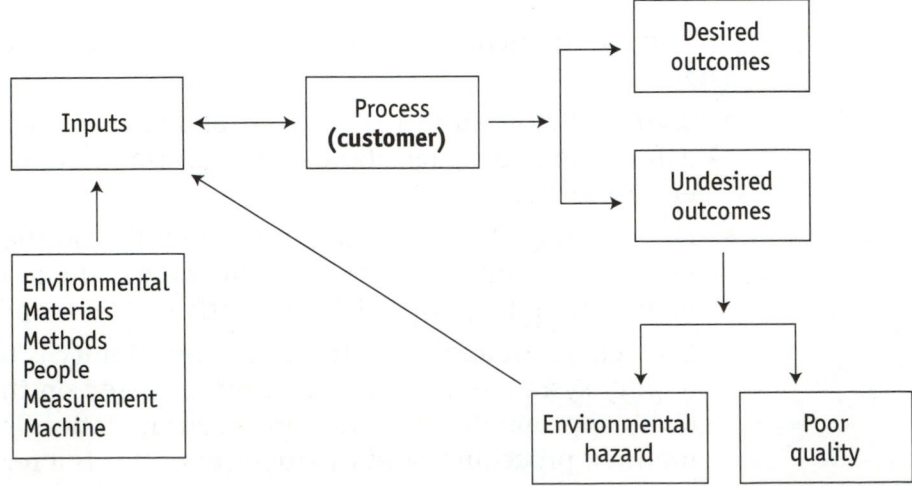

Figure 6.4 A typical process audit

Tools

Just as in the DMAIC model, there are many individual tools that may be used to pursue the design for the six sigma methodology. Here, however, we present the tools in a table format, along with the individual stage of the DCOV model. There is not much discussion with the specific tools, since that information is quite abundant and may be found in many textbooks, including Michalski (2003), training materials, and so on. Some of the most common tools used in the process of implementing DFSS, in addition to the ones already mentioned in chapter 4, are shown in Table 6.4.

Table 6.4 Typical tools used in implementing DFSS

Tool/method	Define	Characterize	Optimize	Verify
Automated data acquisition	X			X
Automation controls				X
Calibration certifications				X
Certification				X
Customer documents	X			
Customer surveys	X			
Defect data	X			X
Design simplification		X		
Discrete data			X	
Engineering changes		X	X	
Engineering specifications			X	X
Expert judgment	X	X	X	X
Graphing package	X	X	X	X
Inspection history files	X			
Industry standards	X	X		X
Inspection and test procedure				X
Literature reviews	X	X	X	
Operator certification				X
Operator training				X
Poka-yoke methods				X
Process audits				X
Process simplification			X	
Qualitative interpretation	X	X	X	X
Quality function deployment	X	X		
Quality program documents				X
Test certification				X
Vendor feedback surveys	X	X	X	
Worst case analysis		X	X	X

(Continued on next page)

Table 6.4 (*Continued*)

Tool/method	Define	Characterize	Optimize	Verify
2 level: fractional factorial design		X	X	
2 level: full factorial designs		X	X	
3 level: fractional factorial designs		X	X	
3 level: full factorial design		X	X	
Advanced control charts				X
Analysis of covariance			X	
Analysis of variance		X	X	
Auto-correlation		X	X	
Chi square methods		X	X	
Correlation studies		X	X	X
Cross tabulation methods			X	X
Cube plots		X	X	
Defect probability	X	X		
Distribution goodness-of-fit	X	X	X	
EVOP designs			X	
F tests		X	X	
Finite element analysis		X	X	
Fractional factorials with outer arrays		X	X	
Full factorials with outer arrays		X	X	
GR&R (gauge repeatability and reproducibility) control chart method		X	X	X
GR&R statistical DOE		X		
Interaction plots		X	X	X
Mathematical models		X	X	
Mixture designs			X	
Monte Carlo simulation			X	
Multi-level full factorial designs		X	X	
Non-parametric tests		X	X	
OR programming methods			X	X
Physical models			X	
Random sampling	X	X	X	
Random strategy designs		X	X	X
Realistic tolerancing		X	X	X
Regression		X	X	X
Response surface designs		X	X	
Taguchi designs		X	X	
Time series analysis			X	

References

— ISO 9000:2000. Quality system. International organization for standardization. Milwaukee, WI: ASQ.

Akao, Y. *Quality Function Deployment*. Cambridge, MA: Productivity Press, 1990.

ANSI/ISO/ASQC A8402. *Quality Vocabulary*. Milwaukee, WI: ASQC, 1994.

Arter, D. R. *Quality Audits for Improved Performance*. 2nd ed. Milwaukee, WI: Quality Press, 1994.

Bank, A., Henderson, M., and Eu, L. *A Practical Guide to Program Planning: A Teaching Models Approach*. New York: Columbia University, 1981.

Brinkerhoff, R. O. *Achieving Results From Training*. San Francisco: Jossey Bass, 1987.

Campbell, A., and G. Katona. "The Sample Survey: A Technique for Social-Science Research." In L. Festiger and D. Katz, *Research Methods in the Behavioral Science*. New York: Holt, Reinhart, and Winston, 1953, pp.115–131.

Delbecq, A. L., and A. H. Van de Ven. *Group Techniques for Program Planning*. Middleton, WI: Green Briar Press, 1986.

Delbecq, A. L., A. H. Van de Ven, and D. H. Stamatis. *Group Techniques for Program Planning: A Guide for Nominal and Delphi Processes*. Glenview, IL: Scott-Foresman, 1975.

Eppinger, S. D., M. Nukala, and D. E. Whitney. "Generalized Models Of Design Iteration Using Signal Flow Graphs." *Research in Engineering Design* 9(2), pp. 112–123.

Forsha, H. I. *Show Me: The Complete Guide to Storyboarding and Problem Solving*. Milwaukee, WI: Quality Press, 1995.

Forsha, H. I. *Show Me: Storyboard Workbook and Template*. Quality Press. Milwaukee, WI, 1995a.

Keeney, K. A. *The ISO9000 Auditor's Companion*. Milwaukee, WI: Quality Press, 1995.

Keeney, K. A. *The Audit Kit*. Quality Press. Milwaukee, WI.

Kerlinger, F. N. *Foundations of Behavioral Research*. 2nd ed. New York: Holt, Reinhart and Winston, Inc., 1973.

Kish, L. *Survey Sampling*. New York: New York: John Wiley & Sons, 1965.

Madaus, G. F., M. Scriven, and D. L. Stufflebeam, (eds). *Evaluation Models*. Boston: Kluwer-Nijhoff Publishing, 1983.

Michalski, W. J. *Six Sigma Tool Navigator: The Master Guide for Teams*. New York: Productivity Press, 2003.

Mills, C. A. *The Quality Audit*. Milwaukee, WI: Quality Press, 1989.

Mintzberg, H. *The Rise and Fall of Strategic Planning*. New York: Free Press, 1994.

Parsowith, B. S. *Fundamentals of Quality Auditing*. Milwaukee, WI: Quality Press, 1995.

Russell, J. P. *Quality Management Benchmark Assessment*. 2nd ed. Milwaukee, WI: Quality Press, 1995.

Scriven, M. *Evaluation Thesaurus*. 4th ed. Newbury Park, CA: Sage Publications, 1991.

Suh, N. P. *The Principles of Design*. New York: Oxford University Press, 1990.

Stamatis, D. H. *Six Sigma and Beyond: Design for Six Sigma*. Boca Raton FL: St. Lucie Press, 2003.

Stamatis, D. H. *Total Quality Service*. Delray Beach, FL: St. Lucie Press, 1996.

Stamatis, D. H. *Documenting and Auditing for ISO 9000 and QS-9000*. Burr Ridge, IL: Irwin Professional, 1996a.

Stamatis, D. H. *Advanced Quality Planning. A Commonsense Guide to AQP and APQP*. New York: Quality Resources, 1998.

Chapter 7

Roles and Responsibilities

I n any project, philosophy or program, decisions must be made along the way. However, these decisions, more often than not, are diffused because of the project's, philosophy's, or program's complexity. Therefore, the implication is that control and coordination must be critical items of concern. Given that assumption then, three axioms are required for successful implementation. They are:

- People are the project's, philosophy's and/or program's most important asset.
- The focus should be more on people than on techniques.
- The project manager (black belt) is not the boss in the traditional sense–but rather a facilitator and a coach.

To facilitate and optimize these axioms every organization defines the specific roles and responsibilities for the specific project, philosophy or program implementation. For the six sigma methodology, this definition of roles and responsibilities is also important. There are several levels of roles in the methodology. However, none of them are mandatory and some of them may be called by a different name in some organizations. (There is a difference between functions and titles. The functions and responsibilities are always important, whereas the titles may or may not be important.) Table 7.1 shows the variation in names.

Table 7.1 Different role names used in the six sigma methodology

Generic name	Other name
Process owner	Sponsor or champion
Team member	Team member or green belt
Team leader	Black belt or green belt or project manager
Coach	Master black belt or shogun or black belt
Implementation leader	Six sigma director, quality leader, master black belt
Sponsor	Champion or process owner
Executive management	Six sigma steering committee, quality council, leadership council

In the six sigma methodology, all the roles and responsibilities for all levels presuppose several prerequisites. The specific prerequisites, of course, depend on the level. However, there are some prerequisites that are common to all levels and they are:

- Having process or product knowledge.
- Being willing and able to learn mathematical concepts.
- Knowing the organization.
- Having communication skills.
- Being a self-starter and being self-motivated.
- Being open-minded.
- Being eager to learn new ideas.
- Having a desire to drive change.
- Possessing project leadership skills.
- Being a team player.
- Being respected by others.
- Having a track record on results.

In conjunction with these prerequisites, there is also an implied responsibility that is of paramount importance on the part of the executives. After all, it is the executives who are in charge of the change. Therefore, it is important for them to accelerate the change process by being a visible advocate of the six sigma methodology. Specifically, the executives must get involved. That means that they have to work closely with the champions and the shoguns to mobilize commitment and make change last. The commitment must be translated into the following actions:

- Identify and remove the barriers and roadblocks to achieving high performance with six sigma.
- Ensure that only the best are nominated to be black belts.
- Ask the black belts many questions to ensure that they are focused appropriately.
- Demand follow-up and monitoring activities.
- Establish the six sigma scorecard. Make six sigma reviews a regular part of your management process.
- Align six sigma results and business strategic objectives.
- Drive functional ownership and accountability.
- Manage your attention. Be proactive to ensure that the change is documented and verified.
- Develop and demonstrate personal competence with the breakthrough strategy.
- Celebrate successes and recognize accomplishments.

Now let us look at some traditional roles and their specific contribution to the six sigma methodology.

Executives

The executives legitimize the changes about to happen because of the six sigma implementation methodology through their actions to:

- Establish the vision—why we are doing six sigma.
- Articulate the business strategy—how six sigma supports the business strategy.
- Provide resources.
- Remove roadblocks and buffer conflicts.
- Support the culture change by encouraging others to take the risk and make the change.
- Monitor the results by defining the scorecard for six sigma and holding others accountable for the results.
- Align the systems and structures with the changes taking place.
- Participate with the black belts through project reviews and recognition of results.

Champions

The champions implement the changes as a result of the six sigma methodology by taking action to:

- Develop a vision for the organization.
- Create and maintain passion.
- Develop a model for a perfect organization.
- Facilitate the identification and prioritization of projects.
- Develop the strategic decisions in the deployment of six sigma around timing and sequencing of manufacturing, transactional and new product focus.
- Extend project benefits to additional areas.
- Communicate and market the breakthrough strategy process and results.
- Share best practices.
- Establish and monitor a team process for optimum results.
- Recruit, inspire and "free up" black belts—pick the best people.
- Develop the reward and recognition program for black belts.
- Remove barriers for black belts.
- Coach and develop black belts.
- Provide the drum beat for results by reviewing projects and keeping score through metrics.
- Develop a comprehensive training plan for implementing the breakthrough strategy.

Master black belt (shogun)

The master black belt (shogun) assists the champion and/or guides the black belt as needed by taking action to:

- Be the expert in the tools and concepts.
- Develop and deliver training to various levels of the organization.
- Certify the black belts.
- Assist in the identification of projects.
- Coach and support the black belts in project work.
- Participate in project reviews to offer technical expertise.

- Partner with the champions.
- Demonstrate passion around six sigma.
- Share best practices.
- Take on leadership of major programs.
- Develop new tools or modify old tools for application.
- Understand the link between six sigma and the business strategy.

Black belt

The black belt serves as the project manager for the six sigma project. Fundamentally, the black belt is the individual who receives the change and makes sure that the change is institutionalized throughout the organization by taking some form of action in the following categories:

- *Mentoring.* Cultivate a network of experts in the factory and/or site.
- *Teaching.* Provide formal training to local personnel in new strategies and tools.
- *Coaching.* Provide one-on-one support to local personnel.
- *Transferring.* Pass on new strategies and tools in the form of training, workshops, case studies, local issues and so on.
- *Discovering.* Finding application opportunities for breakthrough strategies and tools, both internal and external.
- *Identifying.* Surfacing business opportunities through partnerships with other organizations.
- *Influencing.* Selling the organization on the use of breakthrough strategies and tools.

On the other hand, because the black belt is so important to the process, it is imperative that the individual who carries this title must have the following specific requirements and knowledge to be able to:

- Understand how to implement the breakthrough strategy application.
- Prepare initial project assessment to validate benefits.
- Lead and direct the team to execute projects.
- Determine the most effective tools to apply.

- Show the data.
- Identify barriers.
- Identify project resources.
- Determine appropriate and applicable input from knowledgeable functional experts/team leaders/coaches.
- Report progress to appropriate leadership levels.
- Present the final report.
- Deliver results on time.
- Solicit help from the champions when needed.
- Influence without direct authority.
- Be a breakthrough strategy enthusiast.
- Stimulate champion thinking.
- Teach and coach breakthrough strategy methods and tools.
- Manage project risk.
- Ensure the results are sustained.
- Document learning.

Green belt

The green belt is the individual who assists black belts with completing projects and applies the six sigma breakthrough strategy (DMAIC or DCOV) on the job. The specific details regarding the deployment and the role of any green belt is determined by each organization.

Other roles

Team members. They are the people who provide the everyday requirements for execution of the DMAIC and DCOV model. They also help spread the word about six sigma tools and processes and ultimately they become part of the reservoir of human resources available for future projects.

Process owner. This is the person who takes on a new, cross-functional responsibility to manage all the steps that provide value to the internal as well as external customer. The sponsor and the process owner may be the same person.

Chapter 8

Six Sigma Applied in Non-manufacturing

Six sigma focuses on translating requirements to the functionality needs and expectations of the customer. In manufacturing the process is quite simple because the outputs are tangible and long lasting. On the other hand, in service organizations this is not as easy, as the outcome is very short lived and intangible. Therefore, if we are to apply the six sigma methodology in non-manufacturing organizations, we must reexamine some of the issues and concerns that contribute to dissatisfaction as well as satisfaction.

First, in service organizations we must recognize early on (preferably in the Kano or QFD stage) that there are words or phrases that provoke the customer into negative behavior. Therefore, we must plan and recognize our procedures so that these words or phrases are avoided. Some of the words or phrases are:

- Sorry, there is nothing I can do.
- I can't do anything about that.
- I am not authorized to . . .
- Wrong.
- Why?
- Impossible.
- No, absolutely not.

- Should have.
- Wait.
- Listen.
- What?
- Our policy is . . .

Obviously, we all know that language is important in the service domain, so how do we plan for a particular service for a six sigma performance? To begin the process and apply either the DMAIC or DCOV models, we must plan and/or design with trust in mind.

Stephen R. Covey, author of the best-selling business book, *The Seven Habits of Highly Effective People*, is encouraging organizations to examine the impact trust has on the bottom line:

"Trust—or the lack of it—is at the root of the success or failure in relationships and the bottom line results of business, industry, education and government," says Covey. "If you have no or low trust, how are you going to manage people? When you don't have trust, you have to control people. But if you have high trust, you don't supervise them—they supervise themselves."

The six sigma methodology helps suppliers, employees and customers to develop and sustain trust. This trust, especially in the service domain, becomes *the key to high performance*, as well as increased productivity, increased satisfaction and increased in profitability.

According to *The Loyalty Effect* by Frederick Reichheld, U.S. corporations, on average, now lose half of their customers within five years, half of their employees within four years and half of their investors within less than one year. Disloyalty at current rates stunts corporate performance by 25 to 50 percent. Reichheld found that firms earning superior levels of customer, employee and investor loyalty and retention, also earn consistently higher profits.

When trust is low, organizations decay, relationships deteriorate and divisive politics, turf wars and in-fighting escalate. The results are low profitability and dissatisfaction. An employee's commitment to his or her organization's vision and strategy plummets, product quality declines, customers leave, employee turnover skyrockets and noncompliance increases. The following are some ways six sigma can help in the service sector:

1. Keep promises and honor commitments. If you promise something, deliver it. Period!

2. Share information, both positive and negative, with the people who need it. Do not be afraid of the truth. People can take it! There is nothing worse than a cover up.

3. Don't talk with co-workers about other co-workers who are not present. Gossip will act as a negative force to improvement. If you have something to say go to the source. However, make sure that the organization has implemented the "elimination of fear," and remove the "retaliation and intimidation" principles from its culture.

4. Acknowledge and apologize for mistakes. No one is perfect. When mistakes are made, own up to them and try to correct them. Honesty is always the best policy and it works. People will understand and appreciate your efforts to make amends.

5. Involve people in decisions that affect them. This is of great importance in service organizations espcially. Make sure everyone has a say in the expected outcomes. Try to explain the reasoning behind the decision. Some people have talked about "insight" into the customer, which is to say that it is your obligation to find out how and why employees and customers behave toward a particular program and or purchase.

6. Give credit where credit is due. We all like recognition. In fact, psychologists have found that recognition is the number one motivator, followed by challenging work and money. Recognition is the credit we all long for. However, that credit may be in many forms including but not limited to monetary rewards, publishing your photograph in the corporate newsletter or local newspaper, and so on. Recognition goes a long way toward building trust and as a consequence it will have a direct influence on many items including but not limited to:
   - Improved quality of products and services.
   - Increased commitment to the organization's strategy and vision.
   - Better client relations and enhanced customer loyalty.
   - More effective, cohesive work teams.
   - Decreased employee turnover.
   - Decreased frustrations caused by dysfunctional relationships.
   - Drastic reduction or elimination of office politics or infighting.
   - Reduction in the cost of customer complaints

To somewhat repeat ourselves, six sigma can and does provide the methodology for improvement. For example, the New York State Electric and Gas company some years ago found that the following costs were related to customer complaints:

- Phone complaint: $10.00
- Written complaint: $20.00
- Meter check: $80.00
- High bill investigation: $125.00
- Public Service Commission complaint: $400.

Eliminate just one Public Service Commission complaint a day would save $146,000 (365 × 400) a year (and these figures are old, savings would be even more today). How much are customer complaints costing you?

Six sigma prides itself on supplying the customer with what they want. However, we must be careful, especially in the service sector, because the intangible aspects of the service itself may make the difference. For example, customers expect accuracy, a service representative who is not rude and thanks for their purchase. Provide these three aspects of customer service and you have done nothing unusual. That is what is expected and that is what is delivered. To astonish customers and build their loyalty, consider the following:

- *Speed.* Saving the customers time is very important. Time savers include express lanes, pre-approved credit, databases that already hold key customer information and order history, free assembly and overnight or same-day delivery. If you serve a customer in his or her physical presence, visibly hustling shows you clearly respect the value of the customer's time.

- *Sincerity.* Many customer service reps act like drones, speaking in a mechanical voice. When you hold eye contact for several extra seconds, smile and use the customer's name, you have sent a clear message showing sincerity. When speaking over the phone, put a smile in your voice and speak to the person as if he or she was a member of your own family.

- *The unexpected.* Offer unexpected services like a free upgrade, free information, free delivery or free assembly and installation. Customer extras need not even be tangible. Provide a joke of the day, an interesting newsletter clipping or the latest industry chatter. When you give something unexpected, you are telling the customer you really value him or her.

Obviously, there is a cost associated with these three elements, but with the aid of the six sigma methodology, we can optimize the service, satisfaction and profitability. After all, the aim is to correct and/or improve service mistakes. A prerequisite to implementing the six sigma methodology is to:

- *Admit.* Immediately tell the customer what went wrong and why. Accept responsibility and sincerely apologize for the problem.

- *Inform.* Tell the customer what you are doing to repair the situation and what actions and time frames are expected during the recovery.

- *Mitigate.* Show empathy for the customer's inconvenience, correct the situation and offer a significant extra to help dim the memory of the original error.

Once these preliminary steps are taken, pursue the investigation with rigor to find out if there is a systematic problem and, if so, begin the process of six sigma. Always remember that some problems are unique and happen so infrequently that perhaps no action is necessary. If the problem is systematic and recurring, or is of high impact (e.g., a government regulation or safety issue) then six sigma will be worth the effort.

If a service organization is committed to six sigma, they have to meet or exceed the expectations of their customers, which are demanding. They must want their customers to enjoy a premier ownership experience in addition to a premier product. To be committed to such aims, one must have the right attitude. It begins with simple things: always tell the truth, keep your word, do not make any promises you personally cannot keep and treat the customer as you would treat yourself. These basic characteristics will lead to the following philosophy: no customer inquiry or problem will go unanswered. When this philosophy is internalized in any organization then unique and effective solutions are the result.

Six sigma forces the organization to challenge everything. The world we live in is changing rapidly and is very complicated. You have to keep asking what your customer wants and constantly question the procedure. Is there a way we could simplify things for the customers? Are we servicing customers on their terms?

Six sigma allows an organization to constantly explore new, better and more creative ways to satisfy customer needs and requests. The way to challenge and probe is to make it very clear to employees that you encourage dialogue with customers. Make it easy for customers to contact you. Provide an 800-number and Internet access. Send relationship marketing mailings and surveys to solicit customer input. Finally, always encourage your representatives to make sure they can deliver on any promise they make.

Success is measured in many ways depending on the goals of the organization, however, one sure way to be successful is to make sure that your customers become the ambassadors and advocates of your products and or services. They will do that if they are satisfied with the product, service and experience. There is no need to elaborate on the difference between ambassodor and advocate. The distinction is inherent in their functions and approach: One is benevolent the other aggressive.

Six sigma and safety

Perhaps as a subsystem to service, one may include the issue of safety as part of the concerns and anticipated expectations of a program that is supposed to deliver perfection. Much time and effort is being spent on safety from both the organization's and government's perspective. In fact, OSHA's (Occupational Safety and Health Administration's) responsibility and function are precisely to overview and provide approaches to safety. One such compliance methodology is program safety management (PSM). Of course, compliance is a requirement of PSM, but it is not the only one. In addition, PSM is interested in establishing programs that demonstrate return, not only through enhanced safety culture and performance, but through the improvement of process reliability and operability.

Therefore, an important objective of PSM is the minimization of unwanted deviations from normal process operations. Improved process reliability, measured for example, as decreased process downtime, should be a collateral benefit of the program. The objective of achieving this benefit can be explicitly incorporated into the program through process hazard analyses procedure, and the way in which risk and reliability criteria form the basis for the mechanical integrity program.

In developing PSM programs we:

- Show what has and has not worked for peers by reviewing precedents set by OSHA in the interpretation and enforcement of the PSM standard.

- Establish a dynamic, flexible program addressing activities, record keeping and accountabilities, that can be systematically and conveniently revised as improvements in practice are identified.

- Fully integrate the program with other safety and reliability programs in place at the site, such as an EPA risk management program (RMP), or other related OSHA, EPA, corporate or industry standard-based programs.

- Support specific technical needs under the program, related to areas such as emergency response planning, mechanical integrity program, development, written operating procedures, process hazard analyses, compliance audits, training, evaluation of safety instrumented systems and facility siting assessment.

By comparison, the fundamental objective of the six sigma methodology is to implement a measurement system that will facilitate strategy of continual process improvements, with tremendous sensitivity to deviations from standardized values. In this section, therefore we want to take the opportunity and do a cursory comparison between the six sigma methodology and the OSHA PSM standard, to identify similarities between the two approaches, and to demonstrate that the OSHA PSM standard is consistent with the fundamentals of six sigma.

As we already have discussed, the six sigma methodology derives its goals by addressing customer satisfaction and not product quality, as derived by other traditional quality systems. Therefore, measuring quality on an absolute scale, rather than referring to one standard or another, is one of the great innovations in the development of six sigma. Six sigma also provides tools for measurement and control of processes. In addition, six sigma is as much about changing attitudes as it is about introducing a systematic analytical approach to performance measurements. A zero defects quality attitude is very demanding and it is not compromising in issues such as long-term management commitment, involvement of all employees, intensive training, outsource usage, high levels of communication and massive allocations of internal resources.

In the six sigma methodology, the evaluation is conducted by using the DMAIC and the DCOV models (as before). The difference is that now we may want to focus even more on customer satisfaction and effectiveness.

Six sigma and the PSM program

Just like a six sigma program, pursuing a PSM program is a very complicated mission, and should be carried out with great care. Furthermore, PSM program implementation is a much tougher mission to accomplish, and it can be done in several ways. The OSHA PSM regulation specifies 14 elements to be taken into consideration when writing, implementing and maintaining PSM program. They are:

1. Employee participation.
2. Process safety information.
3. Process hazard analysis.
4. Operating procedure.
5. Training.
6. Contractors.
7. Pre-startup safety review.
8. Mechanical integrity.
9. Hot work permit.
10. Management of change.
11. Incident investigation.
12. Emergency planning and response.
13. Compliance audits.
14. Trade secrets.

PSM is much more difficult to implement than six sigma. However, a comparison of the six sigma methodology with the OSHA PSM regulations reveals a high level of similarity. Identifying six sigma elements in the OSHA PSM regulation requires substitution of the PSM program in a SIPOC (supplier of input to a process that adds values and delivers output to customer) map. This can be broken down as follows: The supplier inputs are operating the plant OSHA regulations. The process from start to stop is writing, implementing and maintaining the PSM program. The customer outcomes are no near-misses, no incidences, which is equivalent to six sigma's "zero defects."

A simple comparison of the PSM implementation with the DMAIC and DCOV models is shown in Table 8.1.

Table 8.1 Comparison of PSM, DMAIC and DCOV models

PSM	DMAIC	DCOV
Define goals	Define	Define
Evaluate current status	Measure	Characterize
	Analyze	
Develop	Improve	Optimize
Monitor	Control	Verify

The critical OSHA PSM Elements

To better make the comparison between the elements of PSM and those of the six sigma methodology, one must clearly understand the critical PSM elements:

- *Employee participation.* Section 304 of the Clean Air Act Amendment (CAAA) states that employees and their representatives should take part in the decision making regarding the efforts that the employer should make in order to create a safe workplace. It is also required that the employer train and educate his employees and inform them of the findings of any incident investigation. Furthermore, the employer is required to consult with the employees' representatives regarding the conducting and development of hazard assessments and the development of accident prevention plans. This is parallel to six sigma, which recommends initiating personnel meetings to promote the acceptance of the program among the employees, to reduce resistance to change (Tennant 2001).

- *Process safety information.* OSHA requires compiling of process safety information before conducting a process hazards analysis. The process safety information is classified into three categories:
  - Information on the dangers of any highly hazardous chemical used or produced by the processes.
  - Information on the technology of the process.
  - Information on the equipment utilized in the process.

- *Process hazard analysis.* Process hazard analysis (PHA) is the most thorough element among the OSHA PSM elements. PHA is a sequence that systematically examines equipment, procedures and systems, handling regulated substance to identify hazards and to define solutions and corrective actions. The owner should initiate PHA and is required to determine priorities for conducting PHA according to the complexity of the process, its age and its history, and to document them. The rule determines the need for using methodologies in the analysis, and lists minimal methods, as what-if, checklist, what if/check list, HAZOP (hazard and operability study) as an examination procedure. Process hazard analysis' purpose is to identify all possible deviations from the way in which a design is expected to work and to identify all the hazards associated with these deviations. Where deviations arise that result in hazards, actions are generated that require design engineers to review and suggest solutions to either remove the hazard or reduce its risk to an acceptable level. These solutions are reviewed and accepted by the HAZOP team before implementation, by using FMEA (failure mode and effect analysis) and FTA (fault tree analysis) or other equivalent methods. The PHA shall address the following:

♦ The hazards of the process.
♦ The identification of any previous incident that had a likely potential for significant offsite consequences.
♦ Engineering and administrative controls applicable to the hazards and their interrelationship and appropriate application of detection methodologies to provide early warning of releases. (Acceptable detection methods might include process monitoring and control instruments with alarms and detection hardware such as hydrocarbon sensors.)
♦ Consequences of failure of engineering and administrative controls.
♦ Stationary source siting.
♦ Human factors.
♦ A qualitative evaluation of a range of possible safety and health effects of failure of controls on public health and the environment.

A PHA conducting team is required to consist of:
♦ Members with expertise in engineering and process operation.
♦ A member with specific knowledge in the process to be evaluated.
♦ A member familiar with the specific PHA methodology.

The management is required to verify that the findings will be addressed, and that the solution implementation will be scheduled. An update stage of the PHA is required every five years, at least. A typical update review will include:

- The PHA element covers the measurement stage, the analysis stage and the improvement stage in the six sigma methodology. The PHA sequence is parallel to the following sub-processes of the DMAIC.
- The measurements and the root cause analysis in the six sigma methodology are the results from the first part of the PHA (for instance, the FTA results of the current processes).
- The clarification of the project scope (in the six sigma's analyzing stage) is the determination of the ways to solve the findings, to generate solution, to select the ideal solution and to implement the solution. These subelements are also subelements in the OSHA PSM.
- Process standardization and remeasure that are taking place in the control stage of the six sigma methodology are equivalent to the documentation and the requirement for the periodic update of the PHA element of OSHA PSM regulation.

- *Operating procedures.* This element requires documentation of the proper and safe way of operating processes and equipment, and the proper way of handling chemicals that are regulated. The documentation should have detailed instructions as to the different operating stages (normal operation, start–ups, temporary and emergency operation and shutdowns), operating limits, safety and health considerations, and safety systems and their functions. The procedures are required to be reviewed when necessary, so that they will always reflect the current status. The operating procedure is an act of standardization and is equivalent to the control stage in the six sigma methodology.

- *Training.* An effective training program will significantly reduce the number of incidences and their severity. OSHA PSM regulations address training in order to practice the operating procedures. The regulations distinguishes between different cases of training:
  - Initial training.
  - Process overview to new assigned employees with special emphasis on scenarios that impact safety.
  - Refresher training.

The importance of training is easily understood. A contribution of six sigma to the training element can be achieved by developing systems to measure training performance and effectiveness. The human resource department, with the help of a consulting firm and the master black belt, can take ownership of that process. (Training documentation, evaluation of training program effectiveness and schedules for reviewing and revising the program are also required.)

- *Contractors.* The employer must obtain and evaluate information regarding the contract employer safety performance programs and must inform the contract employer regarding the variety of hazards that characterize the area of work. Furthermore, the employer must ensure that the contract employer and its employees will be provided with appropriate information and training and will be familiar with the plant emergency response plan. (The contractor element is not applicable to six sigma implementation).

- *Mechanical integrity.* The mechanical integrity element fills a missing part in the PHA element. The maintenance program ensures that the equipment will perform according to the appropriate reliability information. The program must include documentation regarding the preventive maintenance routine, capability, inspections and tests needed to verify its in operation condition. Any six sigma aspect that is valid to PHA is valid to mechanical integrity.

- *Pre-startup review.* The pre-startup review's purpose is to verify that new equipment installed, or modifications made, are ready to operate properly and safely. The review should verify the following:
  - Construction and equipment are in accordance with design specifications.
  - Safety, operating, maintenance and emergency procedures are in place and are adequate.
  - PHA has been performed to new stationary sources, and that resolutions have been implemented.
  - Modifications meet the management of change requirements.
  - Training has been completed, including training for new emergency response procedures.

- *Management of change.* A management of change (MOC) program is an administrative procedure that verifies that all aspects of changes and modifications have been considered, and that the appropriate managerial level has authorized the change. (A pre-startup review and management of change are processes that can always be improved and do not have direct relevancy to six sigma).

- *Compliance audits.* Re-measurement, impact evaluation and process standardization take place in the six sigma control stage. An audit process is a periodic examination of the process safety management program. Audit is a control stage that ensures compliance with OSHA PSM regulations by an overall program evaluation and is similar to the control stage in the six sigma methodology. The difference is on emphasis—the six sigma methodology is more interested in the effectiveness of the system, rather than compliance.

- *Accident investigation.* An accident investigation is a self-corrective element that addresses the prevention of the accident reoccurring. The investigation is required to begin within less than 48 hours following the accident and should be conducted by a team that is composed of persons with certain relevancy to the event, and at least one person knowledgeable with the process. Usually, documentation is required. The accident investigation is related to the six sigma improve stage.

- *Emergency planning and response.* The purpose of an emergency response program is to prepare to respond to, and the mitigation of, accidental releases and their impact on the public health and environment. The process's owner is required to establish and implement an emergency response plan for responding to, and for the mitigation of, the accidental release of regulated substances. (Note that all employees must be trained for emergency response and practice drills of the emergency response to evaluate the effectiveness.) The program is required to include the following:
  - Evacuation routes or protective actions for employees who are not directly involved in the process.
  - Procedure for employees responding to the release, including protective equipment use.
  - Technologies available for responding.
  - Procedures to inform the public and emergency response agencies about releases.
  - Procedures to inspect, test and maintain the emergency response equipment.

♦ Documentation of first aid and emergency medical treatment for each of the substances that are under regulation.

It is required that the emergency response will be coordinated with the local emergency response plans. Emergency response planning is different from other elements in the OSHA PSM regulations in terms of six sigma implementation. Two parameters influencing the plan's effectiveness are time and accuracy of response. Since both parameters are simply measurable, and since there are a variety of measures to improve the process of emergency response, it is applicable to the six sigma methodology.

- *Hot permit work.* Issuing a hot permit work is required for all hot work operations performed near covered processes. The permit lists all work's safety impacts and specifies the steps necessary to perform the work safely. Hot permit work is an element that can be improved by the six sigma methodology. Cutting and welding operations (commonly referred to as "hot work") are associated with machine shops, maintenance, and construction activities, as well as certain laboratory-related activities, such as glass blowing and torch soldering. Potential health, safety, and property hazards result from the fumes, gases, sparks, hot metal and radiant energy produced during hot work. Hot work equipment, which may produce high voltages or utilize compressed gases, also requires special awareness and training on the part of the worker to be used safely. The hazards associated with hot work can be reduced through the implementation of effective control programs. On the other hand, hot work permits should be developed by departments where cutting or welding is performed. Hot work permits can help minimize the risk of fire during cutting and welding activities by serving as a checklist for operators and those performing fire watch duties. The person responsible for issuing permits should be qualified to examine the work site and ensure that appropriate protective steps, such as those listed in this section, have been taken. A hot work permit should be issued at the beginning of each shift for each specific operation.

- *Trade secrets.* A trade secret indirectly contributes to six sigma, by forcing the organization to look at benchmarking and to be vigilant about the best in class.

PSM sigma metric

Process safety performance measurements are a hot topic in the safety industry. The purpose of the development of process safety performance measurements is to measure the contribution of a proactive approach and the efforts invested in that approach to the prevention of incidences. A process safety performance metric is an important issue. Six sigma is inherent in the PSM standard, but the missing part of six sigma is the sigma metric. Six sigma needs to calculate the quality of an absolute scale. In order to calculate the six sigma metric of an entity, the defects and the opportunity for defects must be defined.

Defect definition and data collections are easy. Each accident and each near miss are defects. The definition of the opportunities is more complicated. An opportunity can be a very simple operation of the process, like opening a cooling water valve to the reactor's jacket or inserting an agitator into work (opening a drinking water valve is not an opportunity). In addition, any maintenance working order will consist of at least one opportunity. The same is true for raw materials handling. By screening the entire operating procedure and other procedures, it is possible to count the opportunities created every day and to use an annual average for the six sigma calculation. Although it is possible that the computer will make an online counting of the opportunities, accidents and near misses should be counted manually, since there are only a few of them. Therefore, the sigma metric can be obtained by converting the DPMO, according to the table in Appendix B.

A calculation of the current sigma metric will probably reveal a surprising sigma metric value, that will be higher than this value in the production line.

ISO 14000 and six sigma

Environmental Management Systems (ISO 14001)

ISO 14001 specifies the requirements of the environmental management system (EMS). EMS, like six sigma and PSM, needs to have senior management commitment and to be structured and integrated within the management system to be effective. The requirements are applicable to all kinds of organizations, be it a manufacturing industry or a service industry. The EMS model consist of five categories:

- Environmental policy.
- Planning.
- Implementation and operation.
- Checking and corrective action.
- Management review.

Project team. The first step in implementing ISO 14001 together with six sigma is to establish a project team. The project team, which can be named the EMS-six sigma implementation committee or steering committee, steers the sequence of adopting both ISO 14001 and six sigma. An employee from the environmental department is the best choice to lead this process. This employee should be trained to a level of master black belt (MBB) in the six sigma methodology. Another two employees should be assigned to the committee, one from the engineering division and one from the budget department.

Environmental policy. Environmental policy has an important role in the implementation of ISO 14001. The definition of the policy shall ensure the following:

- The policy is appropriate to the nature, and scales the environmental impact, of the organization's activities.
- The policy shall contain a commitment to continual improvement and pollution prevention.
- The policy shall contain a commitment to comply with relevant environmental legislation and regulations, and to other requirements to which the organization has subscribed.
- The policy shall define a framework for the setting and the reviewing of environmental objectives and targets.
- The policy shall be documented, implemented, maintained and communicated to all employees.
- The policy shall be available to the public.

Planning. The organization is required to establish and to maintain a procedure to identify activities that have environmental aspects. These aspects are to be considered in defining environmental objectives. The framework of these objectives should be sensitive to changes in legislation, and to perform activities to meet the requirement derived from legislation changes. Objectives and targets are expected to be defined in the planning stage and to be documented. The establishment of a program to achieve the objective and its targets is part of the planning stage and it should include the following:

- Designation of responsibility for achieving objectives and targets at each relevant function and level of the organization.
- A time frame and means to achieve these objectives and targets.

In this category, the process is studied in order to determine the changes that will lead to the improvements.

Structure and responsibilities. Definition of roles, responsibilities, and authorities are among the first steps in the implementing of ISO 14001. A representative from top management shall be assigned to that mission, irrespective of his other responsibilities. The steering committee analyzes the framework and obtains the requirements for sources allocation. (If the implementation of ISO 14001 is in order to became certified, a registrar firm should be contacted for the registration.)

Training, awareness and competence. All employees whose work will significantly impact the environment must be appropriately trained. The steering committee prepares a training program for the employees that will address the awareness of the following:

- The importance of conformance with the environmental policy and the requirements of EMS.
- The significant impact of the employees' activities on the environment, and the benefits of personal performance improvement.
- The roles and responsibilities of the different functions in achieving conformance with the environmental policy, and the requirements from EMS, including emergency preparation and response.
- The potential consequences of departing from specified operating procedures.

Communication. The steering committee shall establish a procedure for internal communication between the different levels of functions, and for receiving, documenting and responding to external interested parties.

EMS documentation and document control

A documentation of the interaction among the core elements of an EMS is required. Establishing a document control procedure ensures that:

- Documents can be located.
- Documentation will be reviewed periodically and revised if necessary and approved by the authorized personnel.
- The current documents are available, should they be needed.
- Obsolete documents will be removed and retained in a way that they can be identified.

Operational control. Activities that are associated with significant impact on the environments have to be redesigned to ensure the following conditions:

- Scenarios, which deviate from normal operation conditions, will be covered.
- Operational criteria will be stipulated.
- The environmental aspects of organization goods and services will be identified.

Emergency preparedness. Scenarios of accident and emergency situations should be treated in the following sequence:

- Identify potential scenarios.
- Apply activities to prevent and mitigate the scenarios.
- Establish responding programs to treat real time events.
- Establish procedures for recovery after the occurrence of accidents or an emergency situation.
- Periodically drill and test responding programs and recovery procedure.
- Review and revise all the aspects, procedures and emergency preparation programs after the occurrence of an accident.

Checking and corrective actions

Monitoring and measurement. Monitoring and measuring activities that have significant impact on the environment are key elements in maintaining environmental policy. Documented procedures for measurements and monitoring are required by the ISO. The information revealed from this monitoring and measuring shall be recorded in order to track conformance performance. Monitoring equipment should be calibrated and a record of this process should be retained.

Corrective and preventive actions. The international standard (ISO14000) requires the establishment of procedures that define the responsibility and authority of handling, investigating and taking corrective actions to mitigate and prevent nonconformance.

EMS audit. The purpose of auditing is to verify the process conforms to the planning, and proper implementing of EMS. The results of the auditing process should be presented to the management.

Management review. Management review is required to verify EMS's continual improvement, adequacy and effectiveness, and to address changes in policy needed to maintain continual improvement.

Environmental performance evaluation (ISO 14031)

ISO 14031, environmental performance evaluation (EPE), identifies the key elements of evaluation for any organization that does not have EMS. Typical items are:

- Identifying the organization's environmental aspects.
- Determining which aspects it will treat as significant.
- Setting criteria for its environmental performance.
- Assessing its environmental performance against these criteria (later, when EMS is established and it's in its operation stage).

ISO describes two categories of indicators:

1. Environmental performance indicators (EPIs).
2. Environmental condition indicators (ECIs).

EPE is a performance indicator. The EPIs are divided into two groups:

- Management performance indicators (MPIs) reflect management's efforts to influence environmental performance.
- Operational performance indicators (OPIs) reflect the organization's operation environmental performance.

ECIs reflect the environmental condition and help in understanding the potential impact that the organization's activities have on the environment.

The information generated by an EPE can assist in the following:

- Determining any necessary actions to achieve the organization's environmental performance criteria.
- Identifying significant environmental aspects.
- Recognizing opportunities for better management of the organizational environmental aspects (e.g., prevention of pollution).
- Identifying trends in its environmental performance.
- Increasing the organization's efficiency and effectiveness.
- Recognizing strategic opportunities.

EPE process model. EPE is an internal process that uses indicators for the evaluation of the organizational environmental performance. EPE methodology consists of four stages that follow the plan-do-check-act (PDCA) model where:

- **Plan** involves planning environmental performance evaluation and selecting indicators for environmental performance evaluation.
- **Do** includes using data and information (i.e., collecting data analyzing and converting data, assessing information and results and reporting and communicating findings.
- Check and Act consists of reviewing and improving environmental performance evaluation.

EPE is a very strong measurement tool that can lead to the successful implementation of ISO 14001 and can be a tool to be used by the six sigma methodology.

Comment

The six sigma methodology is inherent in OSHA PSM elements, although the measurement of the bottom line performance on the sigma metric scale is missing. Identifying the PSM sigma metric is not a simple task, but it is applicable. It is possible to measure the sigma metric of subsequences in the PSM with different parameters. Then, the subsequence can be improved to a six sigma level separately, and by that it will contribute to the improvement of the main program.

The six sigma methodology is applicable to environmental management systems. The EMS leads to a state of continual improvement and has the basic features that are essential to any system that is applicable to the implementation of a quality management system. A model of the combined six sigma-EMS system should consist of the different stages of both standards. Table 8.2 is a summary of the combined stages with recommendations to the ownerships of each stage.

Table 8.2 A summary of the six sigma and EMS stages

Stage	Requirements	Ownership
Environmental policy	Management commitment to EMS and six sigma	Champion
	Definition of framework	Steering team
	Communicating the policy with the employees, with third parties and with the local community.	Marketing
	Document environmental policy.	Archive
Planning	Identify activities with environmental aspects.	EH&S*
	Perform process mapping	MBB
	Define customer research procedure	Marketing
	Study customer needs	Marketing
	Derive CTQs	BB
	Calculate customer satisfaction limits	BB
	Calculate the desired average and standard deviation.	BB
	Define objectives and targets	Steering team
	Establish program to achieve objectives and program	EH&S
	Set time-frame	Steering team
	Define allocation of resources	MBB
	Build teams	MBB
	Define training program	EH&S
	Train teams in six sigma aspects	Consulting firm
	Determine criteria	EH&S
	Define and select indicators to EPE	Consulting firm

(Continued on next page)

Table 8.2 (*Continued*)

Stage	Requirements	Ownership
Implementation and operation	Define structure and responsibilities Allocate resources Implement training program	Steering team Champion EH&S
EMS measurements	Collect data Analyze data Assess information Report to top management Perform current sigma metric calculation Perform six sigma data analyzing Perform root cause analyses Define opportunities to improvements Perform documentation	Operations EH&S EH&S EH&S MBB MBB MBB Engineering Archive
Improve	Generate solutions Select solution Design Verify by experiments and pilots (if needed) Implement improvement Perform documentation	Engineering EH&S EH&S Engineering Operations Archive
Emergency preparedness	Perform drills of emergency response Evaluate effectiveness Improve program Report Perform documentation	EH&S EH&S EH&S EH&S Archive
Review	Review Evaluate if policy needs changes Redefine environmental policy	Steering team EH&S Champion
Checking and Corrective actions	Perform measurements and monitoring Recalculate sigma metrics Present results on control charts Report Perform improve sequence Perform standardization Audit Perform documentation	Operation BB MBB MBB EH&S Multiple Archive

* EH&S—Environmental, Health and Safety
  MBB—Master black belt
  BB—black belt

References

Tennant, G. *Six Sigma: SPC and TQM in Manufacturing and Service*. Brookfield, VT: Gower Publishing Limited, 2001.

Selected bibliography

Block M. R. *Implementing ISO 14001*. Milwaukee, WI: Quality Press, 1997.

Breyfogle, W. F., M. J. Cupello, and B. Meadows. *Managing Six Sigma: a Practical Guide to Understanding, Assessing and Implementing the Strategy that Yields Bottom Line Success*. New York: John Wiley & Sons, 2001.

Clarke, T., and S. Clegg *Changing Paradigms : The Transformation of Management Knowledge for the 21st Century*. London: Harper Collins, 1998.

Deming, W. E. *Out of Crisis*. Cambridge, MA: MIT, 1986.

Dennison, M. S. *OSHA and EPA Process Safety Management Requirement, A Practical Guide for Compliance*. London: International Thompson Publishing Europe, 1994.

Evans, J. R., and W. M. Lindsay. *The Management and Control of Quality*. New York: West Publishing Company, 1995.

Fuller, H. T. "Observation About the Success and Evolution of Six Sigma at Seagate" *Quality Engineering Journal* 12, No. 3 (2000), pp. 311–315.

Hahn, J. G., N. Doganaksoy, and R. Hoerl. "The Evolution of Six Sigma." *Quality Engineering Journal* 12, No. 3 (2000), pp. 313–326.

Harry, M., and R. Schroeder. *Six Sigma, The Breakthrough Management Strategy Revolutionizing the World's Top Corporations*. New York: Doubleday, 2000.

Haskett, J. *Service Breakthroughs*. New York: Free Press, 1990.

Hoyle, D. *ISO9000 Quality Systems Handbook*. Bodenham, England: Butford Technical Publishing, 1994.

ISO 14000: International Environmental Management Standards.

ISO 14001: Environmental Management System—General Guidelines on Principles for Use.

ISO 14004: Environmental Management System—General Guidelines on Principles, Systems, and Supporting Techniques.

ISO 14010: Guidelines for Environmental Auditing—General Principles on Environmental Auditing.

ISO 14011/1: Guidelines for Environmental Auditing—Audit Procedures Audit of Environmental Management Systems.

ISO 14012: Guidelines for Environmental Auditing—Qualification Criteria for Environmental Auditors.

ISO 14020: Goals and Principles of All Environmental Labeling.

ISO 14024: Environmental Labels and Declaration—Environmental Labeling Type I—Guiding Principles and Procedures.

ISO 14031: Evaluation of Environmental Performance.

ISO 14040: Environmental Management—Life Cycle Analysis—Principle and Framework.

ISO 14041: Environmental Management—Life Cycle Analysis—Life Cycle Inventory Analysis.

ISO 14042: Environmental Management—Life Cycle Analysis—Impact Assessment.

ISO 14043: Environmental Management—Life Cycle Analysis—Interpretation.

Lovelock, C. H. *Managing Services: Marketing, Operations and Human Resources*. Englewood Cliffs, NJ: Prentice-Hall, 1992.

Michaud, P. A. *Accident Prevention and OSHA Compliance*. Boca Raton, FL: CRC Press, 1995.

Prahalad, C. K., and G. Hamel "The Core Competence of the Corporation," *Harvard Business Review* (May–June 1999), pp. 79–91.

Roberts H,. and C. Robinson. *ISO 14001 EMS Implementation Handbook*. Bodenham, England: Butford Technical Publishing, 1998.

Sanders D., and C. Hild. A Discussion of Strategies for Six Sigma Implementation. *Quality Engineering Journal* 12, No. 3 (2000), pp. 303–309.

Svendsen, A. *The Stakeholder Strategy: Profiting from Collaborative Business Relationships*. San Francisco: Berrett Koehler, 1998.

Tennant, G. *Six Sigma: SPC and TOM in Manufacturing and Service*. Brookfield, VT: Gower Publishing Limited, 2001.

Tweeddale, M. *Application of Quality Assurance Principles in Risk Management*. Brisbane, Australia: Risk Management Conference, 1995.

Wheeler, D., and M. Sillanpaa. *The Stakeholder Corporation*. London: Pitman, 1997

Chapter 9

Training and Certification

Training is one of the essential items in any initiative. However, it must be prioritized depending on the goals of the organization, the boss's expectations and certainly on the return on investment (ROI). It also depends on the prerequisites of what is expected to be learned and on so many other conditions such as cost, governmental regulations, safety, etc.

Fundamentally, six sigma training and its objectives are quite different for each of the roles within the six sigma methodology. There are some training strategies, however, that apply in all cases and should be considered an essential part of the organization's strategic plan. If these strategies are not followed, success will be elusive. The components of the strategic training are:

- *Goal setting and planning.* When executives decide to follow the six sigma methodology, they should know how to set goals and how those goals are related to each other. In addition, part of the planning stage in the six sigma implementation process is to decide whether or not the training is going to be on a standard basis or an accelerated approach. Standard training of 16 to 20 days to produce a black belt and 8 to 10 days to produce a green belt has become common in the industry. However, more and more organizations are finding out that accelerated training can produce the same results. With the accelerated training there is an important assumption that relates to the shorter training time. The assumption is that the black or green belt candidate will have previous experience in the use of quality tools such as design of experiments, statistical and root-cause analysis, to help produce a well-developed resource.

- *Basic business skills*. Especially the executives and champions must be aware of the consequences of selecting projects and their ROI, so that smarter and more profitable decisions may be made.

- *Adaptability*. Especially for master black belts and black belts, cross-training is a way to build respect and understanding that results in a more productive environment. Adaptability enhances creativity and encourages outside-the-box thinking.

- *Technical skills*. To be sure, in any six sigma endeavor the need for both supportive and technical skills is necessary. The supportive skill (team dynamics, how to conduct meetings, conflict resolution, project management and others), as important as they are, are not the only ones needed. Technical skills are the engine for conducting analysis and come to a decision that is based on data. In other words, these skills are the unique requirements that will make or break the project. Without appropriate knowledge of what technological solutions are available and how you can use what is available, six sigma will not be reached.

- *Problem-solving tools and skills*. This is the component that most organizations committed to six sigma should emphasize, and ensure that all employees have a good understanding of critical thinking, root-cause analysis, and applied statistics. These skills can eliminate inertia when employees come upon obstacles that might paralyze less educated employees.

- *Interpersonal skills*. These are also known as communication skills. Speaking, listening and conflict management are the foundations of interpersonal skills and very important elements in the pursuit of the six sigma methodology.

- *Ability and style of mental processing and external interaction*. An effective training and development strategy without this component would be like conducting an orchestra without knowledge of which instruments the musicians play and how well they play them. It is imperative for executives and champions in the six sigma methodology to know their players (master black belts and black belts) so that they can help, not only in developing training, but also in making smarter choices in terms of project assignment.

Now that we have examined the strategic aspects of training in the six sigma environment, let us summarize some of the key ingredients that the training for each role requires.

Green belts. Their function is primarily dependent on others to acquire data. In order for them to fulfill their anticipated tasks, they must:

- Demonstrate competence on a portion of a larger project.
- Be competent at detailed and routine tasks.
- Show directed creativity and initiative.
- Be able to perform well under time and budget pressure.
- Be able to learn how "we" do things.

Black belts. Their function is based on the principle of contributing independently and applying the appropriate and applicable techniques in the process of resolving problems and issues in the organization. In order for them to fulfill their anticipated tasks, they must:

- Assume responsibility for definable projects.
- Rely less on supervision, work independently and produce significant results.
- Develop credibility and a positive reputation.
- Posses technical competence and ability.
- Build an internal network for problem resolution.

Master black belts. Their function is to motivate others so that they contribute. Their contribution in the six sigma process is to make sure that they contribute through others based on appropriate and applicable leadership. To fulfill their anticipated guidance and leadership qualities they must:

- Have technical breadth.
- Know how to stimulate others through ideas and knowledge.
- Be involved as a manager, mentor or idea leader in developing others.

- Represent the organization effectively to clients and external bodies.
- Build a strong network.

Executives and champions. Their function is to lead through vision. Their role in the six sigma process is to make sure that their contribution will shape the future of their organization, as well as facilitate and appropriate resources as required. Specifically, the executive team focuses on the overall vision whereas the champions focus on the strategy. To fulfill their responsibilities, however, both must:

- Provide direction to the organization.
- Exercise power to influence decisions or obtain resources.
- Represent the organization in critical strategic issues.
- Sponsor promising individuals to prepare them for leadership roles in the organization.

This is indeed an awesome responsibility! Because the responsibility is so great and the expectations are so high, especially for the executives and champions, there must be a provision in the training to address the change process. This material is needed so that the level of frustration, shock and defensiveness often associated with change is minimized, or even eliminated. Typical items of coverage should be:

- Understanding change and the reasons for change:
  - Directed and undirected change.
  - Characteristics of change.
  - External drivers of changes.
  - Internal drivers of changes.
  - The cycles of change.
- Planning for change:
  - Using teamwork as a structure for change.
  - Establishing roles and responsibilities.
  - Developing the change plan.
- Helping change occur and reinforcing new behaviors:
  - Establishing a sense of urgency.
  - Communication.
  - Reinforcing change using the reward and recognition system.

- Managing change:
  - Major change inhibitors.
  - Working through change.
  - Guiding principles for managing change.
  - Dealing with setbacks, slow-downs and uncertainty.
  - Tools for managing change.
- Documenting the business process:
  - Document the relationships between the mainstay and enabling processes.
  - Identify the process owners and metrics.
- Selecting projects that support the strategic goals and objectives of the organization:
  - Select six sigma projects that support the corporate objectives.
  - Identify the champion and black belts.
- Performing active as opposed to passive six sigma reviews:
  - Participate in the project reviews by asking questions and providing constructive feedback.
- Actively cultivate the six sigma culture:
  - Help in removing roadblocks.
  - Help in securing appropriate and applicable resources on time.
  - Manage the leverage of change.
  - Assess the commitment of each key executive and manager.
  - Provide enthusiasm and motivation about the six sigma methodology.
  - Provide hints and encouragement as to sustain six sigma progress.
- Take responsibility for implementing six sigma.

Now that we have understood the primary functions of each major role within the six sigma methodology, we have to decide what the specific elements of their training are, and how we should prioritize the training. Unfortunately "required" training is usually performed first only because it is required. However, even in the six sigma methodology we have to be very careful not to neglect training that is essential and beyond the basic requirements. For example, to train selected individuals in the six sigma process obviously is a requirement. On the other hand, it may also be a requirement to train those selected individuals in mistake-proofing, measurement system analysis, axiomatic designs, specific statistical methodologies and so on. Again, in a summary form let us examine the content of a typical training curriculum:

Green belt. Six sigma green belts work directly with six sigma black belts, the cross-functional project leaders, to carry out identified improvement projects. As such, green belts need to be able to implement all of the appropriate tools of six sigma and to lead independent local projects when necessary. Generally, this training is a five-day duration. This five-day training prepares the green belt to provide key support to six sigma breakthrough and process improvement projects by working with cross-functional teams to define and measure problems, analyze the root causes, implement improvements and establish control at new levels. Therefore, the training should include information about the following:

- What is six sigma?
- Green belts and black belts.
- Identifying opportunities for improvement.
- Working with an improvement team.
- Mapping the process.
- Removing speed bumps in the process.
- The dangers of variation.
- What is process capability?
- How to collect useful data using the five points of view.
- How to create useful data by making deliberate process changes.
- Getting ideas from simple pictures: tally sheets, trend charts and dot plots.
- Searching for root causes using distinctions and changes. (Note: make sure we are addressing actionable causes and not causes that force us to look at the molecular and or subatomic level.)
- Analyzing root causes using the cause and effect (C and E) matrix.
- How to verify a root cause.
- Developing an action plan using the C and E matrix.
- Selling the action plan.
- How to maintain the gain.

The sample content for a 10-day training program is shown in Figure 9.1.

WEEK ONE
Introduce six sigma concepts
Introduce project management concepts
Selecting a project
Define: the key processes: ensure that processes are aligned and identified; define the cost of quality
Measure: review concept of variation; SPC overview; significance of data; types of data; measuring cost of quality; rational sampling, measurement system analysis; process flowcharting of the as is process
Analyze: focus on detailing the process (the micro-flow diagram); document every important process action; introduce the basic concepts of failure modes and effects analysis; performing a cause and effects analysis, selecting important cause and effects to analyze; an overview of applied statistical and DOE techniques.
Between week one and two, there is a break, so that the participants may work on their projects. Usually the break is between one and three weeks long.

WEEK TWO
Project reports and discussions (each participant briefly reports on the status of their project. Both positive and negative feedback is highly encouraged).
Improve: understanding technical and behavioral solutions; mistake-proofing and error-proofing; procedures and work instructions; significance of continual training when needed; significance of leadership, management and employee constancy, as far as "the project" is concerned; developing the implementation plan; reducing the risk of problems in implementation; significance of formalizing management approval; managing the plan; cost/benefit analysis.
Control: understanding process control; an overview of quality and business system structures; ongoing quality and management systems reviews

Figure 9.1 Sample training program for green belts

Black belt. The training for the black belt candidates is very intensive in quantitative and qualitative analytical skills, project management, group dynamics, team building, and change management. Generally, this training is a four-week long duration. This four-week training consists of one-week training segments, each separated by three weeks back at the site, during which time the trainees work on real-world projects, seeing first-hand how six sigma achieves breakthrough financial results and/or productivity gains. Specifically, the training of each week should cover the DMAIC model in a project format from beginning to end. Figure 9.2 shows a sample training program for black belts.

WEEK ONE

Prerequisite: each participant brings a selected project to work on during the training.

    Introductions, expectations, review of project selection

    Introduce the six sigma methodology

    Introduce the significance of the project

    Discuss the significance of the customer

    Introduce the DMAIC model

Define: the key as is process; understanding the key process in relation to inputs and outputs; recognition of the voice of the customer; introduce the concept of process-mapping and the difference/significance of macro/micro flow diagram; the value of procedures and work instructions; the value and main contributions of the team-concept and team-member participation; define cost of quality; introduce basic calculations, i.e., for cost of quality, defects per million, defects per million opportunities; identify the preliminary should be process; defining the project; establish a project charter.

Measure: variation; significance of data; types of data; rational sampling; measurement system analysis and evaluation; measuring cost of quality; strategy for developing data collection; statistical process control.

Therefore, in week one:

    Project: define an opportunity for improving your business; measure what you are doing now.
    Deliverable: real problems causing real pain are identified and prioritized.

Between each week there is a break, so that the participants may work on their projects. Usually the break is between three and four weeks long.

WEEK TWO

Project reports and discussions (each participant briefly reports on the status of their project).

    Analyze: process-mapping the process; the significance of the micro-flow diagram (document every important process action); how to determine the important from the significant. Analyzing the process (performing a process failure modes and effects analysis); analyzing product designs (performing a product failure modes and effects); performing a cause and effects analysis (selecting important cause and effects to analyze); introduction to simple applied statistics; introduction to reliability statistics; introduction to design of experiments (factorial, fractional factorial, location effects, variance effects, and yield effects, parameter design and tolerance design); developing a scientific verification plan

Therefore, in week two:

    Project: use the tools to analyze data and measurements and convert them to information leading to a solution.

    Deliverable: a plan of action and timeline is developed to solve a real problem.

Figure 9.2 Sample training program for black belts

WEEK THREE
Project reports and discussions (each participant briefly reports on the status of their project).

Improve: defining technical solutions; understand the difference between technical and managing behavioral solutions; mistake-proofing and error-proofing; design for assembly/manufacturing; quality function deployment and other product/process design solution strategies; design for reliability; procedures and work instructions; ongoing employee training; leadership, management, and employee constancy; developing the implementation plan; reducing the risk of problems in implementation; formalizing management approval and managing the plan; cost and benefit analysis.

Therefore, in week three:

Project: implement and deploy the improvements.

Deliverable: improvement begins and measurable gains are realized.

WEEK FOUR
Project reports and discussions (each participant briefly reports on the status of their project).

Control: understanding process control; planning for quality; quality and business system structures; ongoing quality and management systems reviews; quality system and six sigma audits; closing the project; how to keep six sigma alive and healthy in your organization; prepare for project closure.

Therefore, in week four:

Project: use the techniques learned to control and continue the improvements.

Deliverable: long-term results are maintained, producing ongoing, measurable savings.

Figure 9.2 (*Cont.*)

Master black belt. The master black belt undergoes the same training as the black belt with an additional week to include the following:

- Extensive knowledge of the core business of the organization and enabling processes.
- Knowledge of tools that help in selection of a viable project.
- Knowledge about teams and how they operate.
- Methodology of how to acquire and verify customer needs.
- Extensive knowledge of process-mapping.
- Selling skills—especially as they relate to six sigma.
- Conflict resolution.
- Extensive statistical knowledge.
- Project management.

Sponsors (champions). The sponsors of six sigma undergo one week of training, which covers the following items:

- Knowledge of current culture.
- Vision as to where they want the organization to be.
- Project management skills.
- Risk management.
- Financial background–cost-related.
- Leadership skills.

Executives. Executives participate in a one- or two-day training session that includes the following topics:

- What is six sigma?
- What is new and different about six sigma?
- Enterprise CEOs driving six sigma.
- Ten times (order of magnitude) improvements.
- Integrated strategic plan.
- Key measures relative to business plan.
- Balanced customer requirements/business results.
- Process focused.
- Methods, tools and sequence to meet business plan.
- Full-time black belts.
- Coaches, mentors and champions.
- Senior executive process.
- The implementation steps to six sigma.

Design for six sigma training:

As we have already said, the approach of DFSS is quite different from the DMAIC model. Therefore, the training is also different. Fundamental issues for this training are:

- Understand and employ the DCOV process.
- Define and select a six sigma project for design, or redesign, of goods or services.
- Correlate customer needs with the specific features of a product or service.
- Analyze the potential effect of failures on the selected design.

- Achieve robust design levels that will function over the environmental areas of use.

Generally, the training for DFSS is of five-day duration, and it provides an overview of the six sigma approach to planning and design. The DCOV strategy emphasizes design for manufacturability of goods and/or the repeatability of services. Each phase is discussed together with the methods and tools typically used. A typical roll out follows the following steps:

- Explain the roles and responsibilities of the black belt, DFSS engineer and green belts in the DFSS process.
- Identify the DFSS training sequence for those involved in DFSS process sequence.
- Explain the DFSS, DCOV model/process.
- Demonstrate how the assessment measures the DCOV process.
- Identify the selection criteria for design projects.

Typical overall objectives of DFSS training are to:

- Apply coaching tools to support the engineering processes for DFSS.
- Select the appropriate customer satisfaction variables.
- Explain a transfer function and the relationship to improving customer satisfaction.
- Select the appropriate tools for applying the DCOV process.
- Explain robustness improvement strategies that will improve customer satisfaction.
- Identify resources available for assistance.

Specific training objectives for each phase of the DCOV model are as follows:

- **Define.** To capture the voice of the customer, trainees must learn to:
  - Establish the scope and goals of the project.
  - Develop the six sigma project plan.
  - Flow the macro process.
  - Describe the DCOV process and its associated steps.
  - Describe the relationship between DFSS activities and organizational timing.
  - Describe the relationship between DFSS and six sigma processes.

- ◆ Establish balanced metrics.
- ◆ Establish critical to customer metrics.
- **Characterize.** Trainees learn about system design, including how to:
  - ◆ Validate the measurement systems.
  - ◆ Identify process options that will satisfy customer requirements.
  - ◆ Identify weaknesses of the process actions.
  - ◆ Develop and understand the cause and effect matrix.
  - ◆ Employ statistics, experiments and observations to verify cause and effect.
  - ◆ Apply functional structure methods for flowing CTS big Ys down to lower level technical metrics, the small ys.
  - ◆ Determine critical little ys from list of technical metrics.
  - ◆ Select the appropriate tools for evaluating and generating new design concepts.
  - ◆ Explain evaluation criteria and assessment for this step.
- **Characterize.** Trainees learn about the functional mapping aspect of the DCOV model, including how to:
  - ◆ Determine method for relating little ys to critical to quality (CTQ) design parameters.
  - ◆ Describe how to flow little ys down to design parameters (xs) and noise factors (ns) using the transfer function.
  - ◆ Determine critical xs and ns.
  - ◆ Characterize robustness opportunities.
  - ◆ Explain evaluation criteria and assessment for this step.
- **Optimize.** Design for robustness is the topic of training for this aspect of the DCOV model. Trainees learn how to:
  - ◆ Characterize the present long time in service robustness for the product.
  - ◆ Select methods for improving product and process robustness by further minimizing product sensitivity to manufacturing and usage conditions—as required.
  - ◆ Explain the relationship of robustness and producibility.
  - ◆ Identify the appropriate tools to use when designing to be insensitive to variation.
  - ◆ Explain the process of robust assessment.

- ◆ Explain the function, criteria for selection as a tool and interpretation of outputs of parameter design, tolerance design, statistical tolerancing and analytical reliability and robustness.
- ◆ Explain the evaluation criteria and assessment for this step.
- **Optimize.** For the design for productivity function of the DCOV model, trainees must learn to:
  - ◆ Select process and product characteristics that will meet customer requirements.
  - ◆ Characterize capability and stability of present process.
  - ◆ Minimize process sensitivity to product and manufacturing variations—as required.
  - ◆ Explain the relationship of this step and the organization's milestone timing for product development as well as robustness.
  - ◆ Explain the purpose and selection criteria for determining the appropriate tools to make the product insensitive to noise.
  - ◆ Explain the purpose and selection criteria for each of the countermeasure tools as appropriate, including dynamic control plan, poka-yoke, sequence modeling and selective assembly.
  - ◆ Explain the evaluation criteria and assessment for this step.
- **Verify.** The verify step in the DCOV model involves assessment and testing, and training therefore focuses on how to:
  - ◆ Estimate sigma for process capability and product function at job one and over time.
  - ◆ Explain the evaluation criteria incorporated in the assessment.
  - ◆ Explain the use of the assessment in processing through the DFSS process.
  - ◆ Identify tools for assessing actual performance, reliability and manufacturing capability.
  - ◆ Explain what is meant by demonstrating customer correlated performance over time.
  - ◆ Explain the relationship between establishment of a transfer function, ys, xs and ns, and the development and execution of a quality design and verification plan.
  - ◆ Explain the evaluation criteria and assessment of this step.
  - ◆ Verify that the design can satisfy customer requirements.

Selected topics are covered in greater detail as needed. The typical content is:
- Why the DFSS approach is different.

- What does six sigma mean to a designer.
- Capability indices and their use.
- The DCOV strategy and when to apply it.
- How to define a six sigma project.
- Principles to apply in establishing metrics for a project.
- Correlating the voice of the customer with product features (QFD).
- The analysis phase and conceptual design.
- Concurrent design.
- Principles of experimentation.
- Statistical tolerancing.
- Concept of reliability.
- Decision matrices.
- Failure modes and effects analysis (FMEA).
- Fault trees.
- What constitutes an adequate pilot program.
- Planning for control.

Certification

Certification presupposes not only some knowledge by the holder of the certification, but also that the knowledge has been verified by some means and has been found to be within acceptable standards through a third party.

So how has the current state of six sigma certification come about? Motorola first developed six sigma during the late 1980s. In the early days, the focus of six sigma was actually plus or minus three standard deviations (or C_{pk} of 1.0). As the process evolved through the 1990s, the need for improved processes caused the concept of six sigma to move to plus or minus six standard deviations (or C_{pk} of 2.0). At the same time, the idea of certifying individuals was also being discussed. That discussion was based on the American Society for Quality (ASQ) experience with certifications especially the CQE certification. (The certified quality engineer (CQE) certification is one of several certifications that the ASQ provides.) It started in 1968, thus making the certification one of the oldest in the business. As successful as the CQE was—and continues to be—the process of certification even during the 1990s tended to be very technical and manufacturing oriented and was not suitable for other business practitioners.)

As the self-proclaimed six sigma consultants and practitioners were trying to use the basic tools and process of total quality in service areas as well as manufacturing, they claimed that the CQE was not meeting their requirements and was not appropriate for their needs. Today, various training organizations (see www.isixsigma.com), have grown in number and are eagerly pushing the envelope of propaganda to stand out in the general business community.

On the other hand, business managers want to have some assurance that the people they hire will bring the six sigma process into their organizations and improve customer satisfaction and profitability. Already, two professional societies now have certification processes for the six sigma methodology and many companies have self-certifications for their own black belts. However, the other levels of champion, master black belt and green belt have yet to be addressed by the professional organizations.

In the case of ASQ, the National Certification Board researched the idea of a black belt certification for nearly two years and held a number of meetings to discuss the need for such a process. They decided to go forth with the idea and they began formulating their own Body Of Knowledge (BOK) and ultimately commenced with certification. Their process of certification is to ensure at least a minimum knowledge of what is described in the BOK.

To receive certification from the ASQ, the following are the minimum requirements:

- Proof of professionalism.
- Two completed six sigma projects documented by signed affidavits, or one project with a signed affidavit and three years of work experience, as it pertains to the BOK (no education waiver is given).
- Successful passage of a four-hour, 150 multiple-choice question examination.

The other professional organization that is offering a certification is the International Quality Federation (IQF). Their exam is computer-based and can be offered to anyone on demand. The major difference between ASQ's and IQF's certification is the emphasis of the organization. For IQF it is imperative that the certification be based on tangible results. As such, the candidate's own organization is in the best position to determine how effective the candidate is in applying the six sigma methodology. Thus, the IQF certification model requires that the individual be co-certified by both the IQF and a "sponsoring organization" (Pyzdek 2002).

On the other hand, we also see a trend in individual organization certifying their own black belts under the leadership of General Electric (GE). This is a very interesting phenomenon, since even at GE, many do not realize that there are many divisions within GE that have their own way applying six sigma within their unit. Thus even at GE, there is limited standardization as to how and what certification consists of. However, since many managers do not know of, or seem to care about, the nuances of what the six sigma practitioners are doing, there seems to be a common belief that if GE trained someone, then they are truly the experts in the field.

Even though there are no direct studies conducted for the specific purpose of evaluating six sigma certification, there is a body of research in regards to certification in general that we may use as surrogate data. For example, nearly all existing research on teacher qualifications or state regulations demonstrates that they have no significant relation to student performance. In fact, teacher qualification requirements have no positive correlation with teacher performance. In the end, as the Coleman Report (U.S. Office of Education, 1964) pointed out, families are the most important factors in determining students' academic performance.

No one will deny that competency is an admirable goal in any discipline and certainly in the six sigma methodology. Certification, if done correctly, can provide standardization of knowledge, but that is all. The problem is not only that most organizations, executives/managers and/or professional societies (and society at large) have accepted certification that persistently blur the distinction between good and outstanding performance, while they award certifications for passing examinations and/or being politically correct within their own organizations—even when their own personal performance is marginal and the selected project is of questionable merit. Competency is indeed very difficult to measure. Several of the problems associated with six sigma certification are outlined in the following sections.

False security about knowledge. We have, in the last three to four years, indicated that black belts and shoguns (master black belts) are the new superheroes of the organizations. We expect them to deliver fixes for problems that are causing discomfort on many levels, internal and external to the organization. We emphasize statistical thinking and statistical analysis with a sprinkling of interdisciplinary themes and hope that these items will resolve the concerns of the current organizations. We have forgotten the lessons that the scientists have taught us over the years that it is a mistake to bury one's head in the statistical sand. On average, oil tankers make it to their destinations, but the Exxon Valdez did not; on average, the world gets enough rainfall, but for a whole decade, the African Sahel did not; and on average, problem-solvers do solve problems, but sometimes they do not or, even worse, they provide the wrong solution. Certification, at this time, subverts the primary function of competency, as well as the overall quality goal of any organization. After all, a certification is a go/no go measurement and it does not represent the holder's true knowledge or performance.

Wrong emphasis on the learning process. We now believe that, with a specific affirmation, we can indeed reach perfection or specific competence. We believe that certification provides a specific piece of paper that enables us to boost our ability for that particular knowledge. Certification is such an affirmation, a false hope. Why? Because certification does not address the real issue of knowledge and competence in that order. Furthermore, by certifying someone at this time, for going through the motions of learning, we are, by default, adapting a scheme of professional promotion that has no credibility. (The proof of this statement is in the announcements of the last month's financial results from several six sigma companies. Unprecedented losses, no bonus for their employees, and thousands of lay-offs from both management and non-management ranks. If indeed all these experts on six sigma were following the six sigma methodology for their organization, would the results be so bad?) We continue to generate notions that are patently absurd, and many of those silly ideas produce not disbelief or rejection, but repeated attempts to show that they might be worthy of attention. Rather than focusing on the basic causes of competency, we look at effects. The irony here is that the entire methodology of six sigma is based on "root cause" and the certification is on the "effect." Rather than emphasizing the appropriate education and training in the school environment, we try to cram knowledge in a very limited time frame. We hire graduates from universities with statistics or engineering degrees, and then we expect them to pass a certification exam. Something is wrong here. If the university did their job, there should be no need for further certification. On the other hand, if they did not, then they should not graduate such students.

Political ploy. There is a huge difference between reputation and prestige, but it seems to us that certification, as it stands today, is nothing more than an issue of prestige. The issue of reputation is not even addressed. That makes it a political issue and in the long-term it will affect six sigma in a negative way. Lack of absolute scales will be the demise of the current certification process. For the sake of everyone involved and the integrity of certification, the fight for certification needs to be joined at the international, national, regional, institutional and individual levels.

Subjective. How can anyone talk about certification without first addressing the body of knowledge (BOK)? We know of at least four sources that define the BOK quite differently: the six sigma academy, the American Society for Quality, the International Quality Federation and the one proposed in Stamatis (2002). All of them have common points, however, not all of them agree on all issues. So the question becomes, to what BOK are you certified? Is one better than the other one?

Who certifies the certifiers? How can we believe that the certification means anything at all, since the certifiers themselves are self-proclaimed? The certifiers have forgotten that only other specialists can properly evaluate other specialists. In the case of the six sigma, arbitrarily the organizations mentioned above got together, they saw a financial bonanza and they went ahead with tests that are not even based on common knowledge. What do they measure? Do they imply that different organizations have different criteria and different base knowledge for certification? (It is amazing that "discipline envy" has clouded our thinking to the point where some individual organizations have different certifications between their own divisions and do not recognize each other's certification.)

Where is the accountability? By way of comparison, allow us to be provocative. From 1997 to 2000 McMurtrie (2001) reports that out of 2,896 accredited colleges only five have lost their accreditation, 43 have been given probation and 11 have show cause. In the field of quality: how many companies do you know that have been issued a revocation of their ISO 9000 or QS-9000 certification? How many certified lead auditors or auditors or quality professionals or professional engineers have been issued a revocation of their certification? Our point is: what is the ramification of foul play within certification? Or what can happen if there is no certification? The answer, unfortunately, is nothing. There is no accountability, because as we already mentioned there are two very important unresolved issues: there is no uniform BOK and no standardized training. Accountability implies standardization of process, knowledge, delivery and maintenance. In the current state of the six sigma certification, none of these exist.

To be sure, the research on certification is surrogate at best. For some specific studies see University of Rochester 1990; Peavey 1990; Erickson 1990; Heath and Nielson 1984; and Ray 1990. However, the surrogate research does imply (indicate) that the focus of six sigma certification may be overrated and it needs to be reexamined. Taking a test based on a lucid—as yet—body of knowledge does not guarantee success for either the individual certified or the organization that hires that certified individual.

Professionalism does not rest on a certification. It rests on experience and the application of tools to solve problems. It is unfortunate that the emphasis seems to be on protecting certain rights on credentials and not on the overall performance of the organization as a result of the six sigma methodology.

What we can hope for is the quality societies and individual organizations will push for more appropriate and applicable education and training as well as consistent base knowledge. What we would wish to see is a profession that did a better job of teaching everyone how to distinguish for himself or herself between scholarship that moves things forward (truly improve the process and customer satisfaction) and scholarship that just shakes things up (a revolutionary program that changes the direction of our misunderstandings about customer satisfaction and organizational profitability—a true $100\times$ improvement). On a more subjective level we would like to see great emphasis to be given between the *ascesis* or self transformation that produces integrity, honesty, flexibility, and moral independence, so that we are indeed free to tell the Emperor that "he is not wearing any clothes." Currently we are in a limbo state, as a profession because we are afraid to speak; our self transformation has become like a loss of self. A shift in this direction may happen in the next few years, if for no other reason than that integrity, honesty, flexibility and moral independence are qua ities whose value comes into high relief during a time of "high stakes."

We believe that the pressures of the current certification frenzy will converge with the pressures of an already latent dissent within the profession to produce some change, though whether the transformation will be more than superficial, we cannot predict. We hope that part of the change will involve a revived conversation about what it is to be six sigma certified. The debate for certification will continue for sure, but for right now there are more questions than answers to the process, the content and the value of six sigma certification.

References

American Society for Quality. *Certified Six Sigma Black Belt.* Milwaukee, WI: ASQ, 2001.

Erickson, D. "The ABCs of Reform: Give Parents a Chance." *Insight* (September 24, 1990), p. 13.

Hanushek, E. "The Impact of Differential Expenditures on School Performance." *Educational Researcher* (May 1990).

Heath, R. W., and M. A. Nielson. "The Research Basis for Performance-based Teacher Education." *Review of Educational Research.* Vol. 44. 1984. pp 463–484

Pyzdek, T. "Six Sigma Needs Standardization." *Quality Digest* (March 2001), p. 16.

Marash, S. A. *Fusion Management.* New York: McGraw-Hill, 2002.

McMurtrie, B. "Regional Accreditors Punish Colleges Rarely and Inconsistently." *The Chronicle of Higher Education* (January 12, 2001), pp. A27–A30.

Peavey, S. Hearing of September 30, 1998 on Compulsory Education Study Committee of the Iowa Legislature on the Subject of Teacher Qualifications. Also reported in *Insight* (September 24, 1990, p. 13.

Ray, B. A *Nationwide Study of Home Education: Family Characteristics, Legal Matters and Student Achievement.* Seattle, WA: National Home Educational Research Institute, 1990, pp. 53–54

Shewhart, W. *Economic Control of Quality of Manufactured Product.* Milwaukee, WI: ASQ, 1931.

Stamatis, D.H. *Six Sigma: Foundations of Excellent Performance.* Volume 1. Boca Raton, FL: St. Lucie Press, 2002.

University of Rochester. "The Impact of Differential Expenditures on School Performance." *Educational Researcher* (May 1990) pp. 234–256.

Chapter 10

Implementing Six Sigma

There is no one right way to implement six sigma successfully in an organization. Due to the variation of organizational cultures, each organization is quite unique, so there can be no guaranteed recipe for success across the board. The implementation strategy proposed here is a synthesis of approaches used successfully by organizations across all industries. It is offered only as a guide in developing strategies and associated plans to carry out these strategies. The intent of this approach is to demonstrate a flexible method that an organization can use to mobilize its strong points and capitalize all available energy, so that it is focused on key improvement opportunities.

Step 1. Recognize straight away that your organization is unique. As a consequence, do not borrow someone else's experience and try to fit into it. It would not work, even though the organization that you borrowed the plan from had great success with it.

Step 2. Conduct a needs assessment. Unless you know where you currently are, there is no way that you can measure your progress, or for that matter, develop improvement plans. The needs assessment will serve as the springboard for your organization to develop a strategy for improvement by identifying those vital processes to be targeted for change and it will provide a baseline measurement for judging progress.

Step 3. Start small. The best plans are those that result in action— action that improves the processes of the organization and results in better services and products for the customer. A simple plan that generates action and gets results is better than an elaborate plan that collects dust. Some initial six sigma actions might consist of specific projects designed to address systemwide problems that have the potential for expanding to other processes of the organization; or they might be efforts to implement six sigma in one or more organizational components. Examples of such efforts might include:

- Conducting customer identification efforts and customer survey and feedback efforts to be reflected in quality and timeliness indicators.
- Designating quality teams to address specific operating problems.
- Conducting organizational assessment, leadership development and group dynamics efforts.
- Getting some line personnel (i.e., non-managers) involved in implementing some form of quality improvement effort reflected in the overall strategic plan.

Step 4. Identify your customers, their requirements and review areas or quality indicators, or both, where six sigma methodology will be appropriate and applicable.

Step 5. Make a plan. The more specific your plans are, the more likely your organization will be successful.

A synthesized implementation process based on these five steps is the following:

- Gain top management commitment.
- Determine an organization's readiness.
- Create a vision and guiding principles.
- Establish the top management quality council.
- If applicable, communicate vision of six sigma with union representatives.

A successful six sigma implementation in any organization pre-supposes several key ingredients on the part of the leaders in the particular entity. Some of the strengths that the leaders must possess are:

- *Vision.* Six sigma is a visionary methodology that demands long-term vision. Without this long-term vision, the leaders may lose track of what the objective is.

- *Market focus.* Six sigma is centered around the needs, wants and expectations of the customer. It is imperative that the customer must be the center of everything that is being done in the organization. Customer satisfaction and loyalty are the driving forces of the methodology. As a consequence, leaders must be very sensitive to customer demands—both spoken and unspoken.

- *Strategic thinking.* By definition the six sigma methodology demands out of the box thinking and, as such, the leaders must be thinking towards long-term profitability.

- *Alignment skills.* Six sigma demands that the ROI and overall benefits, as a result of the implementation, be in congruence with the organizational goal. It is up to the leaders to make sure that that happens.

- *Expertise in deploying human capital.* Work is done through others. Unless leaders develop future leaders through the allocation of appropriate and applicable resources, any initiative in the continual improvement process will be stifled.

- *Superiority in communicating their vision.* Communication is the heart of the six sigma methodology. If done properly (horizontal as well as vertical) success will follow. If not, expect a hot fad to be replaced by something else.

In addition to the characteristics that the organization's leaders possess, it is also imperative to understand the process of how and why this implementation can be successful. We believe that there are six fundamental steps for this implementation. All of them are part of the internal make-up of the organization and its goals. They are:

1. Decide how to create the future. No implementation process can be successful without probing the future. In fact, this probing has to be quite bold. Six sigma proposes such action in their push from five sigma to six sigma. How is this done? By:

- Discovering new ways of thinking and acting to help you handle complexity and ambiguity.

- Examining best practices for leading transitions and building trust while implementing change.
- Modeling and rehearsing the future using the latest simulation techniques.

2. *Determine how to lead your organization.* The pressures of both the competition and the financial quarterly earnings take a toll on any executive. However, it is imperative that the executive, just like a captain in the turbulent sea, must show his or her strengths under extreme pressure. How is an executive supposed to lead the organization? By:

- Assessing his or her own leadership style.
- Leading the organization toward value creating performance.
- Fostering and developing leadership at every level of the organization.
- Creating greater shareholder value.

3. *Learn tips and techniques for formulating strategy.* You must know where you are before you find out where you can go. Executives in a given organization must be able to understand that hunches and intuition will only serve artificial means. For real breakthrough improvements, they must depend on data. Therefore, depending on the data available, the techniques and strategy will follow. Some of the basic issues dealing with the techniques and the strategy are accomplished by being able to:

- Identify the organization's core competencies.
- Make better strategic decisions and identify priorities and "actionable" tasks or projects.
- Formulate proactive strategies that anticipate market demand.

4. *Develop human capital for outstanding performance.* Organizations are a reflection of the people who work in them. Over time, organizations develop their own cultures and performance standards for excellence. For the executive, however, it is imperative to cultivate the human relations with a steady hand, yet compassion and understanding. A balance must be in the organization at all times between the demands of the employees, the customers and the financial world. To do that, the executive must:

- Recruit and retain multifaceted and diverse talent.
- Develop staff competencies that align with the organization's goals.
- Create a climate of trust and respect for greater efficiency, productivity and profit.

5. Manage the culture. Culture is a dynamic entity—it changes over time. The executives of the organization must be able to control the change by making sure that the strategy that they choose is complementary to the culture. It is imperative that these strategies must be communicated constantly throughout the organization, and they must be realistic and attainable within the constraints of the organization. This may be done with:

- Aligning the organization's culture and strategy.
- Harnessing the power of shared values to meet corporate goals.
- Understanding how corporate cultures drive decision-making.

6. Identify the drivers of peak organizational performance. Everything that we do has key parameters. That means that some things are more important than others. In organizational cultures there is no difference—the Pareto principle applies. How does the executive go about identifying and knowing some of the peak organizational performance? By:

- Allocating resources to maximize competencies and capabilities.
- Designing appropriate performance measurements and systems.
- Using innovation as a strategic tool to enhance profitability.

Now that we have identified some of the key issues in any organization for improvement, as well as the responsibility of management in this improvement effort, let us attempt to formalize the implementation process for the six sigma methodology. The process identified here is the same for manufacturing and non-manufacturing. It is defined in the following steps:

1. Recognize the need for improvement.
2. State goals and objectives.
3. Gain management commitment to those goals and objectives.
4. Select consultants.
5. Select champions.

6. Select candidates for black belts.
7. Authorize training to create a critical mass for a change.
8. Select green belts.
9. Provide generic training.
10. Provide additional training on an as-needed basis.
11. Provide guidelines for appropriateness in the project selection.
12. Allow for review and follow up.

The role of the consultant

Some of us may have experienced or heard horror stories about consultants, especially in recent years, now that so many people have been downsized into consulting rather than choosing it voluntarily. This is too bad, because consultants can be very valuable—that is, those consultants who do have the knowledge and experience to contribute that extra method, approach or knowledge, that will make the difference. By definition, consultants are hired to give advice in broad general terms, rather than really display the instruments of their profession.

Most consultants enjoyed some measure of success early in their careers. The reputations they gained from those early triumphs enabled them to survive professionally. Times have changed, however, and so has the formulae for achieving results. Too many consultants tend to apply the same solution to every problem. A classic example of this is the usage of process mapping. Whereas, it is very important to know your process, that does not mean that by only understanding the process the specific solution may be identified. The consultant and/or experimenter must know, in addition to the process mapping, the appropriate usage of tools and methodologies for the specific issue and/or problem at hand. Another example is the classic transition of corporate individuals who, after terminating their professional work, become consultants based on a specific success story of their career. In other words, in my experience, most tend to rest on their laurels. I would say that almost 70 percent of consultants are sorely lacking in both knowledge, experience and/or integrity. Thirty percent are worth their weight in gold—and charge that way, too.

Why am I so rough on my own profession? All of a sudden, many individuals and organizations began to claim expertise in six sigma.

How did that expertise come about? Was it because someone attended one, or two or even three training sessions and they found out the minimum requirements of the six sigma methodology? Or was it because somebody self-affirmed the knowledge of six sigma due to the monetary rewards? Or is it because many consultants have jumped on the bandwagon of success in previous programs such as ISO, FMEA, TQM and SPC? There are consultants out there who have claimed in national and reputable magazines that they have the experience to consult on ISO 9000, QS-9000, TS 16949, or even the six sigma before these standards and/or methodology were officially released.

Do you need a consultant? This question is very difficult to answer, because it depends on many variables. However, strictly speaking, you do not need a consultant to implement a quality system and/or the six sigma methodology. On the other hand, a consultant with knowledge and experience will help you get to your destination much faster and help you avoid mistakes. When you hire a consultant, make sure that their services are to coach and direct you in becoming self-sufficient in the tasks that you need the help. Do not fall in the trap of allowing the consultant to do it for you. If they do it for you, not only is more expensive, but you did not learn anything from the experience.

How do you connect with a reliable consultant? You must be resourceful and do an enormous amount of homework. Get and check references of previous clients—particularly recent clients. Ask specific questions. You need to know exactly what services were performed and what results were achieved. Agreements prevent disagreements, so once you've made your choice, enter into a written contract with your consultant. Make sure that you can terminate it at any time, no questions asked, with a fixed price to exit. Also, make sure that all the work and development for a project that the consultant did under your contract is your property.

The key ingredients for a six sigma consultancy are: extensive experience in statistics, extensive experience working with project teams, and perhaps the most important, they must have years of tactical (hands-on) and strategic (planning) experience. Unless there are some other mitigating circumstances, do not hire a consultant just because you must, or just because the price is right, or worse still, just because company XYZ hired him. A good six sigma consultant is expensive, but worth it.

Epilogue

For centuries, we thought Neanderthals were brutish, ape-like proto-humans. The most recent work on Neanderthals suggests they were very human in most ways, so it is time to change our popular icon of them. Every school child is taught that atoms are made up of visible electrons that revolve around a nucleus, and the famous Atomic Energy Commission seal shows this as fact. Today, however, the atom is seen as more of a concentric cloud. Human evolution is usually depicted as a fairly straight tree, showing a direct progression from knuckle-dragging beast to erect and noble humankind. But the icon more acceptable today is a complex and growing bush-like image with many branches, some withering and others enlarging over time. These changes are basically from simple to complex, or from linear to geometric.

So it is with the improvement movement. We have seen many programs, tools and methodologies come and go. Some have worked for a long time, some have not. In all cases, however, each new methodology, tool or program, in the process of displacing an old one, has contributed new knowledge and new approaches. The six sigma methodology provides us with a new systematic twist of a process in identifying and resolving issues, in addition to integrating the business strategy as part of the organizational vision. An integral part of this process is the project, which of course, provides specificity for the ROI and accountability for those assigned to it. This is indeed new and worth pursuing, for as long as it lasts!

We need to update the icons or models that we use to represent how we perceive relationships between technology, people and business strategy. Evolution, even in quality, is a way of life. Six sigma is the way to help us accomplish our goal. However, we do not have to improve every process and every product. Some things are good enough as they are.

Appendix A.

Core Competencies for the Six Sigma Methodology

Customer and organizational

- Provide a definition of the term *customer satisfaction*.
- Understand the need-do interaction and how it relates to customer satisfaction and business success.
- Provide examples of the Y and X terms in the expression $y = f(x)$ and or $y = f(x,n)$.
- Interpret the expression $Y = f(x)$ and or $Y = f(x,n)$.
- Define the nature of a performance metric.
- Identify the driving need for performance metrics.
- Explain the benefit of plotting performance metrics on a log scale.
- Provide a listing of several key performance metrics.
- Identify the fundamental contents of a performance metrics manual.
- Recognize the benefits of a metrics manual.
- Understand the purpose and benefits of improvement curves.
- Explain how a performance metric improvement curve is used.
- Explain what is meant by the phrase six sigma rate of improvement.
- Explain why a six sigma improvement curve can create a level playing field across an organization.
- State some problems (or severe limitations) inherent to the current cost of quality theory. Identify and define the principle categories associated with quality costs.
- Compute the cost of quality (COQ), given the necessary background data. Provide a detailed explanation of how a defect can impact the classical cost of quality categories.

Six sigma fundamentals

- Recognize the need for change and the role of values in a business.
- Recognize the need for measurement and its role in business success.
- Understand the role of questions in the context of management leadership.
- Provide a brief history of six sigma and its evolution.
- Understand the need for measuring those things which are critical to the customer, business and process.
- Define the various facets of six sigma and why six sigma is important to a business.
- Identify the parts-per-million defect goal of six sigma.
- Define the magnitude of difference between three, four, five and six sigma.
- Recognize that defects that arise from variation.
- Define the three primary sources of variation in a product.
- Describe the general methodologies that are required to progress through the hierarchy of quality improvement.
- Define the phases of breakthrough in quality improvement.
- Identify the values of a six sigma organization as compared to a four sigma business.
- Understand the key success factors related to the attainment of six sigma.
- Understand why inspection and test is non-value-added to a business and serves as a roadblock for achieving six sigma.
- Understand the difference between the terms *process precision* and *process accuracy*.
- Provide a very general description of how a process capability study is conducted and interpreted.
- Understand the basic elements of a sigma benchmarking chart.
- Interpret a data point plotted on a sigma benchmarking chart.
- Understand the difference between the idea of benchmark, baseline and entitlement cycle time.
- Provide a brief description for the outcome $1 - Y.rt$.
- Recognize that the quantity $1 + (1 - Y.rt)$ represents the number of units that must be produced to extract one good unit from a process.
- Describe how every occurrence of a defect requires time to verify, analyze, repair and re-verify.
- Understand that work-in-process (WIP) is highly correlated to the rate of defects.
- Describe what is meant by the term *mean time between failure* (MTBF).
- Interpret the temporal failure pattern of a product using the classical bathtub reliability curve.
- Explain how process capability impacts the pattern of failure inherent to the infant mortality rate.

- Provide a rational definition of the term *latent defect* and how such defects can impact product reliability.
- Explain how defects produced during manufacture influence product reliability which, in turn, influence customer satisfaction.
- Rationalize the statement: The highest quality producer is the lowest cost producer.
- Understand the fundamental nature of quantitative benchmarking on a sigma scale of measure.
- Recognize that the sigma scale of measure is at the opportunity level, not at the system level.
- Interpret an array of sigma benchmarking charts.
- Understand that global benchmarking has consistently revealed four sigma as average, while best-in-class is near the six sigma region.
- Draw first-order conclusions when given a global bench-marking chart.
- Provide a brief description of the five sigma wall—what it is, why it exists and how to get over it.
- State the general findings that tend to characterize or profile a four sigma organization.
- Explain how the sigma scale of measure could be employed for purposes of strategic planning.
- Recognize the cycle time, reliability and cost implications when interpreting a sigma benchmarking chart.
- Understand how a six sigma product without a market will fail, while a six sigma product in a viable market is virtually certain to succeed.
- Provide a qualitative definition and graphical interpretation of the standard deviation.
- Understand the driving need for breakthrough improvement versus continual improvement.
- Define the two primary components of process breakthrough.
- Provide a brief description of the four phases of process breakthrough (i.e., measure, analyze, improve, control).
- Provide a synopsis of what a statistically designed experiment is and what role it plays during the improvement phase of breakthrough.
- Understand the basic nature of statistical process control charts and the role they play during the control phase of breakthrough.
- Explain the interrelationship between the terms *process capability*, *process precision* and *process accuracy*.
- Explain how statistically designed experiments can be used to achieve the major aims of six sigma from a quality, cost, and cycle time point of view.
- Understand that the term *sigma* is a performance metric that only applies at the opportunity level.

Appendix B

Traditional Sigma (Abridged) Conversion Table

Long-Term Yield	Long-Term Sigma	Short-Term Sigma	Defects Per 1,000,000	Defects Per 10,000	Defects Per 100
99.99966%	4.5	6.0	3.4	0.034	0.00034
99.9995%	4.4	5.9	5	0.05	0.0005
99.9992%	4.3	5.8	8	0.08	0.0008
99.9990%	4.2	5.7	10	0.1	0.001
99.9980%	4.1	5.6	20	0.2	0.002
99.9970%	4.0	5.5	30	0.3	0.003
99.9960%	3.9	5.4	40	0.4	0.004
99.9930%	3.8	5.3	70	0.7	0.007
99.9900%	3.7	5.2	100	1.0	0.01
99.9850%	3.6	5.1	150	1.5	0.015
99.9770%	3.5	5.0	230	2.3	0.023
99.9670%	3.4	4.9	330	3.3	0.033
99.9520%	3.3	4.8	480	4.8	0.048
99.9320%	3.2	4.7	680	6.8	0.068
99.9040%	3.1	4.6	960	9.6	0.096
99.8650%	3.0	4.5	1,350	13.5	0.135
99.8140%	2.9	4.4	1,860	18.6	0.186
99.7450%	2.8	4.3	2,550	25.5	0.255
99.6540%	2.7	4.2	3,460	34.6	0.346
99.5340%	2.6	4.1	4,660	46.6	0.466
99.3790%	2.5	4.0	6,210	62.1	0.621
99.1810%	2.4	3.9	8,190	81.9	0.819
98.930%	2.3	3.8	10,700	107	1.07
98.610%	2.2	3.7	13,900	139	1.39
98.220%	2.1	3.6	17,800	178	1.78
97.730%	2.0	3.5	22,700	227	2.27
97.130%	1.9	3.4	28,700	287	2.87
96.410%	1.8	3.3	35,900	359	3.59
95.540%	1.7	3.2	44,600	446	4.46
94.520%	1.6	3.1	54,800	548	5.48
93.320%	1.5	3.0	66,800	668	6.68

Long-Term Yield	Long-Term Sigma	Short-Term Sigma	Defects Per 1,000,000	Defects Per 10,000	Defects Per 100
91.920%	1.4	2.9	80,800	808	8.08
90.320%	1.3	2.8	96,800	968	9.68
88.50%	1.2	2.7	115,000	1,150	11.5
86.50%	1.1	2.6	135,000	1,350	13.5
84.20%	1.0	2.5	158,000	1,580	15.8
81.60%	.9	2.4	184,000	1,840	18.4
78.80%	.8	2.3	212,000	2,120	21.2
75.80%	.7	2.2	242,000	2,420	24.2
72.60%	.6	2.1	274,000	2,740	27.4
69.20%	.5	2.0	308,000	3,080	30.8
65.60%	.4	1.9	344,000	3,440	34.4
61.80%	.3	1.8	382,000	3,820	38.2
58.00%	.2	1.7	420,000	4,200	42
54.00%	.1	1.6	460,000	4,600	46

Note: Sigma level is typically reported as short-term sigma. When the shift between long-term and short-term capability can be determined, six sigma methodology requires the team to calculate and report short-term sigma based on the actual shift. For reference purposes, this abridged chart uses the generally accepted shift of 1.5 to approximate short-term sigma value when long-term sigma is known.

Appendix C
The Process of QFD

This appendix is based on the work of Akao (1990), Hauser and Clausing (1988) and Sulivan (1986). Its purpose is to show the application of each matrix as part of the design process.

Phase 1—Innovation targets

To set innovation targets, QFD uses the quality and design of experiments. It records these targets on several charts. See the pencil example in Figure C.1.

Figure C.1 Innovation targets for a pencil example

A-1 Innovation

A-1 pencil	Length	Time between sharpening	Lead dust generated	Hexagonality		Rate of importance (A)	Company now (2)	Competitor x (Plan)	Competitor y (Plan)	Plan (X)	Rate of improvement (B)	Sales point (C)	Absolute wt. (D)	Demand wt.
Easy to hold	○ 42			○ 42		3	4	3	3	4	1		3	14
Does not smear		○ 69	◎ 207			4	5	4	5	5	1	○	4.8	23
Point lasts	△ 44	◎ 396	○ 132			5	4	5	3	5	1.25	◎	9.4	44
Does not roll	△ 19			◎ 171		3	3	3	3	4	1.33		4	19
Total	105	465	339	213	1122							Total	21.2	100
%	9	41	30	19	99									
Company now	5"	3pgs	3g	70%										
Competitor x	5"	5pgs	4g	80%										
Competitor y	4"	2.5	3g	60%										
Plan	5.5"	6pgs	2g	80%										

Main Correlations
◎ 9 = Strong correlation
○ 3 = Some correlation
△ 1 = Possible correlation

Sales points ◎=1.5 ○1.2

$D = A \times B \times C$

$B = \frac{X}{2}$

B-2 Costs

Chart B-2 Pencil Example	Company	Competitor x	Competitor y	Plan
Market price	55¢	58¢	54¢	56¢
Sales volume	14M	13M	18M	55M
Market share	26%	22%	42%	28%
Profit	12¢	13¢	12¢	14¢
Cost	43¢	45¢	42¢	42¢
				Target

Other charts include A-2, A-3, A-4, B-3, B-4, C-2, C-3, C-4, and D charts.

Phase 2—Generate innovation ideas

Innovation ideas are developed and recorded (see Figure C.2).

Figure C.2 Generate innovation ideas for a pencil example

C-1 New Technology

First level of detail mechanisms

New techology		Writing mechanism	Erasing mechanism	Lead holding mechanism	Chewing mechanism
	Molded plastics	◯	◯		
	Polymer technology	◎	◎		△
	Plastic erasers		◎		
	New assembly methods	△			

E-1 New Concepts

New concepts

Customer demands		Spring loaded lead	Retractable lead	Datum best in class	Friction fit eraser	Pocket clip	China pencil
	Easy to hold			Quill		-	
	Does not smear		+	E.F.			-
	Point lasts	+	+				-
	Does not roll					+	-
	Cost	-	-		+	-	+
	+'s	1+	2+		1+	1+	
	-'s	1-	1-			1-	3-

Other charts include E-2, E-3, E-4, and F-1.

Phase 3—Innovation engineering

Figure C.3 Innovation engineering for a pencil example

F-1 Value Engineering

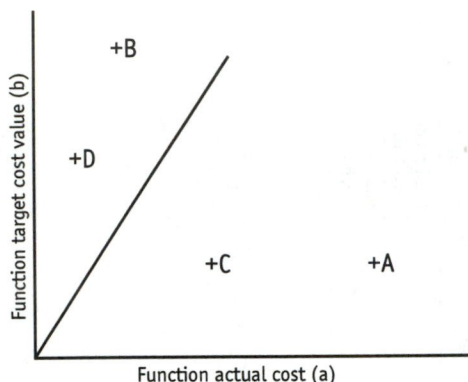

F-2 Revised

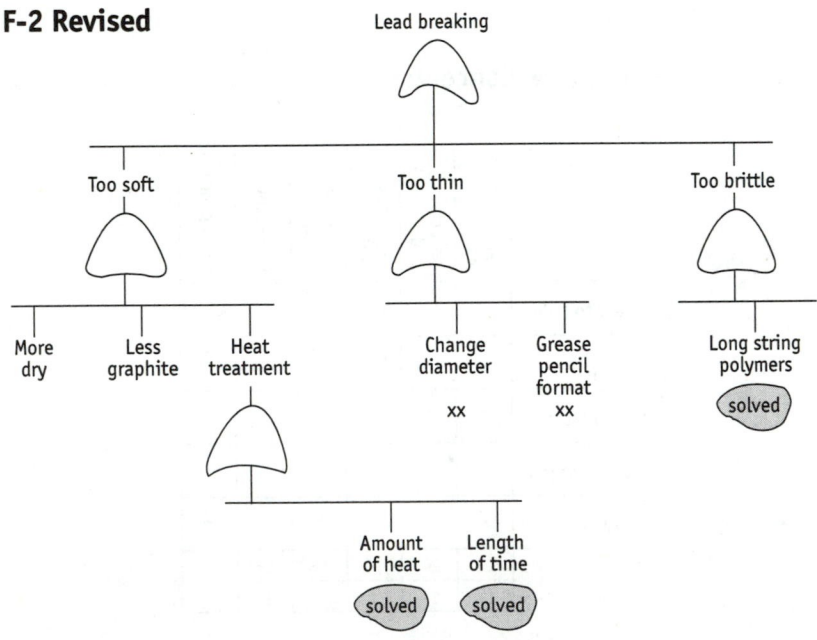

Other charts include F-3.

Phase 4—Manufacturing controls

Some charts help develop manufacturing controls (see Figure C.4).

Figure C.4 Manufacturing controls for a pencil example

G-3 Process Planning Chart

No.	Process	Conditions of manufacturing		Parts characteristics	Control points of process
		Equipment	Index		
1	Obtain steel			Freedom from rust	Incoming observation
2	Form wire	Extruder		Diameter flex	O.D. dimension degree of flex
3	Coil wire	Coiler		Tension	Amount of spring level of recoil
4	Cut spring	Crimp		Smooth	Degree of smoothness

G-6 Q.C. Process Chart

Date Name / # **QFD / 101**	Section head **D. Stamatis**
Date prepared **8/16/03**	Preparer **Aristea**
Revisions **10/22/03**	

Part name/number	Flow Chart		Process name	Work instruction sheet #	Process control item	Control Method								Inspection Method					
	Raw material	Process				Person in charge	Place	When	Measurement	Sampling method	Standard	Control data	Inspection item	Person in charge	Sensory data	Instruction sheet #	Sampling	Record kept	In charge of action
Spring	1		Obtain steel																
	2		Store steel	102	Lot #s	A	Warehouse k	1 month	Count	100%	Zero defects	Check sheet	Rust	C	---	---		Log sheet	E
		3	Form wire																
		4	Coil wire	104	Temp.	E	Coiler 6	Every 30 mins.	Temp. gage	Once every 30 mins.	F degrees	Control chart	Spring tension	D	Feel	Tension tester	5 every 20 mins.	Control chart	F
		5	Cut spring																
		6	Inspection																

Other charts include G-1, G-2, G-4, and G-5.

Appendix D

Example of Using the Quality Charts in the QFD Process for Each of the Stages

Design stage 1—Advanced engineering

Phase 1—Innovation targets for systems

Task / Chart	Purpose / Comments
I – 1 Matrix data	Decide what business you are in.
I – 2 New concept Selection chart	"Blue Sky" New directions for product.
I –3 Market research Kano 3 arrows and survey Results matrix	Determine voice of customer.
I – 4 K-J and Tree 2 Levels (see Figure D.1)	Understand voice of customer.

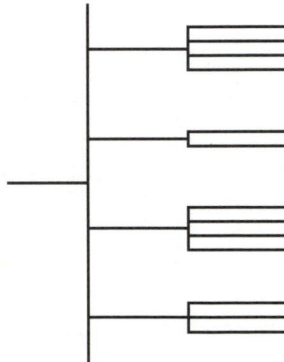

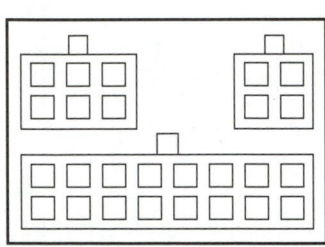

Figure D.1 K-J and tree 2 levels

I – 5
A-1 Part 1
House of quality

Learn customer priorities.

I – 6
A-1 Quality characteristics

Purpose
- Identify key items to measure and control.
- Benchmarking/competitive analysis.
- Preliminary targets.

I – 7
A-2 Voice of engineer (function)
vs. Quality characteristics

- Identify missing quality characteristics.
- Identify over-design.

B-1 Part 1
Voice of engineering vs.
Voice of customer

- Learn engineering priorities (Saaty method).
- Learn conflicts between voice of engineer and voice of customer.
- Alternate approach to learn engineering priorities.

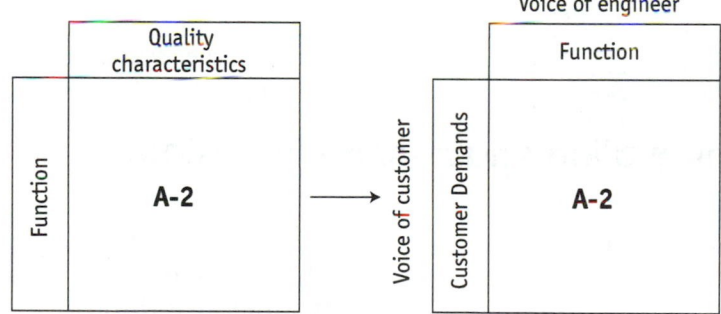

I – 8
B-3 Factor analysis (Taguchi)

Breakthrough targets

In the light of combined voice of customer and voice of engineer.

- Analyze needed breakthroughs (factor analysis).
- Set preliminary breakthrough targets.

Phase 2 – Innovation ideas for systems

I – 9
C-1 New technology vs. systems

In light of breakthrough targets
* Identify potential new technology.
* Select system changes based on new technology.

I – 10
C-2 Part 1
Systems vs. functions

Identify key systems based on voice of engineer (functions).

I – 11
C-3 Part 1
Systems vs. Quality characteristics

Identify key systems based on quality characteristics.

I – 12
B-2 Cost analysis
Total product
(Preliminary)

In light of key systems and potential new technology, do preliminary cost targets.

I – 13
B-1 Part 2

Identify target functions for cost reduction.

I – 14
C-2 Part 2

Identify target systems for cost reduction.

Phase 3 – Innovation engineering for systems

I – 15
F-2 Reviewed dendogram

Draw a diagram of potential system and cost improvements based on data from I – 8 through I – 14 and record on reviewed dendogram.

I – 16
F-1, F-2, F-3 Value engineering
Factor analysis, finite element method

Develop engineering breakthroughs on systems and cost using value engineering, factor analysis, finite element method and other tools of engineering breakthrough.

I – 17
Revise cost analysis B-2 based on engineering breakthroughs

Evaluate competitive cost position based on eng. breakthroughs.
If satisfactory, go on to step I – 18.
If not satisfactory, review steps I – 13,
I – 14, I – 15, and I – 16 for alternatives.

I – 18
Revise targets
A-1 based on engineering and
cost breakthroughs

Check to see how new systems and
new technology stack up against
competitors.

I – 19
Cost / Benefit Analysis (see Figure D.2)

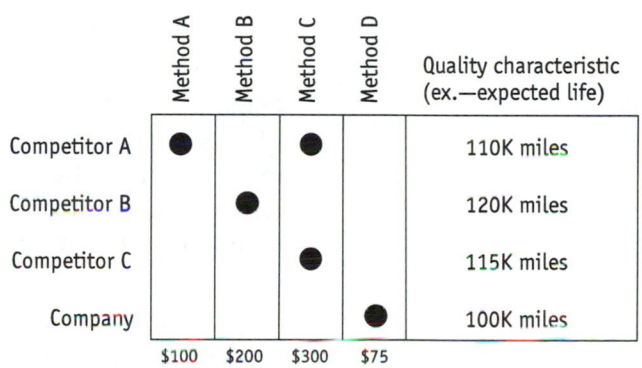

Figure D.2 Cost/Benefit analysis

Stage 2—Project definition
(QFD and new product development)

Phase 1—Innovation targets for subsystems

II – 1
Review charts from Segment I

A-1 Key customer demands, key quality characteristics

A-2 Voice of the engineer, key quality characteristics

B-1 Voice of the customer vs. voice of the engineer

B-2 Cost targets for product

B-3 Preliminary breakthrough targets

C-1 System changes suggested by new technology

C-2 System changes suggested by voice engineer

C-3 System changes suggested by quality characteristics

F-1 Cost reductions of functions and systems

F-2 System changes based on process decision program chart and finite element method

F-3 System changes based on factor analysis and reviewed dendogram

II – 2
A-4 Subsystem chart

Purpose
Identify the key subsystems for improvement based on the ones that have strong relationship with key (top two or three) quality characteristics.

II – 3
B-4 Subsystem chart
Key subsystems and key quality characteristics

Purpose / Comments
Identify the key functions and key quality characteristics for each of the key (top two or three) subsystems and capability indices.

Phase 2 – Innovation ideas for subsystems

II – 4
C-4 Subsystems vs. systems

- Identify subsystems that relate to key systems.
- Identify targets for subsystem cost reduction.

II – 5
D-1 Fault tree analysis vs. customer demands

- Prioritize reliability problems to work on based on customer demands.

II – 6
D-2 Fault tree analysis vs. functions

- Prioritize reliability problems to work on based on voice engineer (functions).

II – 7
D-3 Fault tree analysis vs. quality characteristics

- Prioritize reliability problems to work on based on critical quality characteristics.

II – 8
D-4 Subsystem failure modes vs. parts

- Prioritize the development of subsystem product FMEAs based on an analysis of subsystem failure modes.

II – 9
E-1 New concepts for subsystems vs. customer demands

- Preselect new subsystem concepts based on meeting voice of customer.

II – 10
E-2 New concepts for subsystems vs. voice of the engineer (functions)

- Preselect new subsystem concepts based on meeting voice of engineer.

II – 11
E-3 New concepts for subsystem vs. critical quality characteristics

- Preselect new subsystem concepts based on critical quality characteristics.

II – 12
E-4 New concepts for subsystems summary

- Identify strengths and weaknesses of new concepts based on whether they are better or worse than existing product or best in class product when compared to customer demands, functions, and critical quality characteristics.

Phase 3 – Innovation engineering for subsystems

II – 13
F-2 Reviewed Dendogram
(see Figure D.3)

- Draw a diagram of potential subsystem and cost improvements based on data from steps II – 2 through II – 12.

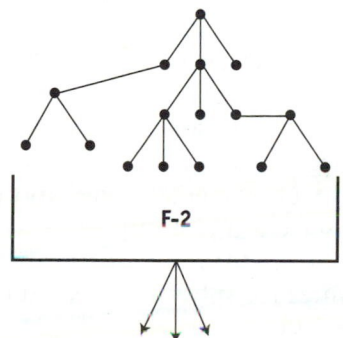

Figure D.3 Dendogram

II – 14
F-1, F-2, F-3

- Develop engineering breakthroughs on systems and cost using value engineering, factor analysis, finite element method, process decision program chart, and other engineering breakthrough tools.

II – 15
B-2 Revise cost analysis based on engineering breakthroughs

- Evaluate competitive cost position based on engineering breakthroughs. If satisfactory, go on to II-16. If not, review steps 13 and 14.

II – 16
A-4 Critical quality characteristics vs. new subsystems

- Redo chart A-4 based on new subsystems developed in steps II-9 through II-14.

II – 17
B-4 Quality characteristics, functions, and C_p vs. key subsystems

- Analyze key new subsystems for function and quality characteristics.

Stage 3—Detailed design
(QFD and new product development)

Phase 1—Innovation targets for parts and components

III – 1 Review charts from Segment II

A-1 Charts	Voice of customer, key quality characteristics, key system changes and approaches, competitive analyses
A-2 Charts	Voice of engineer, key quality characteristics
A-3	Subsystem trade-offs/conflicts
A-4	Key old subsystems, key new subsystems
B-1	Conflicts between voice of customer and voice of engineer
B-2	Cost targets—competitive analysis
B-3	Breakthrough targets for key quality characteristics
B-4	Subsystem quality characteristics, old and new cp targets, etc.
C-1, 2, 3, 4	System priority selection reasons
B-1, C-2, C-4	Cost reduction targets for functions, systems and subsystems
D-1, 2, 3, 4	Reliability priorities for subsystems based on customers, engineers, and quality characteristics
E-1, 2, 3, 4	New subsystem concept priorities based on voice of customers, engineers, and critical quality characteristics
F-1, 2, 3	Subsystem changes developed through value-engineering, factor analysis, finite element method, etc.

III – 2
A-4 Parts, components, and raw materials vs. key quality characteristics

- Identify key parts, components, and raw materials to be improved based on strong relationship to key quality characteristics.

III – 3
B-4 Key parts, components, and raw materials vs. quality characteristics

- Identify key functions, key quality characteristics, and capability indices for each of the key parts, components, and raw materials.

Phase 2—Innovation ideas for parts and components

III – 4
C-1 New technology vs. subsystems

- Identify potential subsystem changes based on new technology.

III – 5
C-2 Subsystems vs. voice of engineer functions

- Identify potential subsystem changes based on voice of the engineer (functions).

III – 6
C-3 Subsystems vs. key quality characteristics

- Identify potential subsystem changes based on key quality characteristics.

III – 7
C-4 Subsystems vs. parts, components, and raw materials

- Identify priority parts, components, and raw materials for cost reduction.

III – 8
D-4 Parts, components, and raw material failure modes vs. parts, components, and raw materials

- Prioritize development of parts, components, and raw material product FMEAs based on strong relationships with failure modes of same.

III – 9
E-1 New concepts for parts and components vs. customer demands

- Preselect new concepts for parts and components based on meeting voice of the customer.

III – 10
E-2 New concepts for parts and components vs. voice of engineer

- Preselect new concepts for parts and components based on meeting voice of the engineer.

III – 11
E-3 New concepts for parts and components vs. key quality characteristic

- Preselect new concepts for parts and components based on meeting key quality characteristics.

III – 12
E-3 New concepts for parts and components summary

- Identify strengths and weaknesses of new concepts for parts and components based on whether they are better or worse than existing product or best in class product when compared to customer demands, functions, and critical quality characteristics.

Phase 3—Innovation engineering for parts and components

III – 13
F-2 Reviewed dendogram

- Draw a diagram of potential part, component, and raw material improvements based on data from steps II – 2 through II – 12.

III – 14
F-1, F-2, F-3

- Develop engineering breakthroughs on subsystems parts, and components using VE, PDPC, FEM, factor analysis, etc.

Task / Chart

III – 15
F-4 Summary of engineering breakthroughs

Purpose / Comments

- Summarize engineering breakthroughs regarding subsystems, parts, components and raw materials, cost savings vs. target, and items crucial for function, reliability and assembly.

III – 16
B-2 Review cost analysis based on engineering breakthroughs

- Evaluate competitive cost position based on engineering breakthroughs.
- If acceptable, go on to III – 17. If not, review III – 9 through III – 14.

III – 17
A-4 Critical quality characteristics vs. new parts, components, and raw materials

- Redo Chart A-4 based on new parts, components, and raw materials developed in steps III – 8 through III – 14.

III – 18
B-4 Functions, quality characteristics and C_p vs. key new parts, components, and raw materials

- Analyze key new parts, components, and raw materials for function, quality characteristics, and C_p.

Phase 4—Manufacturing controls for parts and components

III – 19
G-1 QA Table

- Identify key quality designs, quality characteristics, and reasons for key parts and components.

III – 20
G-2 Purchasing chart

- Select best supplier based on quality, cost and other appropriate measures.

III – 21
G-3 Process planning chart

- Identify the parts, characteristics and conditions of manufacturing (equipment and settings and control of the process).

III – 22
G-4 Process fault tree analysis

- Identify potential process failure modes.

III – 23
G-5 Process failure mode and effect analysis

- Identify the level of occurrence, severity, and detection of failure modes.

III – 24
G-6 QC Process chart

- Identify the plan for process controls and inspection controls.

Stage 4—Prototype/Test: Revise manufacturing controls (QFD and new product development)

Task / Chart	Purpose / Comments

IV – 1
Review A, B, C, D, E, F charts from Phase III and make technical changes based on prototypes and tests. Save breakthroughs and inventions for next model unless savings is considerable, in which case seek appropriate waivers.

IV – 2
G-1 QA Table

- Update QA table based on data from prototype/tests.

IV – 3
G-2 Purchasing chart

- Update purchasing charts based on data from prototype/tests.

IV – 4
G-3 Process planning chart

- Update process planning chart based on data from prototype/tests.

IV – 5
G-4 Process fault tree analysis

- Update process fault tree analysis based on data from prototype/tests.

IV – 6
G-5 Process failure mode and effect analysis

- Update process FMEA based on data from prototype/tests.

IV – 7
G-6 QC Process chart

- Update QC process based on data from prototype/tests.

Appendix E

Using Binomial and Poisson Distributions

This appendix is intended to break through the fear often associated with the use of the binomial and Poisson probability distributions. It provides an introduction to the theory of probability and the mathematics involved in making decisions based upon these distributions. It also introduces easy-to-use charts to simplify calculations. Furthermore, this appendix illustrates the practical application of probability theory to quality control decision-making.

Introduction to discrete distributions

There are two basic types of distributions—continuous and discrete. Continuous distributions are used to make predictions based upon variables data. The most familiar continuous distribution is the "normal" distribution, characterized by the bellcurve. Discrete distributions are used to make predictions based upon attribute data. It is two of these discrete distributions that we will be dealing with in this appendix.

The terms *probability*, *binomial distribution* and *Poisson distribution* generally elicit fear in non-statisticians. However, the mystique surrounding these concepts shrouds some fairly simple and useful decision-making tools and concepts. By far the most important is probability, which may be defined as the ratio of the chances of an event occurring to the total number of possibilities. For example, in the simplest terms, a coin has two sides. When flipped it could land on either heads or tails. The probability of it landing with the head side up is 1/2 or 50 percent.

Before plunging headlong into the binomial and Poisson distributions, let us take a quick look at some very familiar applications of probability theory:

Example 1. What is the probability of drawing an ace from a regulation deck of 52 playing cards?

4/52 = 1/13 or 8 percent

Example 2. What is the probability of drawing two consecutive aces from that deck (assuming that the first ace is *not* returned to the deck)?

4/52 x 3/51 = 12/2,652 or 0.5 percent

These applications are fairly straightforward and unimposing. We intuitively know that the chances of drawing two consecutive aces are much lower than drawing the first ace. But simple mathematical calculations allow us to quantify those chances, or risks.

Binomial distribution

The binomial distribution is composed of independent trials having dichotomous outcomes and a constant probability of occurrence. For example, coin flipping. The mathematical formula defining the binomial distribution is:

$$P(x) = (n!)/\, x!\, (n-x)!\, (p^x\, q^{n-x})$$

Where:

n = number of trials
x = number of occurrences
p = probability of occurrence
q = 1–p

Example 3. Using coin-flipping, suppose we were to flip a coin 10 times.   What is the probability of obtaining 3 heads?

$$n = 10 \quad x = 3 \quad p = 1/2 \text{ or } 0.5 \quad q = 1 - 0.5 = 0.5$$

$$P(3) = (10!)/\, 3!(10-3)!\, (.5^3)\, (.5^7) = 0.117 \text{ or } 11.7 \text{ percent}$$

That looks fairly simple when someone else is doing the calculating. However, the opportunities for errors are great and such calculations can become tedious. An easier approach is to use a set of precalculated tables—see the tables at the end of this appendix. For example, in the previous problem, simply find the section for the number of trials (n) and the number of occurrences (x). Read across this row to where it intersects with the column corresponding to the probability of occurrence (p). Read the value at that intersection –the value of 0.117. Very easy!

You will note that there is also a number in parentheses at the intersection. This is the cumulative probability of occurrence. In other words, this represents the probability of obtaining heads 3 or fewer times in the course of flipping the coin 10 times. This probability is 0.172.

Example 4. What would be the probability of drawing a heart on 4 consecutive draws, assuming that each card is returned to the deck after drawing?

$$n = 4 \quad x = 4 \quad p = 13/52 = 0.25 \quad q = 1 - .25 = .75$$

$$P(4) = 0.004 \text{ or } 0.4 \text{ percent}$$

Remember, the binomial distribution is generally applicable only in cases where there is a constant probability of occurrence. This is also known as the concept of sampling with replacement.

Poisson distribution

The Poisson distribution is similar to the binomial, except that it applies when the number of trials (n) is high, over 20, and/or the probability of occurrence (p) is small. It is defined by the mathematical expression:

$$P(x) = ((np)^x \, e^{-np})/ \, x! \text{ ; where } e = 2.71$$

Example 5. In our coin-flipping example, let's increase our number of flips to 20.

$$n = 20 \qquad x = 3 \qquad p = 0.5$$

$$P(3) = ((20 \times .5)^3 \, (2.71)^{-(20 \times .5)}) \, / \, 3! = 0.007 \text{ or } 0.7 \text{ percent}$$

Again, the calculations are not overly simplistic, rather they can be ominous and very difficult to calculate. Therefore, a set of Poisson tables have been developed to facilitate making such predictions. Using the same problem, first we must calculate an "np" value. This simply involves multiplying "n" times "p" – (20 × 0.5) = 10.0. We find the column under the "np" of 10.0 and read across at the row for our "x" (3). These intersect at 0.007 or 0.7 percent. The reader will also note that we have provided a number in parentheses, which is the cumulative probability of occurrence. Therefore, the probability of 3 or fewer heads in 20 flips is 0.009 or 0.9 percent.

Example 6. Going back to our friendly deck of cards, what would be the probability of drawing four aces in 13 draws?

$$n = 13 \quad x = 4 \quad p = 4/52 \qquad np = 13 \, 4/52 = 1.0$$

$$P(4) = 0.016 \text{ or } 1.6 \text{ percent}$$

Now that we know how to use these two charts, how do we know when to use each chart? The following rule is applicable. Start with the binomial chart. If the exact "n" and "p" values are not there, then calculate "np" and go to the Poisson chart. Let us review this process by solving the next couple of a few problems (#7 and #8).

Example 7. If, on average, a new product produced by a particular company has six defects, what is the probability that the new product you bought from them will have no defects?

$$n = 1 \quad x = 0 \quad p = 6.0$$

Poisson, np = 6.0

$$P(0) = 0.002 \text{ or } 0.2 \text{ percent}$$

Example 8. Suppose that a supplier sends you a lot of material that you find to be 10% defective, but he claims passed his final inspection sampling calling for a sample size of 25 and a reject number of 2. What is the probability that his final inspector properly sampled this lot?

$n = 25$ $x = 2$ $p = 0.10$

Poisson, np = 2.5

$P(2) = 0.287$ or 28.7 percent

In other words, there is nearly a 3 in 4 chance that the final inspection process was flawed.

Conclusion

Despite their forbidding formulae, the binomial and Poisson probability distributions are not difficult to use. They do have limitations. As with any attribute inspection system, they are limited in their application. However, the reader will notice that the potential for these types of examples is unlimited. In fact, these discrete distributions can be valuable, if properly used, in establishing sampling programs such as operating curves (OC) which are developed from the discrete probability formulas, in life testing approximations, or in evaluating the effectiveness of sampling programs. As in Example 8, the results can lead to potential problem areas. The binomial and Poisson distributions are merely two more tools in the toolbox of a professional who deals in quality issues. Too often they have been ignored because we didn't know how to use them. That should never be the case again.

EXAMPLE 3

n	x	.40	.45	.50
10	0	.006(0.006)	.002(0.002)	.001(0.001)
	1	.040(0.046)	.021(0.023)	.010(0.011)
	2	.121(0.167)	.076(0.099)	.044(0.055)
	3	**.215(0.382)**	**.167(0.266)**	**.117(0.172)**
	4	.251(0.633)	.238(0.504)	.205(0.377)
	5	.201(0.834)	.234(0.738)	.246(0.623)
	.	.	.	.
	.	.	.	.
	.	.	.	.
	10	.000(1.000)	.000(1.000)	.001(1.000)

EXAMPLE 4

n	x	.15	.20	.25
4	0	.522(0.522)	.410(0.410)	.316(0.316)
	1	.368(0.890)	.410(0.820)	.422(0.738)
	3	.011(0.999)	.025(0.998)	.047(0.996)
	4	**.001(1.000)**	**.002(1.000)**	**.004(1.000)**

EXAMPLE 5

np	8.0	9.0	10.0
x			
0			
1	.003(0.003)	.001(0.001)	
3	.011(0.014)	.005(0.006)	.002(0.002)
4	**.029(0.043)**	**.015(0.021)**	**.007(0.009)**
2	.000(1.000)	.000(1.000)	.001(1.000)

EXAMPLE 6

np	0.8	0.9	1.0
c			
0	.449(0.449)		
1	.359(0.808)	.406(0.406)	.368(0.368)
2	.144(0.952)	.366(0.772)	.368(0.736)
3	.039(0.991)	.166(0.938)	.184(0.920)
4	**.008 0.999**	**.049 0.987**	**.061 0.981**
5		.011(0.998)	.016(0.997)
	.001(1.000)	.002(1.000)	.003(1.000)

EXAMPLE 7

np	6.0	7.0	8.0
c			
0	**.002(0.002)**	**.001(0.001)**	
1	.015(0.017)	.006(0.007)	.003(0.003)
2	.045(0.062)	.022(0.29)	.011(0.014)
.	.	.	.
.	.	.	.
.	.	.	.
18	.000(1.000)	.000(1.000)	.001(1.000)

EXAMPLE 8

np	2.3	2.4	2.5
c			
0	.100(0.100)	0.91(0.091)	.082(0.082)
1	.231(0.331)	.218(0.309)	.205(0.287)
2	**.265(0.596)**	**.261(0.570)**	**.256(0.543)**
3	.203(0.799)	.209(0.779)	.214(0.757)
.	.	.	.
.	.	.	.
.	.	.	.
9	.000(1.000)	.001(1.000)	.001(1.000)

Table E.1 Poisson probability distribution

np					
c	0.1	0.2	0.3	0.4	0.5
0	.905(0.905)	.819(0.819)	.741(0.741)	.670(0.670)	.607(0.607)
1	.09.1(0.996)	.164(0.983)	.222(0.963)	.268(0.938)	.303(0.910)
2	.004(1.000)	.016(0.999)	.033(0.996)	.054(0.992)	.076(0.986)
3		.010(1.000)	.004(1.000)	.007(0.999)	.013(0.999)
4				.001(1.000)	.001(1.000)
np					
c	0.6	0.7	0.8	0.9	1.0
0	.549(0.549)	.497(0.497)	.449(0.449)	.406(0.406)	.368(0.368)
1	.329(0.878)	.349(0.845)	.359(0.808)	.366(0.772)	.368(0.736)
2	.099(0.977)	.122(0.967)	.144(0.952)	.166(0.938)	.184(0.920)
3	.020(0.997)	.028(0.995)	.039(0.991)	.049(0.987)	.061(0.981)
4	.003(1.000)	.005(1.000)	.008(0.999)	.011(0.998)	.016(0.997)
5			.001(1.000)	.002(1.000)	.003(1.000)
np					
c	1.1	1.2	1.3	1.4	1.5
0	.333(0.333)	.301(0.301)	.273(0.273)	.247(0.247)	.223(0.223)
1	.366(0.699)	.361(0.662)	.354(0.627)	.345(0.592)	.335(0.558)
2	.201(0.900)	.217(0.879)	.230(0.857)	.242(0.834)	.251(0.809)
3	.074(0.974)	.087(0.966)	.100(0.957)	.113(0.947)	.126(0.935)
4	.021(0.995)	.026(0.992)	.032(0.989)	.039(0.986)	.047(0.982)
5	.004(0.999)	.007(0.999)	.009(0.998)	.011(0.997)	.014(0.996)
6	.001(1.000)	.001(1.000)	.002(1.000)	.003(1.000)	.004(1.000)
np					
c	1.6	1.7	1.8	1.9	2.0
0	.202(0.202)	.183(0.183)	.165(0.165)	.150(0.150)	.135(0.135)
1	.323(0.525)	.311(0.494)	.298(0.463)	.284(0.434)	.271(0.406)
2	.258(0.783)	.264(0.758)	.268(0.731)	.270(0.704)	.271(0.677)
3	.138(0.921)	.149(0.907)	.161(0.892)	.171(0.875)	.180(0.857)
4	.055(0.976)	.064(0.971)	.072(0.964)	.081(0.956)	.090(0.947)
5	.018(0.994)	.022(0.993)	.026(0.990)	.031(0.987)	.036(0.983)
6	.005(0.999)	.006(0.999)	.008(0.998)	.010(0.997)	.012(0.995)
7	.001(1.000)	.001(1.000)	.002(1.000)	.003(1.000)	.004(0.999)
8					.001(1.000)
np					
c	2.1	2.2	2.3	2.4	2.5
0	.123(0.123)	.111(0.111)	.100(0.100)	.091(0.091)	.082(0.082)
1	.257(0.380)	.244(0.355)	.231(0.331)	.218(0.309)	.205(0.287)
2	.270(0.650)	.268(0.623)	.265(0.596)	.261(0.570)	.256(0.543)
3	.189(0.839)	.197(0.820)	.203(0.799)	.209(0.779)	.214(0.757)
4	.099(0.938)	.108(0.928)	.117(0.916)	.125(0.904)	.134(0.891)
5	.042(0.980)	.048(0.976)	.054(0.970)	.050(0.964)	.067(0.958)
6	.015(0.995)	.017(0.993)	.021(0.991)	.024(0.988)	.028(0.986)
7	.004(0.999)	.005(0.998)	.007(0.998)	.008(0.996)	.010(0.996)
8	.001(1.000)	.002(1.000)	.002(1.000)	.003(0.999)	.003(0.999)
9				.001(1.000)	.001(1.000)

Table E.1 Poisson probability distribution

np					
c	2.6	2.7	2.8	2.9	3.0
0	.074(0.074)	.067(0.067)	.061(0.061)	.055(0.055)	.050(0.050)
1	.193(0.267)	.182(0.249)	.170(0.231)	.160(0.215)	.149(0.199)
2	.251(0.518)	.245(0.494)	.238(0.469)	.231(0.446)	.224(0.423)
3	.218(0.736)	.221(0.715)	.223(0.692)	.224(0.670)	.224(0.647)
4	.141(0.877)	.149(0.864)	.156(0.848)	.162(0.832)	.168(0.815)
5	.074(0.951)	.080(0.944)	.087(0.935)	.094(0.926)	.101(0.916)
6	.032(0.983)	.036(0.980)	.041(0.976)	.045(0.971)	.050(0.966)
7	.012(0.995)	.014(0.994)	.016(0.992)	.019(0.990)	.022(0.988)
8	.004(0.999)	.005(0.999)	.006(0.998)	.007(0.997)	.008(0.996)
9	.001(1.000)	.001(1.000)	.002(1.000)	.002(0.999)	.003(0.999)
10				.001(1.000)	.001(1.000)

np					
c	3.1	3.2	3.3	3.4	3.5
0	.045(0.045)	.041(0.041)	.037(0.037)	.033(0.033)	.030(0.030)
1	.140(0.185)	.130(0.171)	.122(0.159)	.113(0.146)	.106(0.136)
2	.216(0.401)	.209(0.380)	.201(0.360)	.193(0.339)	.185(0.321)
3	.224(0.625)	.223(0.603)	.222(0.582)	.219(0.558)	.216(0.537)
4	.173(0.798)	.178(0.781)	.182(0.764)	.186(0.744)	.189(0.726)
5	.107(0.905)	.114(0.895)	.120(0.884)	.126(0.870)	.132(0.858)
6	.056(0.961)	.061(0.956)	.066(0.950)	.071(0.941)	.077(0.935)
7	.025(0.986)	.028(0.984)	.031(0.981)	.035(0.976)	.038(0.973)
8	.010(0.996)	.011(0.995)	.012(0.993)	.015(0.991)	.017(0.990)
9	.003(0.999)	.004(0.999)	.005(0.998)	.006(0.997)	.007(0.997)
10	.001(1.000)	.001(1.000)	.002(1.000)	.002(0.999)	.002(0.999)
11				.001(1.000)	.001(1.000)

np					
c	3.6	3.7	3.8	3.9	4.0
0	.027(0.027)	.025(0.025)	.022(0.022)	.020(0.020)	.018(0.018)
1	.098(0.125)	.091(0.116)	.085(0.107)	.079(0.099)	.073(0.091)
2	.177(0.302)	.169(0.285)	.161(0.268)	.154(0.253)	.147(0.238)
	.213(0.515)	.209(0.494)	.205(0.473)	.200(0.453)	.195(0.433)
4	.191(0.706)	.193(0.687)	.194(0.667)	.195(0.648)	.195(0.628)
5	.138(0.844)	.143(0.830)	.148(0.815)	.152(0.800)	.157(0.785)
6	.083(0.927)	.088(0.918)	.094(0.909)	.099(0.899)	.104(0.889)
7	.042(0.969)	.047(0.965)	.051(0.960)	.055(0.954)	.060(0.949)
8	.019(0.088)	.022(0.987)	.024(0.984)	.027(0.981)	.030(0.979)
9	.008(0.996)	.009(0.996)	.010(0.994)	.012(0.993)	.013(0.992)
10	.003(0.999)	.003(0.999)	.004(0.998)	.004(0.997)	.005(0.997)
11	.001(1.000)	.001(1.000)	.001(0.999)	.002(0.999)	.002(0.999)
12			.001(1.000)	.001(1.000)	.001(1.000)

np					
c	4.1	4.2	4.3	4.4	4.5
0	.017(0.017)	.015(0.015)	.014(0.014)	.012(0.012)	.011(0.011)
1	.068(0.085)	.063(0.078)	.058(0.072)	.054(0.066)	.050(0.061)
2	.139(0.224)	.132(0.210)	.126(0.198)	.119(0.185)	.113(0.174)

(Continued on next page)

Table E.1 Poisson probability distribution

c					
3	.190(0.414)	.185(0.395)	.180(0.378)	.174(0.359)	.169(0.343)
4	.195(0.609)	.195(0.590)	.193(0.571)	.192(0.551)	.190(0.533)
5	.160(0.769)	.163(0.753)	.166(0.737)	.169(0.720)	.171(0.704)
6	.110(0.879)	.114(0.867)	.119(0.856)	.124(0.844)	.128(0.832)
7	.064(0.943)	.069(0.936)	.073(0.929)	.078(0.922)	.082(0.914)
8	.033(0.976)	.036(0.972)	.040(0.969)	.043(0.965)	.046(0.960)
9	.015(0.991)	.017(0.989)	.019(0.988)	.021(0.986)	.023(0.983)
10	.006(0.997)	.007(0.996)	.008(0.996)	.009(0.995)	.011(0.994)
11	.002(0.999)	.003(0.999)	.003(0.999)	.004(0.999)	.004(0.998)
12	.001(1.000)	.001(1.000)	.001(1.000)	.001(1.000)	.001(0.999)
13					.001(1.000)

np					
c	4.6	4.7	4.8	4.9	5.0
0	.010(0.010)	.009(0.009)	.008(0.008)	.008(0.008)	.007(0.007)
1	.046(0.056)	.043(0.052)	.039(0.047)	.037(0.045)	.034(0.041)
2	.106(0.162)	.101(0.153)	.095(0.142)	.090(0.135)	.084(0.125)
3	.163(0.325)	.157(0.310)	.152(0.294)	.146(0.281)	.140(0.265)
4	.188(0.513)	.185(0.495)	.182(0.476)	.179(0.460)	.176(0.441)
5	.172(0.685)	.174(0.669)	.175(0.651)	.175(0.625)	.176(0.617)
6	.132(0.817)	.136(0.805)	.140(0.791)	.143(0.778)	.146(0.763)
7	.087(0.904)	.091(0.896)	.096(0.887)	.100(0.878)	.105(0.868)
8	.050(0.954)	.054(0.950)	.058(0.945)	.061(0.939)	.065(0.933)
9	.026(0.980)	.028(0.978)	.031(0.976)	.034(0.973)	.036(0.969)
10	.012(0.992)	.013(0.991)	.015(0.99.1)	.016(0.989)	.018(0.987)
11	.005(0.997)	.006(0.997)	.006(0.997)	.007(0.996)	.008(0.995)
12	.002(0.999)	.002(0.999)	.002(0.999)	.003(0.999)	.003(0.998)
13	.001(1.000)	.001(1.000)	.001(1.000)	.001(1.000)	.001(0.999)
14					.001(1.000)

np					
c	6.0	7.0	8.0	9.0	10.0
0	.002(0.002)	.001(0.001)			
1	.015(0.017)	.006(0.007)	.003(0.003)	.001(0.001)	
2	.045(0.062)	.022(0.029)	.011(0.014)	.005(0.006)	.002(0.002)
3	.089(0.151)	.052(0.081)	.029(0.043)	.015(0.021)	.007(0.009)
4	.134(0.285)	.091(0.172)	.057(0.100)	.034(0.055)	.019(0.028)
5	.161(0.446)	.128(0.300)	.092(0.192)	.061(0.116)	.038(0.066)
6	.161(0.607)	.149(0.449)	.122(0.314)	.091(0.207)	.063(0.129)
7	.138(0.745)	.149(0.598)	.140(0.454)	.117(0.324)	.090(0.219)
8	.103(0.848)	.131(0.729)	.140(0.594)	.132(0.456)	.113(0.332)
9	.069(0.917)	.102(0.831)	.124(0.718)	.132(0.588)	.125(0.457)
10	.041(0.958)	.071(0.902)	.099(0.817)	.119(0.707)	.125(0.582)
11	.023(0.981)	.045(0.947)	.072(0.889)	.097(0.804)	.114(0.696)
12	.011(0.992)	.026(0.973)	.048(0.937)	.073(0.877)	.095(0.791)
13	.005(0.997)	.014(0.987)	.030(0.967)	.050(0.927)	.073(0.864)
14	.002(0.999)	.007(0.994)	.017(0.984)	.032(0.959)	.052(0.916)
15	.001(1.000)	.003(0.997)	.009(0.993)	.019(0.978)	.035(0.951)
16		.002(0.999)	.004(0.997)	.011(0.989)	.022(0.973)

Table E.1 Poisson probability distribution

c	11.0	12.0	13.0	14.0	15.0
17		.001(1.000)	.002(0.999)	.006(0.995)	.013(0.986)
18			.001(1.000)	.003(0.998)	.007(0.993)
19				.001(0.999)	.004(0.997)
20				.001(1.000)	.002(0.999)
21					.001(1.000)

np

c	11.0	12.0	13.0	14.0	15.0
0					
1					
2	.001(0.001)				
3	.004(0.005)	.002(0.002)	.001(0.001)		
4	.010(0.015)	.005(0.007)	.003(0.004)	.001(0.001)	.001(0.001)
5	.022(0.037)	.013(0.020)	.007(0.011)	.004(0.005)	.002(0.003)
6	.041(0.078)	.025(0.045)	.015(0.026)	.009(0.014)	.005(0.008)
7	.065(0.143)	.044(0.089)	.028(0.054)	.017(0.031)	.010(0.018)
8	.089(0.232)	.066(0.155)	.046(0.100)	.031(0.062)	.019(0.037)
9	.109(0.341)	.087(0.242)	.066(0.166)	.047(0.109)	.032(0.069)
10	.119(0.460)	.105(0.347)	.086(0.252)	.066(0.175)	.049(0.118)
11	.119(0.579)	.114(0.461)	.101(0.353)	.084(0.259)	.066(0.184)
12	.109(0.688)	.114(0.575)	.110(0.463)	.099(0.358)	.083(0.267)
13	.093(0.781)	.106(0.681)	.110(0.573)	.106(0.464)	.096(0.363)
14	.073(0.854)	.091(0.772)	.102(0.675)	.106(0.570)	.102(0.465)
15	.053(0.907)	.072(0.844)	.088(0.763)	.099(0.669)	.102(0.567)
16	.037(0.944)	.054(0.898)	.072(0.835)	.087(0.756)	.096(0.663)
17	.024(0.963)	.038(0.936)	.055(0.890)	.071(0.827)	.085(0.748)
18	.015(0.983)	.026(0.962)	.040(0.930)	.056(0.883)	.071(0.819)
19	.008(0.991)	.016(0.973)	.027(0.957)	.041(0.924)	.056(0.875)
20	.005(0.996)	.010(0.988)	.018(0.975)	.029(0.953)	.042(0.917)
21	.002(0.998)	.006(0.994)	.011(0.986)	.019(0.972)	.030(0.947)
22	.001(0.999)	.003(0.997)	.006(0.992)	.012(0.984)	.020(0.967)
23	.001(1.000)	.002(0.999)	.004(0.996)	.007(0.991)	.013(0.980)
24		.001(.1.000)	.002(0.998)	.004(0.995)	.008(0.988)
25			.001(0.999)	.003(0.998)	.005(0.993)
26			.001(1.000)	.001(0.999)	.003(0.996)
27				.001(1.000)	.002(0.998)
28					.001(0.999)

Table E.2 Binomial probability distribution

n	x	0.05	0.10	0.15	0.20	0.25
1	0	0.950(0.950)	0.900(0.900)	0.850(0.850)	0.800(0.800)	0.750(0.750)
	1	0.050(1.000)	0.100(1.000)	0.150(1.000)	0.200(1.000)	0.250(1.000)
2	0	0.902(0.902)	0.810(0.810)	0.722(0.722)	0.640(0.640)	0.562(0.562)
	1	0.095(0.997)	0.180(0.990)	0.255(0.977)	0.320(0.960)	0.375(0.938)
	2	0.003(1.000)	0.010(1.000)	0.022(1.000)	0.040(1.000)	0.062(1.000)
3	0	0.857(0.857)	0.729(0.729)	0.614(0.614)	0.512(0.512)	0.422(0.422)
	1	0.135(0.993)	0.243(0.972)	0.325(0.939)	0.384(0.896)	0.422(0.844)
	2	0.007(1.000)	0.027(0.999)	0.057(0.997)	0.096(0.992)	0.141(0.984)
	3		0.001(1.000)	0.003(1.000)	0.008(1.000)	0.016(1.000)
4	0	0.815(0.815)	0.656(0.656)	0.522(0.522)	0.410(0.410)	0.316(0.316)
	1	0.171(0.986)	0.292(0.948)	0.368(0.890)	0.410(0.819)	0.422(0.738)
	2	0.014(1.000)	0.049(0.996)	0.098(0.988)	0.154(0.973)	0.211(0.949)
	3		0.004(1.000)	0.011(0.999)	0.026(0.998)	0.047(0.996)
	4			0.001(1.000)	0.002(1.000)	0.004(1.000)
5	0	0.774(0.774)	0.590(0.590)	0.444(0.444)	0.328(0.328)	0.237(0.237)
	1	0.204(0.977)	0.328(0.919)	0.392(0.835)	0.410(0.737)	0.396(0.633)
	2	0.021(0.999)	0.073(0.991)	0.138(0.973)	0.205(0.942)	0.264(0.896)
	3	0.001(1.000)	0.008(1.000)	0.024(0.998)	0.051(0.993)	0.088(0.984)
	4			0.002(1.000)	0.006(1.000)	0.015(0.999)
	5					0.001(1.000)
6	0	0.735(0.735)	0.531(0.531)	0.377(0.377)	0.262(0.262)	0.178(0.178)
	1	0.232(0.967)	0.354(0.886)	0.399(0.776)	0.393(0.655)	0.356(0.534)
	2	0.031(0.998)	0.098(0.984)	0.176(0.953)	0.246(0.901)	0.297(0.831)
	3	0.002(1.000)	0.015(0.999)	0.041(0.994)	0.082(0.983)	0.132(0.962)
	4		0.001(1.000)	0.005(1.000)	0.015(0.998)	0.033(0.995)
	5				0.002(1.000)	0.004(1.000)
	6					
7	0	0.698(0.698)	0.478(0.478)	0.321(0.321)	0.210(0.210)	0.133(0.133)
	1	0.257(0.956)	0.372(0.850)	0.396(0.717)	0.367(0.577)	0.311(0.445)
	2	0.041(0.996)	0.124(0.974)	0.210(0.926)	0.275(0.852)	0.311(0.756)
	3	0.004(1.000)	0.023(0.997)	0.062(0.988)	0.115(0.967)	0.173(0.929)
	4		0.003(1.000)	0.011(0.999)	0.029(0.995)	0.058(0.987)
	5			0.001(1.000)	0.004(1.000)	0.012(0.999)
	6					0.001(1.000)
	7					
8	0	0.663(0.663)	0.430(0.430)	0.272(0.272)	0.168(0.168)	0.100(0.100)
	1	0.279(0.943)	0.383(0.813)	0.385(0.657)	0.336(0.503)	0.267(0.367)
	2	0.051(0.994)	0.149(0.962)	0.238(0.895)	0.294(0.797)	0.311(0.679)
	3	0.005(1.000)	0.033(0.995)	0.084(0.979)	0.147(0.944)	0.208(0.886)
	4		0.005(1.000)	0.018(0.997)	0.046(0.990)	0.087(0.973)
	5			0.003(1.000)	0.009(0.999)	0.023(0.996)
	6				0.001(1.000)	0.004(1.000)
	7					
	8					

Table E.2 Binomial probability distribution

n	x	0.05	0.10	0.15	0.20	0.25
9	0	0.630(0.630)	0.387(0.387)	0.232(0.232)	0.134(0.134)	0.075(0.075)
	1	0.299(0.929)	0.387(0.775)	0.368(0.599)	0.302(0.436)	0.225(0.300)
	2	0.063(0.992)	0.172(0.947)	0.260(0.859)	0.302(0.738)	0.300(0.601)
	3	0.008(0.999)	0.045(0.992)	0.107(0.966)	0.176(0.914)	0.234(0.834)
	4	0.001(1.000)	0.007(0.999)	0.028(0.994)	0.066(0.980)	0.117(0.951)
	5		0.001(1.000)	0.005(0.999)	0.017(0.997)	0.039(0.990)
	6			0.001(1.000)	0.003(1.000)	0.009(0.999)
	7					0.001(1.000)
	8					
	9					
10	0	0.599(0.599)	0.349(0.349)	0.197(0.197)	0.107(0.107)	0.056(0.056)
	1	0.315(0.914)	0.387(0.736)	0.347(0.544)	0.268(0.376)	0.188(0.244)
	2	0.075(0.988)	0.194(0.930)	0.276(0.820)	0.302(0.678)	0.282(0.526)
	3	0.010(0.999)	0.057(0.987)	0.130(0.950)	0.201(0.879)	0.250(0.776)
	4	0.001(1.000)	0.011(0.998)	0.040(0.990)	0.088(0.967)	0.146(0.922)
	5		0.001(1.000)	0.008(0.999)	0.026(0.994)	0.058(0.980)
	6			0.001(1.000)	0.006(0.999)	0.016(0.996)
	7				0.001(1.000)	0.003(1.000)
	8					
	9					
	10					
11	0	0.569(0.569)	0.314(0.314)	0.167(0.167)	0.086(0.086)	0.042(0.042)
	1	0.329(0.898)	0.384(0.697)	0.325(0.492)	0.236(0.322)	0.155(0.197)
	2	0.087(0.985)	0.213(0.910)	0.287(0.779)	0.295(0.617)	0.258(0.455)
	3	0.014(0.998)	0.071(0.981)	0.152(0.931)	0.221(0.839)	0.258(0.713)
	4	0.001(1.000)	0.016(0.997)	0.054(0.984)	0.111(0.950)	0.172(0.885)
	5		0.002(1.000)	0.013(0.997)	0.039(0.988)	0.080(0.966)
	6			0.002(1.000)	0.010(0.998)	0.027(0.992)
	7				0.002(1.000)	0.006(0.999)
	8					0.001(1.000)
	9					
	10					
	11					
12	0	0.540(0.540)	0.282(0.282)	0.142(0.142)	0.069(0.069)	0.032(0.032)
	1	0.341(0.882)	0.377(0.659)	0.301(0.443)	0.206(0.275)	0.127(0.158)
	2	0.099(0.980)	0.230(0.889)	0.292(0.736)	0.283(0.558)	0.232(0.391)
	3	0.017(0.998)	0.085(0.974)	0.172(0.908)	0.236(0.795)	0.258(0.649)
	4	0.002(0.999)	0.021(0.996)	0.068(0.976)	0.133(0.927)	0.194(0.842)
	5	0.001(1.000)	0.004(0.999)	0.019(0.995)	0.053(0.981)	0.103(0.946)
	6		0.001(1.000)	0.004(0.999)	0.016(0.996)	0.040(0.986)
	7			0.001(1.000)	0.003(0.999)	0.011(0.997)
	8				0.001(1.000)	0.002(1.000)
	9					
	10					
	11					
	12					

(Continued on next page)

Table E.2 Binomial probability distribution

n	x	0.05	0.10	0.15	0.20	0.25
13	0	0.513(0.513)	0.254(0.254)	0.121(0.121)	0.055(0.055)	0.024(0.024)
	1	0.351(0.865)	0.367(0.621)	0.277(0.398)	0.179(0.234)	0.103(0.127)
	2	0.111(0.975)	0.245(0.866)	0.294(0.692)	0.268(0.502)	0.206(0.333)
	3	0.021(0.997)	0.100(0.966)	0.190(0.882)	0.246(0.747)	0.252(0.584)
	4	0.003(1.000)	0.028(0.994)	0.084(0.966)	0.154(0.901)	0.210(0.794)
	5		0.006(0.999)	0.027(0.992)	0.069(0.970)	0.126(0.920)
	6		0.001(1.000)	0.006(0.999)	0.023(0.993)	0.056(0.976)
	7			0.001(1.000)	0.006(0.999)	0.019(0.994)
	8				0.001(1.000)	0.005(0.999)
	9					0.001(1.000)
	10					
	11					
	12					
	13					
14	0	0.488(0.488)	0.229(0.229)	0.103(0.103)	0.044(0.044)	0.018(0.018)
	1	0.359(0.847)	0.356(0.585)	0.254(0.357)	0.154(0.198)	0.083(0.101)
	2	0.123(0.970)	0.257(0.842)	0.291(0.648)	0.250(0.448)	0.180(0.281)
	3	0.026(0.996)	0.114(0.956)	0.206(0.853)	0.250(0.698)	0.240(0.521)
	4	0.004(1.000)	0.035(0.991)	0.100(0.953)	0.172(0.870)	0.220(0.742)
	5		0.008(0.999)	0.035(0.988)	0.086(0.956)	0.147(0.888)
	6		0.001(1.000)	0.009(0.998)	0.032(0.988)	0.073(0.962)
	7			0.002(1.000)	0.009(0.998)	0.028(0.990)
	8				0.002(1.000)	0.008(0.998)
	9					0.002(1.000)
	10					
	11					
	12					
	13					
	14					
15	0	0.463(0.463)	0.206(0.206)	0.087(0.087)	0.035(0.035)	0.013(0.013)
	1	0.366(0.829)	0.343(0.549)	0.231(0.319)	0.132(0.167)	0.067(0.080)
	2	0.135(0.964)	0.267(0.816)	0.286(0.604)	0.231(0.398)	0.156(0.236)
	3	0.031(0.995)	0.129(0.944)	0.218(0.823)	0.250(0.648)	0.225(0.461)
	4	0.005(0.999)	0.043(0.987)	0.116(0.938)	0.188(0.836)	0.225(0.686)
	5	0.001(1.000)	0.010(0.998)	0.045(0.983)	0.103(0.939)	0.165(0.852)
	6		0.002(1.000)	0.013(0.996)	0.043(0.982)	0.092(0.943)
	7			0.003(0.999)	0.014(0.996)	0.039(0.983)
	8			0.001(1.000)	0.003(0.999)	0.013(0.996)
	9				0.001(1.000)	0.003(0.999)
	10					0.001(1.000)
	11					
	12					
	13					
	14					
	15					

Table E.2 Binomial probability distribution

n	x	0.30	0.35	0.40	0.45	0.50
1	0	0.700(0.700)	0.650(0.650)	0.600(0.600)	0.550(0.550)	0.500(0.500)
	1	0.300(1.000)	0.350(1.000)	0.400(1.000)	0.450(1.000)	0.500(1.000)
2	0	0.490(0.490)	0.423(0.423)	0.360(0.360)	0.303(0.303)	0.250(0.250)
	1	0.420(0.910)	0.455(0.877)	0.480(0.840)	0.495(0.798)	0.500(0.750)
	2	0.090(1.000)	0.122(1.000)	0.160(1.000)	0.203(1.000)	0.250(1.000)
3	0	0.343(0.343)	0.275(0.275)	0.216(0.216)	0.166(0.166)	0.125(0.125)
	1	0.441(0.784)	0.444(0.718)	0.432(0.648)	0.408(0.575)	0.375(0.500)
	2	0.189(0.973)	0.239(0.957)	0.288(0.936)	0.334(0.909)	0.375(0.875)
	3	0.027(1.000)	0.043(1.000)	0.064(1.000)	0.091(1.000)	0.125(1.000)
4	0	0.240(0.240)	0.179(0.179)	0.130(0.130)	0.092(0.092)	0.062(0.062)
	1	0.412(0.652)	0.384(0.563)	0.346(0.475)	0.299(0.391)	0.250(0.313)
	2	0.265(0.916)	0.311(0.874)	0.346(0.821)	0.368(0.759)	0.375(0.688)
	3	0.076(0.992)	0.111(0.985)	0.154(0.974)	0.200(0.959)	0.250(0.938)
	4	0.008(1.000)	0.015(1.000)	0.026(1.000)	0.041(1.000)	0.062(1.000)
5	0	0.168(0.168)	0.116(0.116)	0.078(0.078)	0.050(0.050)	0.031(0.031)
	1	0.360(0.528)	0.312(0.428)	0.259(0.337)	0.206(0.256)	0.156(0.187)
	2	0.309(0.837)	0.336(0.765)	0.346(0.683)	0.337(0.593)	0.312(0.500)
	3	0.132(0.969)	0.181(0.946)	0.230(0.913)	0.276(0.869)	0.312(0.812)
	4	0.028(0.998)	0.049(0.995)	0.077(0.990)	0.113(0.982)	0.156(0.969)
	5	0.002(1.000)	0.005(1.000)	0.010(1.000)	0.018(1.000)	0.031(1.000)
6	0	0.118(0.118)	0.075(0.075)	0.047(0.047)	0.028(0.028)	0.016(0.016)
	1	0.303(0.420)	0.244(0.319)	0.187(0.233)	0.136(0.164)	0.094(0.109)
	2	0.324(0.744)	0.328(0.647)	0.311(0.544)	0.278(0.442)	0.234(0.344)
	3	0.185(0.930)	0.235(0.883)	0.276(0.821)	0.303(0.745)	0.313(0.656)
	4	0.060(0.989)	0.095(0.978)	0.138(0.959)	0.186(0.931)	0.234(0.891)
	5	0.010(0.999)	0.020(0.998)	0.037(0.996)	0.061(0.992)	0.094(0.984)
	6	0.001(1.000)	0.002(1.000)	0.004(1.000)	0.008(1.000)	0.016(1.000)
7	0	0.082(0.082)	0.049(0.049)	0.028(0.028)	0.015(0.015)	0.008(0.008)
	1	0.247(0.329)	0.185(0.234)	0.131(0.159)	0.087(0.102)	0.055(0.063)
	2	0.318(0.647)	0.298(0.532)	0.261(0.420)	0.214(0.316)	0.164(0.227)
	3	0.227(0.874)	0.268(0.800)	0.290(0.710)	0.292(0.608)	0.273(0.500)
	4	0.097(0.971)	0.144(0.944)	0.194(0.904)	0.239(0.847)	0.273(0.773)
	5	0.025(0.996)	0.047(0.991)	0.077(0.981)	0.117(0.964)	0.164(0.938)
	6	0.004(1.000)	0.008(0.999)	0.017(0.998)	0.032(0.996)	0.055(0.992)
	7		0.001(1.000)	0.002(1.000)	0.004(1.000)	0.008(1.000)
8	0	0.058(0.058)	0.032(0.032)	0.017(0.017)	0.008(0.008)	0.004(0.004)
	1	0.198(0.255)	0.137(0.169)	0.090(0.106)	0.055(0.063)	0.031(0.035)
	2	0.296(0.552)	0.259(0.428)	0.209(0.315)	0.157(0.220)	0.109(0.145)
	3	0.254(0.806)	0.279(0.706)	0.279(0.594)	0.257(0.477)	0.219(0.363)
	4	0.136(0.942)	0.188(0.894)	0.232(0.826)	0.263(0.740)	0.273(0.637)
	5	0.047(0.989)	0.081(0.975)	0.124(0.950)	0.172(0.912)	0.219(0.855)
	6	0.010(0.999)	0.022(0.996)	0.041(0.991)	0.070(0.982)	0.109(0.965)
	7	0.001(1.000)	0.003(1.000)	0.008(0.999)	0.016(0.998)	0.031(0.996)
	8			0.001(1.000)	0.002(1.000)	0.004(1.000)

(Continued on next page)

Table E.2 Binomial probability distribution

n	x	0.30	0.35	0.40	0.45	0.50
9	0	0.040(0.040)	0.021(0.021)	0.010(0.010)	0.005(0.005)	0.002(0.002)
	1	0.156(0.196)	0.100(0.121)	0.060(0.071)	0.034(0.039)	0.018(0.020)
	2	0.267(0.463)	0.216(0.337)	0.161(0.232)	0.111(0.150)	0.070(0.090)
	3	0.267(0.730)	0.272(0.609)	0.251(0.483)	0.212(0.361)	0.164(0.254)
	4	0.172(0.901)	0.219(0.828)	0.251(0.733)	0.260(0.621)	0.246(0.500)
	5	0.074(0.975)	0.118(0.946)	0.167(0.901)	0.213(0.834)	0.246(0.746)
	6	0.021(0.996)	0.042(0.989)	0.074(0.975)	0.116(0.950)	0.164(0.910)
	7	0.004(1.000)	0.010(0.999)	0.021(0.996)	0.041(0.991)	0.070(0.980)
	8		0.001(1.000)	0.004(1.000)	0.008(0.999)	0.018(0.998)
	9				0.001(1.000)	0.002(1.000)
10	0	0.028(0.028)	0.013(0.013)	0.006(0.006)	0.003(0.003)	0.001(0.001)
	1	0.121(0.149)	0.072(0.086)	0.040(0.046)	0.021(0.023)	0.010(0.011)
	2	0.233(0.383)	0.176(0.262)	0.121(0.167)	0.076(0.100)	0.044(0.055)
	3	0.267(0.650)	0.252(0.514)	0.215(0.382)	0.166(0.266)	0.117(0.172)
	4	0.200(0.850)	0.238(0.751)	0.251(0.633)	0.238(0.504)	0.205(0.377)
	5	0.103(0.953)	0.154(0.905)	0.201(0.834)	0.234(0.738)	0.246(0.623)
	6	0.037(0.989)	0.069(0.974)	0.111(0.945)	0.160(0.898)	0.205(0.828)
	7	0.009(0.998)	0.021(0.995)	0.042(0.988)	0.075(0.973)	0.117(0.945)
	8	0.001(1.000)	0.004(0.999)	0.011(0.998)	0.023(0.995)	0.044(0.989)
	9		0.001(1.000)	0.002(1.000)	0.004(1.000)	0.010(0.999)
	10					0.001(1.000)
11	0	0.020(0.020)	0.009(0.009)	0.004(0.004)	0.001(0.001)	
	1	0.093(0.113)	0.052(0.061)	0.027(0.030)	0.013(0.014)	0.005(0.006)
	2	0.200(0.313)	0.140(0.200)	0.089(0.119)	0.051(0.065)	0.027(0.033)
	3	0.257(0.570)	0.225(0.426)	0.177(0.296)	0.126(0.191)	0.081(0.113)
	4	0.220(0.790)	0.243(0.668)	0.236(0.533)	0.206(0.397)	0.161(0.274)
	5	0.132(0.922)	0.183(0.851)	0.221(0.753)	0.236(0.633)	0.226(0.500)
	6	0.057(0.978)	0.099(0.950)	0.147(0.901)	0.193(0.826)	0.226(0.726)
	7	0.017(0.996)	0.038(0.988)	0.070(0.971)	0.113(0.939)	0.161(0.887)
	8	0.004(0.999)	0.010(0.998)	0.023(0.994)	0.046(0.985)	0.081(0.967)
	9	0.001(1.000)	0.002(1.000)	0.005(0.999)	0.013(0.998)	0.027(0.994)
	10			0.001(1.000)	0.002(1.000)	0.005(1.000)
	11					
12	0	0.014(0.014)	0.006(0.006)	0.002(0.002)	0.001(0.001)	
	1	0.071(0.085)	0.037(0.042)	0.017(0.020)	0.008(0.008)	0.003(0.003)
	2	0.168(0.253)	0.109(0.151)	0.064(0.083)	0.034(0.042)	0.016(0.019)
	3	0.240(0.493)	0.195(0.347)	0.142(0.225)	0.092(0.134)	0.054(0.073)
	4	0.231(0.724)	0.237(0.583)	0.213(0.438)	0.170(0.304)	0.121(0.194)
	5	0.158(0.882)	0.204(0.787)	0.227(0.665)	0.222(0.527)	0.193(0.387)
	6	0.079(0.961)	0.128(0.915)	0.177(0.842)	0.212(0.739)	0.226(0.613)
	7	0.029(0.991)	0.059(0.974)	0.101(0.943)	0.149(0.888)	0.193(0.806)
	8	0.008(0.998)	0.020(0.994)	0.042(0.985)	0.076(0.964)	0.121(0.927)
	9	0.001(1.000)	0.005(0.999)	0.012(0.997)	0.028(0.992)	0.054(0.981)
	10		0.001(1.000)	0.002(1.000)	0.007(0.999)	0.016(0.997)
	11				0.001(1.000)	0.003(1.000)
	12					

Table E.2 Binomial probability distribution

n	x	0.30	0.35	0.40	0.45	0.50
13	0	0.010(0.010)	0.004(0.004)	0.001(0.001)		
	1	0.054(0.064)	0.026(0.030)	0.011(0.013)	0.004(0.005)	0.002(0.002)
	2	0.139(0.202)	0.084(0.113)	0.045(0.058)	0.022(0.027)	0.010(0.011)
	3	0.218(0.421)	0.165(0.278)	0.111(0.169)	0.066(0.093)	0.035(0.046)
	4	0.234(0.654)	0.222(0.501)	0.184(0.353)	0.135(0.228)	0.087(0.133)
	5	0.180(0.835)	0.215(0.716)	0.221(0.574)	0.199(0.427)	0.157(0.291)
	6	0.103(0.938)	0.155(0.871)	0.197(0.771)	0.217(0.644)	0.209(0.500)
	7	0.044(0.982)	0.083(0.954)	0.131(0.902)	0.177(0.821)	0.209(0.709)
	8	0.014(0.996)	0.034(0.987)	0.066(0.968)	0.109(0.930)	0.157(0.867)
	9	0.003(0.999)	0.010(0.997)	0.024(0.992)	0.050(0.980)	0.087(0.954)
	10	0.001(1.000)	0.002(1.000)	0.006(0.999)	0.016(0.996)	0.035(0.989)
	11			0.001(1.000)	0.004(0.999)	0.010(0.998)
	12					0.002(1.000)
	13					
14	0	0.007(0.007)	0.002(0.002)	0.001(0.001)		
	1	0.041(0.047)	0.018(0.021)	0.007(0.008)	0.003(0.003)	0.001(0.001)
	2	0.113(0.161)	0.063(0.084)	0.032(0.040)	0.014(0.017)	0.006(0.006)
	3	0.194(0.355)	0.137(0.220)	0.085(0.124)	0.046(0.063)	0.022(0.029)
	4	0.229(0.584)	0.202(0.423)	0.155(0.279)	0.104(0.167)	0.061(0.090)
	5	0.196(0.781)	0.218(0.641)	0.207(0.486)	0.170(0.337)	0.122(0.212)
	6	0.126(0.907)	0.176(0.816)	0.207(0.692)	0.209(0.546)	0.183(0.395)
	7	0.062(0.969)	0.108(0.925)	0.157(0.850)	0.195(0.741)	0.209(0.605)
	8	0.023(0.992)	0.051(0.976)	0.092(0.942)	0.140(0.881)	0.183(0.788)
	9	0.007(0.998)	0.018(0.994)	0.041(0.982)	0.076(0.957)	0.122(0.910)
	10	0.001(1.000)	0.005(0.999)	0.014(0.996)	0.031(0.989)	0.061(0.971)
	11		0.001(1.000)	0.003(0.999)	0.009(0.998)	0.022(0.994)
	12			0.001(1.000)	0.002(1.000)	0.006(0.999)
	13					0.001(1.000)
	14					
15	0	0.005(0.005)	0.002(0.002)			
	1	0.031(0.035)	0.013(0.014)	0.005(0.005)	0.002(0.002)	
	2	0.092(0.127)	0.048(0.062)	0.022(0.027)	0.009(0.011)	0.003(0.004)
	3	0.170(0.297)	0.111(0.173)	0.063(0.091)	0.032(0.042)	0.014(0.018)
	4	0.219(0.515)	0.179(0.352)	0.127(0.217)	0.078(0.120)	0.042(0.059)
	5	0.206(0.722)	0.212(0.564)	0.186(0.403)	0.140(0.261)	0.092(0.151)
	6	0.147(0.869)	0.191(0.755)	0.207(0.610)	0.191(0.452)	0.153(0.304)
	7	0.081(0.950)	0.132(0.887)	0.177(0.787)	0.201(0.654)	0.196(0.500)
	8	0.035(0.985)	0.071(0.958)	0.118(0.905)	0.165(0.818)	0.196(0.696)
	9	0.012(0.996)	0.030(0.988)	0.061(0.966)	0.105(0.923)	0.153(0.849)
	10	0.003(0.999)	0.010(0.997)	0.024(0.991)	0.051(0.975)	0.092(0.941)
	11	0.001(1.000)	0.002(1.000)	0.007(0.998)	0.019(0.994)	0.042(0.982)
	12			0.002(1.000)	0.005(0.999)	0.014(0.996)
	13				0.001(1.000)	0.003(1.000)
	14					
	15					

(Continued on next page)

Table E.2 Binomial probability distribution

n	x	0.55	0.60	0.65	0.70	0.75
1	0	0.450(0.450)	0.400(0.400)	0.350(0.350)	0.300(0.300)	0.250(0.250)
	1	0.550(1.000)	0.600(1.000)	0.650(1.000)	0.700(1.000)	0.750(1.000)
2	0	0.202(0.202)	0.160(0.160)	0.122(0.122)	0.090(0.090)	0.062(0.062)
	1	0.495(0.698)	0.480(0.640)	0.455(0.577)	0.420(0.510)	0.375(0.438)
	2	0.303(1.000)	0.360(1.000)	0.423(1.000)	0.490(1.000)	0.562(1.000)
3	0	0.091(0.091)	0.064(0.064)	0.043(0.043)	0.027(0.027)	0.016(0.016)
	1	0.334(0.425)	0.288(0.352)	0.239(0.282)	0.189(0.216)	0.141(0.156)
	2	0.408(0.834)	0.432(0.784)	0.444(0.725)	0.441(0.657)	0.422(0.578)
	3	0.166(1.000)	0.216(1.000)	0.275(1.000)	0.343(1.000)	0.422(1.000)
4	0	0.041(0.041)	0.026(0.026)	0.015(0.015)	0.008(0.008)	0.004(0.004)
	1	0.200(0.241)	0.154(0.179)	0.111(0.126)	0.076(0.084)	0.047(0.051)
	2	0.368(0.609)	0.346(0.525)	0.311(0.437)	0.265(0.348)	0.211(0.262)
	3	0.299(0.908)	0.346(0.870)	0.384(0.821)	0.412(0.760)	0.422(0.684)
	4	0.092(1.000)	0.130(1.000)	0.179(1.000)	0.240(1.000)	0.316(1.000)
5	0	0.018(0.018)	0.010(0.010)	0.005(0.005)	0.002(0.002)	0.001(0.001)
	1	0.113(0.131)	0.077(0.087)	0.049(0.054)	0.028(0.031)	0.015(0.016)
	2	0.276(0.407)	0.230(0.317)	0.181(0.235)	0.132(0.163)	0.088(0.104)
	3	0.337(0.744)	0.346(0.663)	0.336(0.572)	0.309(0.472)	0.264(0.367)
	4	0.206(0.950)	0.259(0.922)	0.312(0.884)	0.360(0.832)	0.396(0.763)
	5	0.050(1.000)	0.078(1.000)	0.116(1.000)	0.168(1.000)	0.237(1.000)
6	0	0.008(0.008)	0.004(0.004)	0.002(0.002)	0.001(0.001)	
	1	0.061(0.069)	0.037(0.041)	0.020(0.022)	0.010(0.011)	0.004(0.005)
	2	0.186(0.255)	0.138(0.179)	0.095(0.117)	0.060(0.070)	0.033(0.038)
	3	0.303(0.558)	0.276(0.456)	0.235(0.353)	0.185(0.256)	0.132(0.169)
	4	0.278(0.836)	0.311(0.767)	0.328(0.681)	0.324(0.580)	0.297(0.466)
	5	0.136(0.972)	0.187(0.953)	0.244(0.925)	0.303(0.882)	0.356(0.822)
	6	0.028(1.000)	0.047(1.000)	0.075(1.000)	0.118(1.000)	0.178(1.000)
7	0	0.004(0.004)	0.002(0.002)	0.001(0.001)		
	1	0.032(0.036)	0.017(0.019)	0.008(0.009)	0.004(0.004)	0.001(0.001)
	2	0.117(0.153)	0.077(0.096)	0.047(0.056)	0.025(0.029)	0.012(0.013)
	3	0.239(0.392)	0.194(0.290)	0.144(0.200)	0.097(0.126)	0.058(0.071)
	4	0.292(0.684)	0.290(0.580)	0.268(0.468)	0.227(0.353)	0.173(0.244)
	5	0.214(0.898)	0.261(0.841)	0.298(0.766)	0.318(0.671)	0.311(0.555)
	6	0.087(0.985)	0.131(0.972)	0.185(0.951)	0.247(0.918)	0.311(0.867)
	7	0.015(1.000)	0.028(1.000)	0.049(1.000)	0.082(1.000)	0.133(1.000)
8	0	0.002(0.002)	0.001(0.001)			
	1	0.016(0.018)	0.008(0.009)	0.003(0.004)	0.001(0.001)	
	2	0.070(0.088)	0.041(0.050)	0.022(0.025)	0.010(0.011)	0.004(0.004)
	3	0.172(0.260)	0.124(0.174)	0.081(0.106)	0.047(0.058)	0.023(0.027)
	4	0.263(0.523)	0.232(0.406)	0.188(0.294)	0.136(0.194)	0.087(0.114)
	5	0.257(0.780)	0.279(0.685)	0.279(0.572)	0.254(0.448)	0.208(0.321)
	6	0.157(0.937)	0.209(0.894)	0.259(0.831)	0.296(0.745)	0.311(0.633)
	7	0.055(0.992)	0.090(0.983)	0.137(0.968)	0.198(0.942)	0.267(0.900)
	8	0.008(1.000)	0.017(1.000)	0.032(1.000)	0.058(1.000)	0.100(1.000)

Table E.2 Binomial probability distribution

n	x	0.55	0.60	0.65	0.70	0.75
9	0	0.001(0.001)				
	1	0.008(0.009)	0.004(0.004)	0.001(0.001)		
	2	0.041(0.050)	0.021(0.025)	0.010(0.011)	0.004(0.004)	0.001(0.001)
	3	0.116(0.166)	0.074(0.099)	0.042(0.054)	0.021(0.025)	0.009(0.010)
	4	0.213(0.379)	0.167(0.267)	0.118(0.172)	0.074(0.099)	0.039(0.049)
	5	0.260(0.639)	0.251(0.517)	0.219(0.391)	0.172(0.270)	0.117(0.166)
	6	0.212(0.850)	0.251(0.768)	0.272(0.663)	0.267(0.537)	0.234(0.399)
	7	0.111(0.961)	0.161(0.929)	0.216(0.879)	0.267(0.804)	0.300(0.700)
	8	0.034(0.995)	0.060(0.990)	0.100(0.979)	0.156(0.960)	0.225(0.925)
	9	0.005(1.000)	0.010(1.000)	0.021(1.000)	0.040(1.000)	0.075(1.000)
10	0					
	1	0.004(0.005)	0.002(0.002)	0.001(0.001)		
	2	0.023(0.027)	0.011(0.012)	0.004(0.005)	0.001(0.002)	
	3	0.075(0.102)	0.042(0.055)	0.021(0.026)	0.009(0.011)	0.003(0.004)
	4	0.160(0.262)	0.111(0.166)	0.069(0.095)	0.037(0.047)	0.016(0.020)
	5	0.234(0.496)	0.201(0.367)	0.154(0.249)	0.103(0.150)	0.058(0.078)
	6	0.238(0.734)	0.251(0.618)	0.238(0.486)	0.200(0.350)	0.146(0.224)
	7	0.166(0.900)	0.215(0.833)	0.252(0.738)	0.267(0.617)	0.250(0.474)
	8	0.076(0.977)	0.121(0.954)	0.176(0.914)	0.233(0.851)	0.282(0.756)
	9	0.021(0.997)	0.040(0.994)	0.072(0.987)	0.121(0.972)	0.188(0.944)
	10	0.003(1.000)	0.006(1.000)	0.013(1.000)	0.028(1.000)	0.056(1.000)
11	0					
	1	0.002(0.002)	0.001(0.001)			
	2	0.013(0.015)	0.005(0.006)	0.002(0.002)	0.001(0.001)	
	3	0.046(0.061)	0.023(0.029)	0.010(0.012)	0.004(0.004)	0.001(0.001)
	4	0.113(0.174)	0.070(0.099)	0.038(0.050)	0.017(0.022)	0.006(0.008)
	5	0.193(0.367)	0.147(0.247)	0.099(0.149)	0.057(0.078)	0.027(0.034)
	6	0.236(0.603)	0.221(0.467)	0.183(0.332)	0.132(0.210)	0.080(0.115)
	7	0.206(0.809)	0.236(0.704)	0.243(0.574)	0.220(0.430)	0.172(0.287)
	8	0.126(0.935)	0.177(0.881)	0.225(0.800)	0.257(0.687)	0.258(0.545)
	9	0.051(0.986)	0.089(0.970)	0.140(0.939)	0.200(0.887)	0.258(0.803)
	10	0.013(0.999)	0.027(0.996)	0.052(0.991)	0.093(0.980)	0.155(0.958)
	11	0.001(1.000)	0.004(1.000)	0.009(1.000)	0.020(1.000)	0.042(1.000)
12	0					
	1	0.001(0.001)				
	2	0.007(0.008)	0.002(0.003)	0.001(0.001)		
	3	0.028(0.036)	0.012(0.015)	0.005(0.006)	0.001(0.002)	
	4	0.076(0.112)	0.042(0.057)	0.020(0.026)	0.008(0.009)	0.002(0.003)
	5	0.149(0.261)	0.101(0.158)	0.059(0.085)	0.029(0.039)	0.011(0.014)
	6	0.212(0.473)	0.177(0.335)	0.128(0.213)	0.079(0.118)	0.040(0.054)
	7	0.222(0.696)	0.227(0.562)	0.204(0.417)	0.158(0.276)	0.103(0.158)
	8	0.170(0.866)	0.213(0.775)	0.237(0.653)	0.231(0.507)	0.194(0.351)
	9	0.092(0.958)	0.142(0.917)	0.195(0.849)	0.240(0.747)	0.258(0.609)
	10	0.034(0.992)	0.064(0.980)	0.109(0.958)	0.168(0.915)	0.232(0.842)
	11	0.008(0.999)	0.017(0.998)	0.037(0.994)	0.071(0.986)	0.127(0.968)
	12	0.001(1.000)	0.002(1.000)	0.006(1.000)	0.014(1.000)	0.032(1.000)

(Continued on next page)

Table E.2 Binomial probability distribution

n	x	0.55	0.60	0.65	0.70	0.75
13	0					
	1					
	2	0.004(0.004)	0.001(0.001)			
	3	0.016(0.020)	0.006(0.008)	0.002(0.003)	0.001(0.001)	
	4	0.050(0.070)	0.024(0.032)	0.010(0.013)	0.003(0.004)	0.001(0.001)
	5	0.109(0.179)	0.066(0.098)	0.034(0.046)	0.014(0.018)	0.005(0.006)
	6	0.177(0.356)	0.131(0.229)	0.083(0.129)	0.044(0.062)	0.019(0.024)
	7	0.217(0.573)	0.197(0.426)	0.155(0.284)	0.103(0.165)	0.056(0.080)
	8	0.199(0.772)	0.221(0.647)	0.215(0.499)	0.180(0.346)	0.126(0.206)
	9	0.135(0.907)	0.184(0.831)	0.222(0.722)	0.234(0.579)	0.210(0.416)
	10	0.066(0.973)	0.111(0.942)	0.165(0.887)	0.218(0.798)	0.252(0.667)
	11	0.022(0.995)	0.045(0.987)	0.084(0.970)	0.139(0.936)	0.206(0.873)
	12	0.004(1.000)	0.011(0.999)	0.026(0.996)	0.054(0.990)	0.103(0.976)
	13		0.001(1.000)	0.004(1.000)	0.010(1.000)	0.024(1.000)
14	0					
	1					
	2	0.002(0.002)	0.001(0.001)			
	3	0.009(0.011)	0.003(0.004)	0.001(0.001)		
	4	0.031(0.043)	0.014(0.018)	0.005(0.006)	0.001(0.002)	
	5	0.076(0.119)	0.041(0.058)	0.018(0.024)	0.007(0.008)	0.002(0.002)
	6	0.140(0.259)	0.092(0.150)	0.051(0.075)	0.023(0.031)	0.008(0.010)
	7	0.195(0.454)	0.157(0.308)	0.108(0.184)	0.062(0.093)	0.028(0.038)
	8	0.209(0.663)	0.207(0.514)	0.176(0.359)	0.126(0.219)	0.073(0.112)
	9	0.170(0.833)	0.207(0.721)	0.218(0.577)	0.196(0.416)	0.147(0.258)
	10	0.104(0.937)	0.155(0.876)	0.202(0.780)	0.229(0.645)	0.220(0.479)
	11	0.046(0.983)	0.085(0.960)	0.137(0.916)	0.194(0.839)	0.240(0.719)
	12	0.014(0.997)	0.032(0.992)	0.063(0.979)	0.113(0.953)	0.180(0.899)
	13	0.003(1.000)	0.007(0.999)	0.018(0.998)	0.041(0.993)	0.083(0.982)
	14		0.001(1.000)	0.002(1.000)	0.007(1.000)	0.018(1.000)
15	0					
	1					
	2	0.001(0.001)				
	3	0.005(0.006)	0.002(0.002)			
	4	0.019(0.025)	0.007(0.009)	0.002(0.003)	0.001(0.001)	
	5	0.051(0.077)	0.024(0.034)	0.010(0.012)	0.003(0.004)	0.001(0.001)
	6	0.105(0.182)	0.061(0.095)	0.030(0.042)	0.012(0.015)	0.003(0.004)
	7	0.165(0.346)	0.118(0.213)	0.071(0.113)	0.035(0.050)	0.013(0.017)
	8	0.201(0.548)	0.177(0.390)	0.132(0.245)	0.081(0.131)	0.039(0.057)
	9	0.191(0.739)	0.207(0.597)	0.191(0.436)	0.147(0.278)	0.092(0.148)
	10	0.140(0.880)	0.186(0.783)	0.212(0.648)	0.206(0.485)	0.165(0.314)
	11	0.078(0.958)	0.127(0.909)	0.179(0.827)	0.219(0.703)	0.225(0.539)
	12	0.032(0.989)	0.063(0.973)	0.111(0.938)	0.170(0.873)	0.225(0.764)
	13	0.009(0.998)	0.022(0.995)	0.048(0.986)	0.092(0.965)	0.156(0.920)
	14	0.002(1.000)	0.005(1.000)	0.013(0.998)	0.031(0.995)	0.067(0.987)
	15			0.002(1.000)	0.005(1.000)	0.013(1.000)

Table E.2 Binomial probability distribution

n	x	0.80	0.85	0.90	0.95
1	0	0.200(0.200)	0.150(0.150)	0.100(0.100)	0.050(0.050)
	1	0.800(1.000)	0.850(1.000)	0.900(1.000)	0.950(1.000)
2	0	0.040(0.040)	0.023(0.023)	0.010(0.010)	0.003(0.003)
	1	0.320(0.360)	0.255(0.278)	0.180(0.190)	0.095(0.098)
	2	0.640(1.000)	0.722(1.000)	0.810(1.000)	0.902(1.000)
3	0	0.008(0.008)	0.003(0.003)	0.001(0.001)	
	1	0.096(0.104)	0.057(0.061)	0.027(0.028)	0.007(0.007)
	2	0.384(0.488)	0.325(0.386)	0.243(0.271)	0.135(0.143)
	3	0.512(1.000)	0.614(1.000)	0.729(1.000)	0.857(1.000)
4	0	0.002(0.002)	0.001(0.001)		
	1	0.026(0.027)	0.011(0.012)	0.004(0.004)	
	2	0.154(0.181)	0.098(0.110)	0.049(0.052)	0.014(0.014)
	3	0.410(0.590)	0.368(0.478)	0.292(0.344)	0.171(0.185)
	4	0.410(1.000)	0.522(1.000)	0.656(1.000)	0.815(1.000)
5	0				
	1	0.006(0.007)	0.002(0.002)		
	2	0.051(0.058)	0.024(0.027)	0.008(0.009)	0.001(0.001)
	3	0.205(0.263)	0.138(0.165)	0.073(0.081)	0.021(0.023)
	4	0.410(0.672)	0.392(0.556)	0.328(0.410)	0.204(0.226)
	5	0.328(1.000)	0.444(1.000)	0.590(1.000)	0.774(1.000)
6	0				
	1	0.002(0.002)			
	2	0.015(0.017)	0.005(0.006)	0.001(0.001)	
	3	0.082(0.099)	0.041(0.047)	0.015(0.016)	0.002(0.002)
	4	0.246(0.345)	0.176(0.224)	0.098(0.114)	0.031(0.033)
	5	0.393(0.738)	0.399(0.623)	0.354(0.469)	0.232(0.265)
	6	0.262(1.000)	0.377(1.000)	0.531(1.000)	0.735(1.000)
7	0				
	1				
	2	0.004(0.005)	0.001(0.001)		
	3	0.029(0.033)	0.011(0.012)	0.003(0.003)	
	4	0.115(0.148)	0.062(0.074)	0.023(0.026)	0.004(0.004)
	5	0.275(0.423)	0.210(0.283)	0.124(0.150)	0.041(0.044)
	6	0.367(0.790)	0.396(0.679)	0.372(0.522)	0.257(0.302)
	7	0.210(1.000)	0.321(1.000)	0.478(1.000)	0.698(1.000)
8	0				
	1				
	2	0.001(0.001)			
	3	0.009(0.010)	0.003(0.003)		
	4	0.046(0.056)	0.018(0.021)	0.005(0.005)	
	5	0.147(0.203)	0.084(0.105)	0.033(0.038)	0.005(0.006)
	6	0.294(0.497)	0.238(0.343)	0.149(0.187)	0.051(0.057)
	7	0.336(0.832)	0.385(0.728)	0.383(0.570)	0.279(0.337)
	8	0.168(1.000)	0.272(1.000)	0.430(1.000)	0.663(1.000)

(Continued on next page)

Table E.2 Binomial probability distribution

n	x	0.80	0.85	0.90	0.95
9	0				
	1				
	2				
	3	0.003(0.003)	0.001(0.001)		
	4	0.017(0.020)	0.005(0.006)	0.001(0.001)	
	5	0.066(0.086)	0.028(0.034)	0.007(0.008)	0.001(0.001)
	6	0.176(0.262)	0.107(0.141)	0.045(0.053)	0.008(0.008)
	7	0.302(0.564)	0.260(0.401)	0.172(0.225)	0.063(0.071)
	8	0.302(0.866)	0.368(0.768)	0.387(0.613)	0.299(0.370)
	9	0.134(1.000)	0.232(1.000)	0.387(1.000)	0.630(1.000)
10	0				
	1				
	2				
	3	0.001(0.001)			
	4	0.006(0.006)	0.001(0.001)		
	5	0.026(0.033)	0.008(0.010)	0.001(0.002)	
	6	0.088(0.121)	0.040(0.050)	0.011(0.013)	0.001(0.001)
	7	0.201(0.322)	0.130(0.180)	0.057(0.070)	0.010(0.012)
	8	0.302(0.624)	0.276(0.456)	0.194(0.264)	0.075(0.086)
	9	0.268(0.893)	0.347(0.803)	0.387(0.651)	0.315(0.401)
	10	0.107(1.000)	0.197(1.000)	0.349(1.000)	0.599(1.000)
11	0				
	1				
	2				
	3				
	4	0.002(0.002)			
	5	0.010(0.012)	0.002(0.003)		
	6	0.039(0.050)	0.013(0.016)	0.002(0.003)	
	7	0.111(0.161)	0.054(0.069)	0.016(0.019)	0.001(0.002)
	8	0.221(0.383)	0.152(0.221)	0.071(0.090)	0.014(0.015)
	9	0.295(0.678)	0.287(0.508)	0.213(0.303)	0.087(0.102)
	10	0.236(0.914)	0.325(0.833)	0.384(0.686)	0.329(0.431)
	11	0.086(1.000)	0.167(1.000)	0.314(1.000)	0.569(1.000)
12	0				
	1				
	2				
	3				
	4	0.001(0.001)			
	5	0.003(0.004)	0.001(0.001)		
	6	0.016(0.019)	0.004(0.005)		
	7	0.053(0.073)	0.019(0.024)	0.004(0.004)	
	8	0.133(0.205)	0.068(0.092)	0.021(0.026)	0.002(0.002)
	9	0.236(0.442)	0.172(0.264)	0.085(0.111)	0.017(0.020)
	10	0.283(0.725)	0.292(0.557)	0.230(0.341)	0.099(0.118)
	11	0.206(0.931)	0.301(0.858)	0.377(0.718)	0.341(0.460)
	12	0.069(1.000)	0.142(1.000)	0.282(1.000)	0.540(1.000)

Table E.2 Binomial probability distribution

n	x	0.80	0.85	0.90	0.95
13	0				
	1				
	2				
	3				
	4				
	5	0.001(0.001)			
	6	0.006(0.007)	0.001(0.001)		
	7	0.023(0.030)	0.006(0.008)	0.001(0.001)	
	8	0.069(0.099)	0.027(0.034)	0.006(0.006)	
	9	0.154(0.253)	0.084(0.118)	0.028(0.034)	0.003(0.003)
	10	0.246(0.498)	0.190(0.308)	0.100(0.134)	0.021(0.025)
	11	0.268(0.766)	0.294(0.602)	0.245(0.379)	0.111(0.135)
	12	0.179(0.945)	0.277(0.879)	0.367(0.746)	0.351(0.487)
	13	0.055(1.000)	0.121(1.000)	0.254(1.000)	0.513(1.000)
14	0				
	1				
	2				
	3				
	4				
	5				
	6	0.002(0.002)			
	7	0.009(0.012)	0.002(0.002)		
	8	0.032(0.044)	0.009(0.012)	0.001(0.001)	
	9	0.086(0.130)	0.035(0.047)	0.008(0.009)	
	10	0.172(0.302)	0.100(0.147)	0.035(0.044)	0.004(0.004)
	11	0.250(0.552)	0.206(0.352)	0.114(0.158)	0.026(0.030)
	12	0.250(0.802)	0.291(0.643)	0.257(0.415)	0.123(0.153)
	13	0.154(0.956)	0.254(0.897)	0.356(0.771)	0.359(0.512)
	14	0.044(1.000)	0.103(1.000)	0.229(1.000)	0.488(1.000)
15	0				
	1				
	2				
	3				
	4				
	5				
	6	0.001(0.001)			
	7	0.003(0.004)	0.001(0.001)		
	8	0.014(0.018)	0.003(0.004)		
	9	0.043(0.061)	0.013(0.017)	0.002(0.002)	
	10	0.103(0.164)	0.045(0.062)	0.010(0.013)	0.001(0.001)
	11	0.188(0.352)	0.116(0.177)	0.043(0.056)	0.005(0.005)
	12	0.250(0.602)	0.218(0.396)	0.129(0.184)	0.031(0.036)
	13	0.231(0.833)	0.286(0.681)	0.267(0.451)	0.135(0.171)
	14	0.132(0.965)	0.231(0.913)	0.343(0.794)	0.366(0.537)
	15	0.035(1.000)	0.087(1.000)	0.206(1.000)	0.463(1.000)

Appendix F

Development Flow for an Automotive Organization

This appendix identifies the flow of development to job one for a typical, large manufacturing organization. It is important to see how the development may be tracked on parallel lines with both the DMAIC and the DCOV model of the six sigma methodology. At any point of this flow, there is an opportunity to apply the six sigma methodology for improvement. If it is done ahead of the problem, the DCOV will apply. On the other hand, if it is done as a corrective action of a problem, then the DMAIC model will apply. So in a typical large (automotive) manufacturing organization, we have:

Concept development

Program start: Basic business plan objectives and constraints are identified and incorporated into the corporate strategic planning.

Deliverables/Requirements
1. Brand vision/marketing plans
    a. Proposed marketing strategy complete
    b. Brand identity model/concept direction alignment complete
    c. Preliminary service readiness plan
2. Program definition
    a. Stable and balanced long-range product plan published
    b. Initial top-down vehicle level targets established
    c. Vision paper complete
    d. Manufacturing and assembly plant alternatives identified business planning and approvals
3. Business planning and approvals
    a. Initial long-lead projects and early funding approval complete
4. Program planning and resource management
    a. Up-front study team established
    b. Resource requirements identified

5. Design and development
   a. Potential product alternatives and concept direction

6. Production preparation
   a. Preliminary part installations assessment

7. Program and process assessment
   a. Program assessment (function, product cost program cost, timing and process conformance)
   b. Lessons learned, documented and shared

Confirm program vision: Basic business plan objectives and constraints confirmed to a elect strategic corporate direction. Strategic plan may be reviewed, modified and/or abandoned at this point.

Deliverables/Requirements

1. Brand vision/marketing plans
   a. Product/process/service customer requirements identified
   b. Unique must-haves for brand differentiation consensed
   c. Service tool requirements identified

2. Program definition
   a. Product/process/service product plan usage and configurations
   b. Initial program vision document
   c. Preliminary product/service functional objectives
   d. Major system initial cost targets derived
   e. Strategy for cost-setting and management documented
   f. If a manufactured product, manufacturing and assembly plants selected

3. Business planning and approvals
   a. Preliminary business requirements and objectives
   b. Program business rules and procedures defined

4. Program planning and resource management
   a. Product/process/service product assurance team established
   b. Initial product/process/service; product assurance plan
   c. Preliminary resource allocation plan

5. Design and development
   a. Preliminary package
   b. Process alternatives
   c. Interchangeability of parts and/or part-sharing across primary brands identified

6. Production preparation
   a. Initial strategy complete

7. Sourcing and logistics
   a. Preliminary sourcing plan for product and process
8. Build and test
   a. Initial product/process/service test strategy and plan
9. Program and process assessment
   a. Program assessment (function, product cost, program cost, timing and process conformance)
   b. Lessons learned, documented and shared

Preliminary program specifications: General product proportion and hard-points, concept direction and preliminary program objectives approved. If necessary, begin multiple theme development.

Deliverables/Requirements
1. Brand vision/marketing plans
   a. Customer requirements updated and component and system customer requirements defined
   b. Product theme research complete
   c. Content trade-off pricing complete
   d. Service parts delivery plan complete
2. Program definition
   a. Preliminary system and component functional objectives and performance standards, and product functional objectives and performance standards complete
   b. Balanced, top-down program targets established
   c. If applicable, product and process technology availability and applicability identified
3. Business planning and approvals
   a. Long lead projects approved for design complete
   b. Program planning and resource management
   c. System and key component product assurance teams established
   d. Initial system and key component product assurance plans
   e. Resource allocation plan complete
4. Design and development
   a. Packaging reviewed and/or updated and basic package hard-points complete
   b. List of new or modified systems and key components
   c. Carryover parts, subsystems from other programs under primary brand complete
   d. Preliminary system and component design FMEAs and key characteristics
   e. Preliminary system and component designs and technical descriptions
   f. If manufacturing, initial manufacturing and assembly process design and analytical studies

5. Production preparation
   a. Manufacturing and assembly systems requirements identified

6. Sourcing and logistics
   a. Preselect packages completed
   b. Material handling strategy
   c. If necessary, material control systems requirements identified
   d. Supplier sourcing plan complete and key suppliers selected
   e. If union representation, program overview and directional sourcing review scheduled

7. Build and test
   a. System and component test plans complete
   b. Preliminary product, system and component engineering design (ED) testing, simulation and analysis results
   c. If applicable, dimensional control plans
   d. If applicable, preliminary product build plans and appropriate tool plan
   e. If applicable, preliminary quality measurement plan

8. Program and process assessment
   a. Program assessment (function, product cost, program cost, timing and process conformance)
   b. Lessons learned, documented and shared

Overlap between concept development and design

Theme selection: Single, broadly feasible product theme selected with allowance for mix and match. All business and functional program objectives affirmed and updated. This is the speed-to-market point in the process.

Deliverables/Requirements
1. Brand vision/marketing plane
   a. Customer requirements complete
   b. Service requirements identified
   c. Public relations plan initiated—as needed

2. Program definition
   a. Functional objectives and performance standards complete
   b. Product and process technology selection complete

3. Program planning and resource management
   a. Component product assurance teams complete
   b. Resource requirement assessment complete

4. Design and development
    a. Design for service efficiency studies complete
    b. All parts disclosed
    c. Packaging themes updated
    d. System and component designs and technical descriptions updated
    e. Theme feasibility complete
    f. Preliminary process failure modes and effects analysis and key characteristics

5. Production preparation
    a. Preliminary process capability estimates

6. Sourcing and logistics
    a. Source packages approved
    b. Supplier selection complete
    c. Supplier initial risk evaluations complete
    d. Initial material handling plan

7. Build and test

8. Program and process assessment
    a. Program assessment (function, product cost, program cost, timing and process conformance)
    b. Lessons learned, documented and shared

Design

Final specifications: All specifications completed. Comprehensively feasible product and process defined. All verification, validation and production plans defined. Action plans in place to meet corporate milestones of development cycle.

Deliverables/Requirements
1. Brand vision/marketing plans
    a. Series line-up and mix price walk finalized
    b. Public relations plan complete

2. Program definition
    a. Program vision document complete
    b. Top-down and detailed (bottom-up) business requirements and objectives reconciled
    c. End-of-life vehicle plan complete

3. Business planning and approvals
    a. Program funding approval complete

4. Program planning and resource management

    a. Product assurance plans complete

    b. Resource requirement assessment complete

5. Design and development

    a. Final packaging theme complete

    b. Comprehensive product and process feasibility

    c. Preliminary workstation designs and operation descriptions

    d. Preliminary gage, fixture, test equipment and mistake-proofing requirements and plans

    e. Preliminary control plans

6. Production preparation

    a. Preliminary systems/controls architecture defined

    b. Establish interface standards team

    c. Preliminary appropriate tooling plan

7. Sourcing and logistics

    a. Production purchase orders issued for top 20 percent of parts

    b. All source packages approved

8. Program and process assessment

    a. Program assessment (function, product cost, program cost, timing and process conformance)

    b. Lessons learned, documented and shared

Product and process design complete: 100 percent production feasible product and process design is complete. All verification, validation and production plans confirmed. This is the speed of execution point in the process.

Deliverables/Requirements

1. Brand vision/marketing plans

    a. Service readiness plan complete

    b. Glove box kit defined

    c. Marketing launch core team established

2. Program definition

    a. Trade-off analysis complete

3. Program planning and resource management

    a. Product assurance plan updated

    b. Resource requirement assessment complete

    c. Launch plan identified

4. Design and development

    a. Product design complete

    b. System and component design FMEAs and key characteristics complete

    c. Design for service efficiency complete

    d. Product and process design release complete

    e. Process design complete

    f. Process FMFAs and key characteristics complete

    g. Workstation designs and operation descriptions complete

    h. Gage, fixture, test equipment, mistake-proofing plans complete

    i. Control plans complete

    j. Feasibility of facilities and plans complete

5. Production preparation

    a. Process capability estimates complete

    b. Tooling and equipment specifications complete

    c. Preliminary diagnostics and service procedures

    d. Appropriate tool plan complete

    e. Facility plans complete

    f. System/controls architecture complete

6. Sourcing and logistics

    a. Material handling plan complete

    b. Production purchase orders issued

7. Build and test

    a. ED testing (engineering design), simulation and analysis complete

    b. All test plans complete

    c. build plan complete

    d. Quality measurement plan complete

8. Program and process assessment

    a. Program assessment (function, product cost, program cost timing and process conformance)

    b. Lessons learned, documented and shared

Overlap between design and execution

Production readiness—I: First pilot program based on product components tools and equipment allowing build to production process intent. Verify the product and process design.

Deliverables/Requirements

1. Brand vision/marketing plans

    a. Advertising positioning clinics complete

    b. Preliminary communication strategy complete

2. Program planning and resource management
   a. Resource requirement assessment complete
   b. All personnel for build at build facility

3. Production preparation
   a. Tooling, equipment, gages, fixtures and mistake-proofing built and installed
   b. Production tooling, equipment, gages, fixtures and mistake-proofing kicked-off
   c. Feasibility of production facilities established
   d. Process description complete for all affected plants

4. Sourcing and logistics
   a. Components and systems received for build
   b. Production intent material handling (racks, containers) received

5. Build and test
   a. Component design verification (DV) complete
   b. Build issue tracking established
   c. Build plans complete

6. Program and process assessment
   a. Program assessment (function, product cost, program cost, timing and process conformance)
   b. Lessons learned, documented and shared

Execution

Production readiness—II: Build of products and properties for design verification. Verification of production build process intent. Determination of product and process issues for resolution. Product and process training of key personnel.

Deliverables/Requirements

1. Brand vision/marketing plans
   a. Final communication strategy

2. Program planning and resource management
   a. Resource requirement assessment complete

3. Production preparation
   a. Assembly plant and supplier process design vented
   b. Initial process performance complete
   c. Preliminary diagnostic and service procedures
   d. Preliminary man-assignments identified
   e. Assembly plant key operator training complete
   f. Vehicle communications software and testing verified

4. Sourcing and logistics
   a. Material handling, material supplied
   b. Process sign-off started

5. Build and test
   a. Products built and assessed
   b. System DV testing complete
   c. Build issues and corrective actions identified
   d. Systems and product dimensional targets verified
   e. Quality tracking measures and process verified

6. Program and process assessment
   a. Program assessment (function, product cost, tooling and process conformances)
   b. Lessons learned, documented and shared

Production readiness—III: Validation of tooling, equipment and verify facilities. Certification test plan is developed.

Deliverables/Requirements

1. Program planning and resource management
   a. Resource requirement assessment complete

2. Production preparation
   a. Control plans for production complete
   b. Man-assignments (individual tasks assigned to individuals) complete
   c. Complete diagnostic and service procedures finalized and validated
   d. Plant training initiated
   e. Production process installed at home plant and certified
   f. Production torque process verified
   g. Containment plan for emergencies complete

3. Sourcing and logistics
   a. Process sign-off complete
   b. Components for build received with PPAP warrant
   c. Production material handling racks and containers required for received product

4. Build and test
   a. Vehicle DV testing complete
   b. Issues identified/resolved and corrective actions verified

5. Program and process assessment
   a. Program assessment (function, product cost, program cost, timing and process conformance)
   b. Lessons learned, documented and shared

Overlap between execution and launch

Production readiness—IV: Home plant facility validation and start of planned ramp-up. Build of saleable products for fast feedback.

Deliverables/Requirements—1st review

1. Production preparation
   a. Assembly plant process validated

2. Build and test
   a. Product build and assessed
   b. Begin product and system process validation (PV) testing
   c. Homologation compliance testing complete

Deliverables/Requirements—2nd review

3. Brand vision/marketing plans
   a. Service scan-tool code and manuals released
   b. Final pacing established

4. Program planning and resource management
   a. Resource requirement assessment complete

5. Production preparation
   a. Control plans for production implemented
   b. Diagnostics and service procedures published
   c. Workstation and launch readiness complete
   d. Home-line installation and validation complete

6. Sourcing and logistics
   a. Material handling validated
   b. Certified components and systems received for build

7. Build and test
   a. Product and system PV testing complete
   b. Issues identified/resolved and corrective actions verified

8. Program and process assessment
   a. Program assessment (function, product cost, program cost, timing and process conformance)
   b. Lessons learned, documented and shared

Launch

Job 1: Continue ramp-up with production of first units for direct sale. All build options introduced.

Deliverables/Requirements—1st review of end milestones
1. Brand vision/marketing plans
   a. Service pans catalog delivered
2. Production preparation
   a. Port operations installation process validated
   b. Assembly plant facilities validated
   c. System fill complete
3. Sourcing and logistics
   a. All production material handling received
4. Build and test
   a. Product built and assessed

Deliverables/Requirements—2nd review of end milestones
5. Brand vision/marketing plans
   a. Flash updates and technical service bulletins issued
6. Program planning and resource management
   a. Resource requirement assessment complete
7. Production preparation
   a. First customer product built
   b. Ramp-up plan executed
8. Build and test
   a. Containment issues identified/resolved and corrective actions verified
9. Program and process assessment
   a. Customer feedback systems implemented
   b. Program assessment (function, product cost, program cost, timing and process conformance)
   c. Lessons learned, documented and shared.

Selected bibliography

Albright, S. C., W. L. Winston, C. J. Zappe, and P. Kolesar. *Managerial Statistics*. Pacific Grove, CA: Duxbury, 2000.

Anderson, N. A. "6 Sigma Producibility Measurement, Thoughts from a Hands-On Engineer," *Alliant Techsystems* (March 1991).

Anderson, V. L., and R. A. McLean. *Design of Experiments*. New York: Marcel Dekker, 1974.

Ayyub, B. Elicitation of Expert Opinions for Uncertainty and Risks. Boca Raton, FL: St. Lucie Press, 2001.

Ayyub, B., and R. H. McCuen. *Probability, Statistics and Reliability for Engineers and Scientists*. 2nd ed.. Boca Raton, FL: St. Lucie Press, 2002.

Bhote, K. R. (1991). *World Class Quality: Using Design of Experiments to Make it Happen*. New York: AMACOM, 1991.

Boothroyd, G., C. Poli, and L. Murch. *Automatic Assembly*. New York: Marcel Decker, 1982.

Bothe, D. R. *Measuring Process Capability*. New York: MacGraw-Hill, 1997.

Box, George E. P., W. G. Hunter, and J. S. Hunter. *Statistics for Experimenters: An Introduction to Design, Data Analysis and Model Building*. New York: John Wiley & Sons, 1978.

Box, G. E. P., W. G. Hunter, and J. S. Hunter. *Statistics for Experimenters*. New York: John Wiley & Sons, 1978.

Brassard, M., and D. Ritter. *The Memory Jogger*. Salem MA: GOAL/QPC, 1994.

Breyfogle, F. W. *Implementing Six Sigma: Smarter Solutions Using Statistical Methods*. New York: John Wiley & Sons, 1999.

Broom, M. F. *The Infinite Organization*. Palo Alto, CA: Davies-Black Publishing, 2002.

Burr, I. *Engineering Statistics and Quality Control*. New York: McGraw-Hill, (1953).

Caldwell, K. "Six Sigma Brings Control to the Shop Floor." *Quality* (August 2002), pp. 28–31.

Carroll, B. J. *Lean Performance ERP Project Management: Implementing the Virtual Supply Chain*. Boca Raton, FL: St. Lucie Press, 2002.

Castrup, H. "Analyzing Uncertainty for Risk Management," *Proc. ASQC 49th Annual Qual. Congress*, Cincinnati, OH (May 1995).

Castrup, H. "Uncertainty Analysis for Risk Management," *Proc. Meas. Sci. Conf.*, Anaheim, CA (January 1995).

Chandra, M. J. *Statistical Quality Control*. Boca Raton, FL: CRC Press, 2001.

Charbonneau, H. C., and G. L. Webster. *Industrial Quality Control*. Englewood Cliffs, NJ: Prentice-Hall, 1978.

Chowdhury, S. *The Power of Six Sigma*. Chicago: Dearborn Trade, 2001.

Cochran, W., and G. Cox. *Experimental Designs*. 2nd ed. New York: John Wiley & Sons, 1957.

Coffman, C. "Make Me A Match: Getting Design and Manufacturing Together-Simultaneously." *Automotive Industries* 167, No. 12 (December 1987), pp 62–64.

Creveling, C. M. *Tolerance Design: A Handbook for Developing Optimal Specifications*. Reading, MA: Addison-Wesley, 1997.

Creveling, C. M., J. L. Slutsky, D. Antis, and J. Slutsky. *Design for Six Sigma in Technology and Product Development*. Englewood Cliffs, NJ: Prentice Hall,2002.

Crowe, D., and A. Feinberg. (2001). *Design for Reliability*. Boca Raton, FL: CRC Press, 2001.

Daniel, C. *Applications of Statistics to Industrial Experimentation*. New York: John Wiley & Sons, 1976.

Deming, W. E. *Quality Productivity and Competitive Position*. Boston: Massachusetts Institute of Technology, Center for Advanced Engineering Study, 1982.

Desatnick, R. L. *Managing to Keep the Customer*. San Francisco: Jossey-Bass Publishers, 1987.

Dhillon, B. S. *Design Reliability: Fundamentals and Applications*. Boca Raton, FL: St. Lucie Press, 1999.

Dhillon, B. S. *Medical Device Reliability and Associated Areas*. Boca Raton, FL: St. Lucie Press, 2000.

Donalson, D. P. On Leadership. *Quality Progress* (August 2002), pp. 24–25.

Duncan, A. J. *Quality Control and Industrial Statistics*, 3rd ed. Chicago: Richard D. Irwin, 1965.

Draper, N. R., and H. Smith. *Applied Regression Analysis*. New York: John Wiley & Sons, 1981.

Eagle, A. "A Method for Handling Errors in Testing and Measuring." *Industrial Quality Control* (March 1954), pp. 10–15.

Eckes, G. *Making Six Sigma Last*. New York: John Wiley & Sons, 2001.

Ehrlich, B. H. (2002). *Transactional Six Sigma and Lean Servicing*. Boca Raton FL: St. Lucie Press, 2002.

Evans, David H. "Statistical Tolerancing: The State of the Art, Part III: Shifts and Drifts." *Journal of Quality and Technology* 7, No. 2 (1975), pp. 72–76.

Feld, W. M. Lean Manufacturing. Boca Raton, FL: CRC Press, 2001

Ferling, J. "The Role of Accuracy Ratios in Test and Measurement Processes." *Proc. Meas. Sci. Conf.*, Long Beach, CA (January 1984), pp 83–102.

Ferling, J. "Uncertainty Analysis of Test and Measurement Processes," *Proc. Meas. Sci. Conf.*, Anaheim, CA (January 1995).

Fisher, K. *Leading Self-Directed Work Teams: A Guide to Developing New Team Leadership Skills*. New York: McGraw Hill, 1993.

Fontenot, G., R. Behara, and A. Gresham "Six Sigma in Customer Satisfaction." *Quality Progress* (December 1994), pp. 73–76.

Frame, J. D. *The New Project Management*. San Francisco: Jossey Bass, 1994.

Franceschini, F. *Advanced Quality Function Deployment*. Boca Raton, FL: St. Lucie Press, 2002.

Garber, P. R. *10 Natural Forces for Business Success*. Palo Alto, CA: Davies-Black Publishing, 2002.

Garber, P. R. *Turbulent Change*. Palo Alto, CA: Davies-Black Publishing, 2002.

Gardiner, P., and R. Rothwell. "Tough Customers: Good Designs." *Design Studies* 6, No. 1. (January 1985), pp. 7–17.

Gitlow, H., S. Gitlow, A. Oppenheim, and R. Oppenheim. *Tools and Methods for the Improvement of Quality*. Homewood, IL: Irwin, 1989.

Grubbs, F., and H. Coon. "On Setting Test Limits Relative to Specification Limits." *Industrial Quality Control* (March 1954), pp. 15–20.

Gunter, B. H. "The Use and Abuse of Cpk, Part 1." *Quality Progress* (January 1989), pp. 72–73.

Gunter, B. H. "The Use and Abuse of Cpk, Part 2." *Quality Progress* (March 1989), pp. 108–109.

Gunter, B. H. "The Use and Abuse of Cpk, Part 3." *Quality Progress* (May 1989), pp. 79–80.

Gunter, B. H. "The Use and Abuse of Cpk, Part 4." *Quality Progress* (July 1989), pp. 86–87.

Hair, J. E., R. E. Anderson, R. L. Tatham, and W. C. Black. *Multivariate Data Analysis*. 5th ed. Upper Saddle River, NJ: Prentice Hall, 1998.

Harry, M. J. "Six Sigma: A Breakthrough Strategy for Profitability." *Quality Progress* 31, No. 5 (May 1998), pp. 60–64

Harry, M., and R. Stewart. *Six Sigma Mechanical Design Tolerancing*. Schaumburg, IL: Motorola, Inc. Motorola University, 1988.

Harry, M., and R. Schroeder. Six Sigma: *The Breakthrough Management Strategy Revolutionizing the World's Top Corporations*. New York: Currency, 2000.

Harry, M. J. Electrical Engineering Application of the Taguchi Design Philosophy, Schaumburg, IL: Government Electronics Group, Motorola, Inc., Motorola University, 1987.

Harry, M. J., and Lawson. J.R. *Six Sigma Producibility Analysis and Process Characterization*. Schaumburg, IL: Motorola University, 1990.

Harry, M. J. The Nature of Six Sigma Quality. Schaumburg, IL: Government Electronics Group, Motorola, Inc., Motorola University, 1987.

Hays, R. H., and S. C. Wheelwright. *Restoring our Competitive Edge: Competing through Manufacturing*. New York: John Wiley & Sons, 1984.

Hays, W. L. *Statistics*. 3rd ed. New York: Holt, Rinehart and Winston, 1981.

Heath, H. H. "Statistical Tolerancing of Engineering Components: Is It Worth It?" *Precision Engineering* 1, No. 3 (1979), pp. 153–156.

Heldt, J. J. *Quality Sampling and Reliability*. Boca Raton, FL: St. Lucie Press, 1998.

Hicks, C. R. *Fundamental Concepts in the Design of Experiments*. New York: McGraw-Hill, 1964.

Hunter, J. S. "Statistical Design Applied to Product Design." *Quality Technology* 17, No. 4 (October 1985), pp. 210–221.

Johnson, W. C. *Designing and Delivering Superior Customer Value*. Boca Raton, FL: CRC Press, 1999.

Juran, J. M., and F. M. Gryna, Jr. *Quality Planning and Analysis*. New York: McGraw-Hill, 1970.

Kackar, R. N. "Off Line Quality Control. Parameter Design, and the Taguchi Method." *Journal of Quality Technology* 17 No. 4 (1985), pp. 176–188.

Kerzner, H. *Project Management: A Systems Approach to Planning, Scheduling and Controlling*. 5th ed. New York: Van Nostrand Reinhold, 1995.

Kliem, R. L., and H. B. Anderson. *The Organizational Engineering Approach to Project Management*. Boca Raton, FL: St. Lucie Press, 2002.

Latino, K. C., and R. J. Latino. *Root Cause Analysis*. Boca Raton, FL: St. Lucie Press, 2002.

Levison, W. A. *Lean Enterprise: A Systematic Approach to Minimizing Waste*. Milwaukee, WI: Quality Press, 2002.

Lippit, M. B. *The Leadership Spectrum*. Palo Alto, CA: Davies-Black Publishing, 2002.

Maier, M. W., and E. Rechtin. *The Art of Systems Architecting*. Boca Raton, FL: CRC Press, 2000.

McCormick, N. J. *Reliability and Risk Analysis*. New York: Academic Press, 1981.

McFadden, F. R. "Six-Sigma Quality Programs." *Quality Progress* (June 1993), pp. 37–42.

Miller, E. J., and C. Casavant. "Continuous Improvement Through Defect Management: A Powerful Technique for Increasing Customer Satisfaction." *Proceedings of ASQC 48th Annual Quality Congress* 1994, pp. 210–217.

Modarres, M., M. Kaminskiy, and V. Krivtsov. *Reliability Engineering and Risk Analysis: A Practical Guide*. New York: Marcel Dekker, 1999.

Montgomery, D. C. *Introduction to Statistical Quality Control*. New York: John Wiley & Sons, 1985.

Montgomery, D. C. *Design and Analysis of Experiments*. New York: John Wiley & Sons, 1976.

Mood, A. M., F. A. Graybill, and D. C. Boes. *Introduction to the Theory of Statistics*. 3rd ed. New York: McGraw-Hill, 1974.

Munro, R. *Six Sigma for the Shop Floor: A Pocket Guide*. Milwaukee, WI: ASQ Quality Press, 2002.

Naumann, E., and S.H. Hoisington. *Customer Centered Six Sigma: Linking Customers, Process Improvement and Financial Results*. Milwaukee, WI: American Society for Quality, 2000.

Neder, J., W. Wasserman, and M H. Kunter. Applied Linear Statistical Models. 2nd ed. Homewood IL: R. D. Irwin, 1985. [Excellent source for studying sample size and power calculations.]

Neuman, R. P., and R. Neuman *The Six Sigma Way Team Fieldbook: An Implementation Guide for Project Improvement Teams*. New York: McGraw-Hill, 2001.

Noguera, J., and T. Nielsen. "Implementing Six Sigma for Interconnect Technology." *1992 ASQC Quality Congress Transactions*, Nashville, pp. 538–544.

Otto, K., and K. Wood. *Product Design: Techniques in Reverse Engineering and New Product Development*. Upper Saddle River, NJ: Prentice Hall, 2001.

Pande, P. S., R. P. Neuman, and R. R. Cavanagh. *The Six Sigma Way*. New York: McGraw-Hill, 2000.

Pande, P. S., R. R., Cavanagh, R. P. Neuman, and R. Neuman. *The Six Sigma Way Team Fieldbook: An Implementation Guide for Project Improvement Teams*. New York: McGraw-Hill, 2001.

Park, R. *Value Engineering*. Boca Raton, FL: St. Lucie Press, 1999.

Peace, G. S. *Taguchi Methods: A Hands-on Approach*. Asian edition. Reading, MA: Addison-Wesley, 1993.

Pecht, M. *Product Reliability, Maintainability and Supportability Handbook*. Boca Raton, FL: St. Lucie Press, 1995.

Pearson, E. S., and H.O. Hartley (eds). *Biometrica Tables for Statisticians*. Vol II. Biometrica Trust. London: Biometrica Trust, 1976. [Excellent source for studying power curves ($v_1 = 1$).]

Pena, E. "Motorola's Secret to Total Quality Control." *Quality Progress* (October 1990), pp. 43–45.

Pyzdek, T. *The Six Sigma Handbook: A Complete Guide for Green Belts, Black Belts and Managers at all Levels*. New York: MacGraw-Hill, 2001 and Tucson: Quality Publishing, 2001.

Rantanen, K. *Simplified TRIZ*. Boca Raton, FL: CRC Press, 2002.

Rath and Strong. *Rath and Strong's Six Sigma Pocket Guide*. Lexington, MA: Rath and Strong Management Consultants, 2002.

Roy, R. K. *Design of Experiments Using the Taguchi Approach*. New York: John Wiley & Sons, 2001.

Savransky, S. D. *Engineering of Creativity: Introduction to TRIZ Methodology of Inventive Problem Solving*. Boca Raton, FL: St. Lucie Press, 2001.

Schonberger, R. J. *World Class Manufacturing: The Lessons of Simplicity Applied*. New York: The Free Press, 1986.

Schragenheim, E., and H. W. Dettmer. *Manufacturing at Warp Speed: Optimizing Supply Chain Financial Performance*. Boca Raton, FL: St. Lucie Press, 2001.

Shillito, M. L. *Acquiring, Processing and Deploying Voice of the Customer*. Boca Raton, FL: St. Lucie Press, 2001.

Shingo, S. *Zero Quality Control: Source Inspection and the Poka-yoke System*. Cambridge, MA: Productivity Press, 1986

Stamatis, D. H.*Six Sigma and Beyond: Problem Solving and Basic Mathematics*. Boca Raton, FL: St. Lucie Press, 2002.

Stamatis, D. H. *Six Sigma and Beyond: Statistics and Probability*. Boca Raton, FL: St. Lucie Press, 2003.

Stamatis, D. H. *Six Sigma and Beyond: Design for Six Sigma*. Boca Raton, FL: St. Lucie Press, 2003.

Stamatis, D. H. *Six Sigma and Beyond: Design of Experiments*. Boca Raton, FL: St. Lucie Press, 2003.

Stamatis, D. H. *Six Sigma and Beyond: Foundations of Excellence*. Boca Raton, FL: St. Lucie Press, 2002.

Stamatis, D. H. *Six Sigma and Beyond: Statistical Process Control*. Boca Raton, FL: St. Lucie Press, 2003.

Stamatis, D. H. *Six Sigma and Beyond: The Implementation Process*. Boca Raton, FL: St. Lucie Press, 2003.

Starinsky, R.W. *Maximizing Business Performance Through Software Packaging*. Boca Raton, FL: CRC Press, 2002.

Suh, N. P. *The Principles of Design*. New York: Oxford University Press, 1990.

Tadikamalla, P. R. "The Confusion over Six-Sigma Quality." *Quality Progress* (November 1994), pp. 83–85.

Taguchi, G. *System of Experimental Design*. Vols. 1 and 2. White Plains, NY: UNIPUB/Kraus International Publications, 1987..

Taguchi, G., S. Chowdhury, and Y. Wu. *The Mahalanobis-Taguchi System*. New York: McGraw-Hill, 2001.

Taylor, G. D., and English, J. R. "A Benchmarking Framework for Quality Improvement." *Quality Engineering* 6, No.1 (1993), pp. 57–69.

Turmel, J., and Gartz, L. "Designing in Quality Improvement: A Systematic Approach to Designing for Six Sigma." *Proceedings of ASQC 51st Annual Quality Congress* (1996), pp. 391–398.

Walpole, R. E., and R. H. Myers. *Probability and Statistics for Engineers and Scientists*. New York: Macmillan Publishing, 1978.

Wheelwright, S. C. and R. H. Haayes. *Restoring our Competitive Edge*. New York: John Wiley & Sons, 1984.

Wolstenholme, L. C. *Reliability Modelling*. Boca Raton, FL: St. Lucie Press, 1999.

Womack, J. P., and D. T. Jones. *Lean Thinking*. New York: Simon and Schuster, 1996.

Web sites:

Six Sigma—What is Six Sigma? http://www.isixsigma.com/sixsigma/six sigma.asp

Optimizing Existing Processes to Achieve Six Sigma Capabilities, http://www.controleng.com/archives/1999/ctIO301.99/03e3Ol.html

Managing Risk Improves Production, http://www.controlen2.com/archives/I 999/ct11201.99/991200wl.html

Patient Safety, Six Sigma & ISO 9000 Ouality Management, http://www.gualitydigest.com/novOO/html/Patient.html

Design for Six Sigma Capability, http://www.controleng.com/archives/1999/ctIO101.99/OlaIO3.html

Environmental Protection Agency Risk Management Plan 3165 Indiana, Executive Summary 1-June -1999, http://db.rtknet.org/E29420T 1092

Managing Risk: Don't Fall Flat, http://www.controleng.com/archives/1999/ctll2Ol.99/991200.html

Index

About the author

Diomidis H. Stamatis, PhD, ASQ-Fellow, CQE, CMfgE, Master Black Belt, is currently president of Contemporary Consultants, in Southgate, Michigan. He received his B.S./B.A. Degree in Marketing from Wayne State University, his Master's Degree from Central Michigan University, and his PhD in Instructional Technology and business/statistics from Wayne State University.

Dr. Stamatis is a specialist in Quality Science, Management Consulting, Organizational Development, and an adjunct faculty in Central Michigan University. He has also taught both undergraduate and graduate courses in Statistics, Operations Management, Technology and Environment and Project Management, for the University of Michigan, Florida Institute of Technology and Central Michigan University.

With more than 30 years of experience in management, quality training and consulting, Dr. Stamatis has served and consulted for numerous industries in the private and public sectors. His consulting extends across the United States, Canada, Australia, Mexico, Brazil, Argentina, Southeast Asia, Japan, China, India, and Europe. Dr. Stamatis has written more than 70 articles in professional and academic journals, and has presented many speeches at national and international conferences on quality. He is a contributing author in several books and the sole author of 20 books. His latest major work is the *Six Sigma and Beyond*, a seven-volume exhaustive study of six sigma methodology, published by St. Lucie Press (2002–2003).

He is an active member of the Detroit Engineering Society, American Society for Training and Development, The American Marketing Association, American Research Association, and the American Society for Quality.